Cecil Scott Forester was born in [illegible] and was educated at Dulwich College and Guy's Hospital Medical School. Before completing his training as a doctor, however, he found that his commitment to becoming a writer was more important than his studies, and he never completed his degree. At twenty he was writing for magazines; at twenty-four he wrote his first bestseller, the classic crime novel *Payment Deferred*. During the next four decades he went on to become one of the most successful authors writing in the English language, publishing a long line of bestselling books which included crime, historical fiction, non-fiction and autobiography, of which the 'Hornblower' novels are perhaps the best known. Several of his novels have been made into films, among them *Payment Deferred*, *The Gun* and *The African Queen*, the Oscar-winning film starring Humphrey Bogart and Katharine Hepburn.

C. S. Forester went to live in California after the war and died in 1966.

'For his account of the naval action between the *Delaware* and the *Calypso* alone, this story is worth reading. But it has many other attractions. I recommend it warmly to all who like reading about ships and ships' companies and naval battles. Captain Peabody is a great creation.' – *The Tatler*

Also by C. S. Forester in Sphere Books:

THE SKY AND THE FOREST
GOLD FROM CRETE
THE GOOD SHEPHERD
THE PEACEMAKER
LIEUTENANT HORNBLOWER
HORNBLOWER AND THE CRISIS
HORNBLOWER AND THE 'ATROPOS'

The Captain from Connecticut

C. S. FORESTER

SPHERE BOOKS LIMITED
30/32 Gray's Inn Road, London WC1X 8JL

First published in Great Britain by
Michael Joseph Ltd 1941

First Sphere Books edition 1979
Reprinted 1980

TRADE
MARK

Set in Intertype Baskerville

Printed in Great Britain by
Hazell Watson & Viney Ltd
Aylesbury, Bucks

CHAPTER ONE

Although it was mid-afternoon it was nearly as dark as a summer night. The ship swayed uneasily at her anchor as the wind howled round her, the rigging giving out musical tones, from the deep bass of the shrouds to the high treble of the running rigging. Already the snow was thick enough on her to blur the outlines of the objects on the deck. On its forward side the square base of the binnacle was now a rounded mound; the flemished coils of the falls were now merely white cylinders. The officer of the watch stood shivering in the little shelter offered by the mizzen mast bitts, and forward across the snow-covered deck a few unhappy hands crouched vainly seeking shelter under the high bulwarks.

The two officers who emerged upon the quarter deck held their hats on to their heads against the shrieking wind. The shorter, slighter one turned up the collar of his heavy coat, and attempted instinctively to pull the front of it tighter across his chest to keep out the penetrating air. As he spoke in the grey darkness he had to raise his voice to make himself heard, despite the confidential nature of what he was saying.

'It's your best chance, Peabody.'

The other turned about, and stood to windward with the snow driving into his face before he answered with a single word.

'Aye,' he said.

'The glass is still dropping. But it can't go much lower,' went on the other. It seemed as if he were talking for the purpose of encouraging himself, not the man he was speaking to. 'The west wind'll veer nor'-easterly tomorrow, but by that time you'll have weathered Montauk, please God.'

'Please God,' echoed Peabody – but it was more like a prayer, in the tone he employed, than the other man's speech.

'Well, goodbye, then. The best of good fortune, Captain Peabody.'

The two men shook hands in their heavy furred gloves. Peabody raised his voice against the storm – it was a penetrant voice, nasal yet with a tenor musical tone which somehow made it more readily audible against the wind.

'Call the Commodore's gig. Pipe the side for the Commodore,' he said.

'Compliments in this weather?' asked the Commodore, a little surprised, but Peabody gave him no explanation. He was not going to allow a blizzard to interfere with the decent and proper routine of his ship.

The figures huddling for shelter under the bulwark came to life and scuttled across the deck and down into the gig. Other figures, black against the snowy deck, came swarming up from below. It was strange and unnatural that their feet made no sound on the deck. They were like ghosts in their noiselessness, treading the thick carpet of snow. Not even the marines, in their heavy shoes, made any sound. Feebly the pipes of the boatswain's mates twittered in the shrieking wind as the Commodore went over the side down into his waiting gig. Peabody watched him down into the boat, saw the bowman cast off the painter, and then turned back to face the wind again.

'Man the capstan, there!' he shouted. 'Mr. Hubbard, fore and main topmast staysails. Three reefs in the tops'ls, ready to sheet home.'

He stood with his hands behind him, facing into the bitter wind, and making no attempt whatever to shelter from it. Forward he could just hear the voice of the boatswain as he gave the word to the men at the capstan bars. Then he heard the clank-clank of the capstan; it was turning slowly – very slowly. It was hard work to drag the big frigate up to the anchor against that wind. There were men aloft, too; their movements disturbed the snow banked against the rigging, and it was drifting astern in big puffs visible through the snow. Another unexpected noise puzzled Peabody for a moment – it was the crackling of the frozen canvas as it was unrolled. And the frozen ropes crackled, too, like a whole succession of pistol shots, as they ran through the sheaves.

Little lumps of ice stripped from them came raining down about him, whirled aft by the wind.

Peabody looked over the starboard quarter. Somewhere in that murk and darkness was the Long Island shore, and Willet's Point, too near to be pleasant, he knew, although invisible. On the larboard bow, equally invisible, lay Throg's Neck. It was only the protection of the guns of Fort Totten and Fort Schuyler on these two points which had enabled him to bring his ship thus far in peace. Beyond them the British Navy cruised unchallenged over the length and breadth of Long Island Sound, yet the watch over the Narrows was stricter still, so strict that in his considered judgment it had been better to make the attempt to reach the open sea by this back door to New York. Were it not for the land batteries the Hudson and Hell Gate would be at the mercy of the British squadrons, just as Long Island Sound was. Hardy – the captain who had kissed the dying Nelson in the cockpit of the *Victory* at Trafalgar – lorded it off New London in the *Ramillies*, burning fishing boats and capturing coasters, and keeping Decatur and Jones blockaded in the port. Peabody thought of the starving seamen and dockyard hands who begged their bread on the waterfronts of New York and Baltimore, of the ruined businesses and the disrupted national economy. Hardy and his brother captains were strangling the Union slowly but certainly. Whether the *Delaware* would help to break their stranglehold in the slightest was more than he could say. He could only carry out his orders, interpreting them as best he could towards that end. If necessary, he could die.

The gale bore back the boatswain's hail from forward.

'Straight up and down, sir!'

'Heave away!' shouted Peabody. 'Sheet home, Mr. Hubbard.'

There were two quartermasters at the wheel beside him; the spokes turned in their hands as the *Delaware* gathered sternway. The canvas slatted wildly as the yards were braced round.

'Hard a-starboard,' said Peabody.

The *Delaware* hesitated and trembled. Her sails filled with a loud report, and Peabody felt the movement of the deck under his feet as the *Delaware* lost her sternway and began to move forward. She was heeling now as the treble-reefed topsails caught the wind. So thickly was the snow driving that it was impossible to see what was happening. Peabody had to rely on his other senses, on the feel of the ship, on his long-trained instincts, to draw his conclusions about what she was doing.

'Keep her to the wind,' he said to the quartermasters. They, too, would have only their long experience to help them in their task. Only by the feel of the wind in their faces, and by the sound of the sails if they steered too close to the wind, could they tell whether they were obeying their orders or not.

Under the pressure of the wind upon her scanty canvas the *Delaware* was moving forward precipitately through the water. The surface was rough enough to give her a distinct motion, and the sound of her bows crashing through the waves was audible through the noise of the wind. She was lying far over with the pressure of the wind, despite the fact that her top-gallant masts had been sent down; she was behaving like a blood horse in the hands of incompetent stable boys. No one save a madman or a blockaded captain would dream of taking a ship to sea in conditions like this, with a treacherous shore under her lee and snow so thick that it was hard to see a dozen fathoms away. But it was only in conditions like this that the *Delaware* stood any chance of evading the attention of Hardy and his watchdogs. She might as well, reflected Peabody bitterly, be piled up on the Long Island shore as lying rotting at Brooklyn.

He bent over the lighted binnacle, and studied the compass, and then turned his face back towards the snow while he made his calculations. His mind worked slowly but with infinite tenacity, and he had no need of paper and pencil as he moved mentally from point to point of the course he had in mind. They would weather Elm Point comfortably, he decided.

'Heave the log every glass, Mr. Hubbard,' he ordered.

'Aye aye, sir,' said Hubbard. Hubbard's breast and the front of his thighs were white with snow as he turned to acknowledge the order; glancing down, Peabody saw that his own clothes were similarly coated. A master's mate and a hand came aft, trudging through the snow on deck, their foothold precarious on that giddy slope. The hand would wet himself thoroughly with the dripping long line as he hauled it in again, and the water would freeze in that biting wind. It would be an uncomfortable night for him, thought Peabody, but discomfort was part of a sailor's life when necessary. The safety of the ship depended on the accurate estimate of her speed and distance travelled. He turned to the quartermasters.

'Are you cold?' he asked.

'A little, sir,' said one of them.

From those tough seamen the two words were the equivalent of a long wail of misery from a landsman. Peabody knew they would be numb and stupid before long.

'Mr. Hubbard!' he said. 'Relieve these men at the wheel every half hour.'

'Aye aye, sir,' said Hubbard.

Hubbard was marking on the traverse board the speed and course.

'What's the speed?'

'Five knots and a bit more, sir.' Even when Hubbard was shouting into a gale his voice bore the faint echo of the South Carolina which had given him birth.

The *Delaware* was showing her good points, doing five knots close-hauled under staysails and close-reefed topsails alone – the Baltimore shipwrights who built her away back in 1800 had left their impress on the shape of her hull, despite the specifications of the Navy Department. Five knots, and it would be more when they had weathered Elm Point and brought the wind abeam. High water at Montauk Point was at two a.m. Peabody stood with the wind whistling round him and the snow banking against his chest while he continued his calculations. In a blizzard like this he could be fairly certain that the British squadron would be blown out to sea; if not, it was so dark that he could hope to get through unobserved. In these conditions his ship was in a hundred times greater danger from the navigational difficulties than from the enemy, and it was only then, as he bitterly realised, that he stood any chance of getting to seat at all.

The relieved quartermasters were stumbling forward now, bent against the wind. He could tell from their gait how numb and stiff they were – they had been standing with their arms extended, holding the wheel, in an attitude which fairly invited the wind to pierce them to the heart. He would be feeling cold himself if he allowed himself to do so, but he would not. He went on facing stubbornly into the wind. They must be abreast of Elm Point by now.

'Nor'-east by east,' he said to the men at the wheel.

'Nor'-east by east, sir,' they echoed.

'Hands to the braces, Mr. Hubbard.'

'Aye aye, sir.'

The *Delaware* steadied herself on her new course, heeling to the wind, rolling rather more now, and pitching far less. Peabody had never known the Sound to be as rough as this – it was the clearest proof of the violence of the blizzard.

'Seven and a half knots, sir,' said Hubbard, marking up the new course and speed.

That was what he had expected. Now they would weather Montauk comfortably before dawn. For a few hours he could relax a little – relax as far as an American captain could possibly relax when sailing in the heart of his own country's waters in the midst of enemies.

The wind that was blowing about him from the Connecticut shore must now – he worked out a neat trigonometrical problem in his head – have passed just over the farm where he was born and spent his childhood. The memory made him shiver a little, although the blizzard did not. It was not often that those memories came back to him, except in nightmares. Against his will they forced themselves into his mind as he stood staring into the darkness. It was not the poverty, or the hunger, or the winter cold, which he hated to remember, although they had been poignant enough at the time. The bare bones of that farm had struck through the skin of the soil, and no one could have hoped to gain more than the barest living from it. There was nothing hateful now about the memory of poverty. But the other memories made him shudder again. That tall, gaunt father of his, with the yellow beard and the blazing blue eyes – he winced a little in the darkness at the vivid mental picture. The bottle beside him and the Bible in front of him, and the furious texts foaming out of his mouth, drunk with rum and the Old Testament – that was one way in which he could remember his father. And then another memory, insidiously creeping into his mind, of his father lurching across the room, still mouthing texts, and unbuckling the heavy belt from his waist; lurching across the room to where a terrified little boy stood cornered, reaching for him with a huge calloused hand, dragging him away from the sheltering walls. How that little boy had screamed under that searing belt! That little boy was now Captain Josiah Peabody, of the frigate *Delaware*.

Those memories had him on their treadmill now, there was no escape from them. There was his mother, dark and beautiful – he had thought her beautiful – who used to take him into her arms and rock with him and pet him; as a big baby, before he became a little boy, he could remember the bliss of those embraces. Then after that he knew that her step was uncertain, that her laugh was too loud and misplaced. He knew the reason for her red cheeks and staring, foolish gaze. After that he shrank from his mother's drunken caresses just as he shrank from his father's clutches – they sickened him equally as much. He remembered the nausea which overtook him when he smelt her breath as her soft arms closed about him.

Then Uncle Josiah, for whom he was named, had come to the farm, very extraordinary in his appearance to the little boy, with his hair tied into a neat queue, and a laced neck-cloth and gloves and riding boots. Uncle Josiah had taken him away – Uncle Josiah was an elegant gentleman, strangely enough; his nephew could guess that queer things had happened to Uncle Josiah during the past few years. Uncle Josiah had a lace handkerchief which wafted the perfumes of Paradise about the room when he applied it delicately to his nose; apparently he was a wealthy man, and the source of his wealth, unbelievable as it might be, was somehow connected with a war which had begun the other side of the ocean.

He was engaged in the most multifarious businesses, obviously, seeing that he received as many as six letters a day at one of the taverns when they stopped on their way to New York. He had friends, too. A mere word from him to one of those friends made young Josiah a boy in the Coastguard Service, where the beatings were not nearly as severe and where the nightmares of a loving mother gradually ceased in intensity. There was the fresh, clean wind of the sea to blow about him, and the boys who berthed with him were not weakly malicious, as had been his younger brothers and sisters. And the cities he visited were vast and intoxicating, from Portsmouth down to Charleston; and somehow the lessons which the master-commandant of the cutter taught him had a peculiar, delicious charm – algebra, when he was introduced to it, gave him pleasure as great as maple syrup or honey had done.

And then, when his voice had broken and his beard had begun to grow, there had come a call for officers in the new Federal Navy. Uncle Josiah said another word for him to another friend, a word which made his nephew a lieutenant at the age of sixteen. It was the last service Uncle Josiah was to do for him, for Uncle Josiah, two months later, paid the penalty of having become a gentleman, and died in Baltimore twelve paces from the pistol of another gentleman who had been his friend until the sudden disclosure of a queer scandal regarding the outfitting of privateers for the war against France.

Josiah knew nothing of his death for some months, for he was at sea in the *Constellation* with Truxtun. Josiah could remember with peculiar vividness those early battles, with the *Insurgente* and the *Vengeance.* He could remember as well the colour and the heat and the rain of the West India islands, where Truxton had displayed the Stars and Stripes – the memories were a little overlayed by others, of Tripoli and Algiers and Malta, but they were still keen enough. He found himself wondering whether he would see those islands again, and then checked himself with a hard smile, for he was under orders to proceed there at present. The immediate problem of weathering Montauk Point and breaking the British blockade had for the moment driven the equally difficult problems of the future clean out of his head. But it was as well that he could smile – most of the time when his weakness had lured him into going back over old memories he could not smile at all.

He shook himself, now that the spell was broken, back into his proper state of mind. He lifted the traverse board into the dim light of the binnacle – he realised that he must have been standing on deck motionless during two or three hours. The *Delaware* had held her course steadily during those hours, and must be well out into the Sound now. New Haven must be on their larboard beam. He could feel his way about Long Island Sound as surely as he could about his own cabin, thanks to his years in the Coastguard Service and to further years commanding one of the gunboats on which Mr. Jefferson had lavished so much of the national income in an attempt to buy security cheap.

The sea had been a second mother to him, and a kinder one than the traditional stepmother had ever been, he reflected, in an unusually analytical mood. The Navy had been his father. Then to continue the analogy the *Delaware* must be his wife, to whom he devoted all his kindly care, and all his waking thoughts. He was more fortunate in his family than most men were. He struggled again against this dangerous habit of brooding. He knew that with advancing age came a tendency to dwell upon the past. Perhaps now that he was thirty-two – close on thirty-three – he was beginning to show signs of it. Realistically he remembered how, as a lieutenant of sixteen, he had looked upon men of twice his age as old; and captains especially so. Truxton, in the *Constellation*, had seemed almost senile, but then Truxton must have been in his fifties or so. On the other hand, Decatur was the same age as himself, practically, and Decatur still seemed young to him. Perhaps, after all, he was not so very old at thirty-two. It was a satisfactory conclusion to reach, especially while he was the most junior captain in the list, and while his country's freedom had still to be defended – and while this very night he had to break a blockade enforced by a squadron of ships of the line.

Enough of this nonsense. He turned to face the snow-covered deck, and was surprised to find that he could hardly move; the bitter cold of the blizzard had stiffened him to such an extent that, now that his attention was called to it, he walked with difficulty. As the *Delaware* heeled before the shrieking wind his feet slipped in the treacherous snow, and he slid away to leeward and cannoned into the bulwarks, his feet struggling to find a foothold in the scuppers. That was the penalty for dreaming, he told himself grimly, as he rubbed his bruises. Uncontrollable shudders shook his body, and his teeth were chattering. It was ridiculous that he should have allowed himself to grow so cold. He struggled up the deck again to the weather side and under the slight shelter of the bulwark, where he flogged himself with his arms, beating off the thick layer of snow which had accumulated on the breast of his pea-jacket. He trudged forward along the spar deck to get his circulation going again; the foremast shrouds on the weather side here were coated completely with ice – the frozen spray taken in over the weather bow – so that shrouds and ratlines were like the frames of windows of ice, hard to see in this shrieking darkness, but plain enough to the touch. A fresh shower of spray blew into his face as he felt about him; there must be a good deal of ice accumulating on the running rigging. Certainly, the anchor at the cathead was welded to the ship's side by a solid block of ice.

He made his way aft again.

'Mr. Murray!'

'Sir!' said the officer of the watch.

'Set the watch to work clearing away the ice. I want twenty hands clearing the running rigging.'

'Aye aye, sir.'

Even with the gale blowing he could hear a few yelps of dismay among the crew as Murray gave his orders. To lay aloft in the blizzard was to face a torture as exquisite as anything the Indians had ever devised, and there would be frost-bite among the crew after this, even if no one broke his neck struggling along the frozen footropes with a precarious hold on the ice-coated yards. Yet it had to be done. The whole safety of the ship depended upon his ability to handle her promptly and to let go the anchor, if necessary. His calculations of her course and run might be faulty. He might find Orient Point close under his lee, when he really intended to give it a wide berth, and the knowledge that he might not be completely infallible gnawed at his conscience. Because of that, he stayed out on the exposed deck, where the blizzard could work its will on him. If the men had to suffer because he could not be sure of his position to within a quarter of a mile he was going to suffer with them; Peabody was not aware of how deeply ingrained into him was the Old Testament teaching of the father whom he had grown to despise.

Something white over the starboard quarter caught his eye – a fleck too big to be a mere breaking wave. He rushed across the deck to look more closely. There it was again – something white in the hurtling grey of the snow. He sprang up into the mizzen rigging, with the wind shrieking round his ears, and the sea hissing beneath his feet. That white fleck was the spray about the bows of a ship. As he leaped back again to the deck he found Murray there – Murray had seen it, too. Murray stabbed at the darkness with a gloved hand, and shouted in his ear, even grabbing his shoulder in the excitement of the moment, for Murray was of an excitable temperament. It was a ship, close hauled under storm canvas on the opposite tack to the *Delaware*. She was close abreast of them. She would cross their stern within a yard of them, Peabody decided; near enough. The bowsprit and martingale which circled in the air under their noses were coated with ice, he noted. Through the snow he could see the curve of her bow with two broad stripes of paint and a double line of checkers – a two decker, then, Hardy's *Ramillies* or Cochrane's *Superb*.

'A Britisher!' shrieked Murray, quite unnecessarily. There were no United States ships of the line. Murray turned away towards the helmsman, and then back to his captain for orders, quite unduly excited. There was nothing to be done. The ships were passing rapidly, and Peabody could be certain that the British guns, like his own, were secured by double breachings. By the time a gun could be loaded and run out the ships would be invisible to each other again; but Murray did not possess the imperturbability of his captain nor his fatalist ability to accept the inevitable.

Already the two decker was passing rapidly – a well-thrown stone would have landed on her deck. The glimmering snow with which she was coated showed up faintly in the darkness; against the whitened decks Peabody thought he could see the dark forms of her officers and crew. The poor devils were having as miserable a time of it as were his own men; worse, probably. Beating about Long Island Sound in a New England blizzard was no child's play, especially in a clumsy, pig-headed ship of the line – Peabody remembered how bluff and inelegant had been the bows she had presented to him when he first caught sight of her.

Now she was gone, engulfed in the darkness. She might put about in pursuit, but it did not matter. At a hundred yards the ships were as invisible to each other as at a hundred miles, and by the time the two decker could go about and settle on her new course she would be a couple of miles at least astern. It was even likely that she had not recognised the *Delaware* as American – there were few enough American frigates, and those all strictly blockaded. It was one of the ironies of history that the last vessel one would expect to see in Long Island Sound was an American frigate.

But on the other hand, the fact that he had been seen at all decided him to take one more risk on his passage to the open sea. It would be high water in Plum Gut in two hours from now, four and a half fathoms at least, and with this wind blowing probably rather more. He would head the *Delaware* through there, and chance all the dangers of Orient Point. Peabody did not think that any British battleship would have the nerve to follow him through.

Peabody studied the compass in the binnacle, and occupied his mind with the fresh problem in mental trigonometry as he worked out the conditions arising from the changed situation.

'Bring her two points farther off the wind,' he said.

'Two points farther off the wind, sir.'

Peabody looked aft into the darkness. The night had most certainly swallowed up the British two decker. He wondered whether there were any parallel mental processes going on in the British captain's mind. Whether there were or were not he could not tell, and certainly he was not going to stop to see. Daylight might perhaps show, and he was quite capable of waiting till daylight.

CHAPTER TWO

Lieutenant George Hubbard was officer of the morning watch. The glass had just been turned for the last time, and seven bells had been duly struck, and Hubbard was beginning to look forward to his relief and to wonder whether he would find any time for sleep during the day, when his captain loomed up beside him. With the cessation of the snow there was enough light now for details to be clearly distinguished.

'You can wear ship now, Mr. Hubbard,' said Peabody. 'Course sou'-west by south.'

'Sou'-west by south, sir,' echoed Hubbard.

'And take those men out of the chains. We won't need the lead again.'

'Aye aye, sir.'

'See that they have something hot to drink.'

'Aye aye, sir.'

The wind had moderated as it veered, but now that they were in the open sea they were encountering the full force of the waves. Close hauled, the *Delaware* had been climbing wave after wave, heeling over to them, soaring upward with her bowsprit pointing at the sky, and then, as she reached the crest, rolling into the wind with her stern heaving upwards in a mad corkscrew roll with the spray bursting over her deck. Now she came round before the wind, and her motion changed. There was not so much feeling of battling with gigantic forces; much more was there an uneasy sensation of yielding to them. The following sea threw her about as if she had no will of her own. Standing by the wheel, Hubbard was conscious of a feeling of relief from the penetrating torture of the wind – so, undoubtedly, were the men at the wheel – but the feeling was conteracted by a sensation of uneasiness as the *Delaware* lurched along before the big grey-bearded waves which came sweeping after her. There was an even chance of her being pooped – Hubbard could tell, by the feel of the deck under his feet, how each of those grey mountains in its turn blanketed the close-reefed topsails, and robbed the ship of a trifle of her way. He could tell it, too, by the way the quartermasters had to saw back and forth at the wheel to meet the *Delaware's* unhappy falling off as each wave passed under her counter. If she once broached-to, then good-bye to the *Delaware*.

'Steer small,' he growled at the quartermasters.

It was unsafe to run before this wind and sea. A cautious captain would have kept the *Delaware* upon the wind for a while longer, or would even heave-to until the sea moderated – provided, that is to say, that a cautious captain would have left port at all on such a night, which was quite inconceivable. As first lieutenant of the ship, and responsible to his captain for her material welfare, Hubbard could never quite reconcile in his mind the jarring claims of military necessity and common sense. He looked with something like dismay about the ship in the growing daylight, at the snow which covered her deck, and the ice which glittered on her standing rigging. The quarter-deck carronades beside him were mere rounded heaps of snow on their forward sides. When the forenoon watch was called he would have to set the hands at work shovelling the stuff away – queer work for a sailorman. The tradition of centuries was that the first work in the morning was washing down decks, not shovelling snow off them.

The captain was still prowling about the deck; Hubbard heard him lift up his voice in a hail.

'Masthead, there! Keep your wits about you.'

'Aye aye, sir.'

The poor devil of a lookout up there was the most uncomfortable man in the whole ship, Hubbard supposed, without much sympathy for him. It was interesting to note that the captain was apparently a little uneasy still about the possible appearance of British ships. Peabody had brilliantly brought the *Delaware* out to sea – the first United States ship to run the blockade for six months – as Hubbard grudgingly admitted to himself, yet with the open Atlantic about him he was still nervous. Hubbard shrugged his shoulders. He was glad that it was not his responsibility.

Here came that pesky young brother of the captain's. During the four weeks that the *Delaware* had lain at Brooklyn, Hubbard had come most heartily to dislike the boy. Captain's clerk, indeed, and he was hardly able to read or write ! It was a pity that the *Delaware's* midshipmen were all young boys. Jonathan Peabody was by several years the oldest of the gunroom mess, and in physique he was as tough as his elder brother, so that there was small chance of his being taught much sense there. He was sly, too; otherwise, as Hubbard was well aware, he would never have contrived for four weeks to avoid trouble in a ship whose First Lieutenant was anxious to make trouble for him.

'Take off your hat to the quarterdeck, you young cub,' snapped Hubbard.

'Aye aye, sir,' said Jonathan Peabody, and obeyed instantly. Yet there was a touch of elaboration about his gesture which conveyed exactly enough contempt both for the ceremony and for the First Lieutenant to annoy the latter intensely, and yet too little to make him liable to punishment under the Naval Regulations issued by command of the President of the United States of America – not even under that all-embracing regulation which decided that 'all other faults disorders and misdemeanours not herein mentioned shall be punished according to the laws and customs in such cases at sea.' The young cub flaunted his excellent clothes with a swagger which smacked of insolence, clothes which, as Hubbard knew, his captain had bought for him only four weeks ago. Until then Jonathan Peabody had been a barefooted follower of the plough, and presumably the furtive Lothario of some Connecticut village. Hubbard disliked him quite as much as he admired his grim elder brother; possibly the dislike and the admiration had some bearing on each other.

There came a yell from the maintopmast crosstrees.

'Sail, ho! Sail to wind'ard, sir.'

The captain appeared from nowhere upon the quarter-deck, leaping on the weather rail, and staring over the heaving sea into the wind over the quarter. Apparently he could see nothing from there, for he hailed the masthead again.

'What d'ye make of her?'

'She's a ship, sir, under tops'ls. Same course as us, sir, or pretty nigh.'

The captain took Hubbard's glass and swung himself into the mizzen rigging, running up the ratlines with the quite surprising agility of a big man. He was back again on deck shortly after, sliding down the backstay despite the handicap of his heavy clothing. Hubbard was not used to captains as athletic as that. The captain's hard face was set like a stone mask.

'That's the two decker we passed last night, Mr. Hubbard,' he said. 'Turn up the hands. I'll have a reef out of those tops'ls, if you please. Set the jib and mizzen stays'l, too.'

'Aye aye, sir.'

All hands came pouring on deck as Hubbard shouted his orders, while Peabody walked aft to the taffrail and stared astern. The fresh canvas as it was spread crackled loudly behind him, and the *Delaware* plunged madly under the increased pressure. Peabody swung round to watch his ship's behaviour. In a full gale like this he was exposing more canvas than he should do in prudence. There was a risk that something might give way, that some portion of the rigging might part – leaving out of all account the possibility that he might run the *Delaware* bodily under. But if he did not take that risk the British ship would overhaul him. It was only under present conditions that a British ship of the line stood any chance in a race with an American frigate. The bigger ship, with her immensely strong gear, could make more sail than he dared, and her buff bows and lofty freeboard which made her so clumsy on a wind were a huge advantage when running before a gale on a rough sea. By ensuring her appearance nearly dead to windward Providence had secured all these advantages for the British ship. But then, on the other hand, if she appeared to leeward, although the *Delaware* could escape from her easily enough close hauled, close hauled she would be headed back for Montauk Point, back to the confinement of blockage – possibly straight into the waiting arms of the blockading squadron. What Providence took away in one fashion she restored in another, keeping an even balance so that a man's success or failure depended entirely on himself, as it should be.

Hubbard was looking up at the straining topmasts. There was a distinct sign of a whip there – they were bending, very slightly, but perceptibly to the naked eye. What the strain was upon backstays and preventer braces could only be imagined; the tautness of the rigging had driven the perennial Aeolian harping of the wind quite a semitone up the scale. Hubbard turned to meet his captain's eye, and went as far in protest as to open his mouth, and then thought better of it, and shut his mouth and resumed his pacing of the deck, where the hands were at work shovelling away the snow. Peabody watched the antics of his ship for a moment longer, noting how low she lay in the water when the pressure of the wind forced her downwards in certain combinations of waves, noticing how the water boiled away from her bows, and then turned back to stare over the taffrail again. The *Delaware* rose upon a wave, heaving up her stern above the mad flurry of grey water, climbing higher and higher as she pitched, and in the very instant of her stern's highest ascent Peabody saw, far astern, on the very limit of the grey horizon, a tiny square of white. It was gone in a flash as the *Delaware* plunged down the farther slope, but Peabody knew it for what it was – the foretopsail of the British ship hoisted above the horizon for a moment. He had seen that foretopsail for a moment the night before; he had stared at it through his glass for two full minutes this morning, and he would recognise it again at any time in any part of the world. The sight of it from the deck meant that it was nearer, that his pursuer was overhauling him.

'Set the mizzen tops'l, Mr. Hubbard, with two reefs.'

'Aye aye, sir.'

'Have the relieving tackles manned, if you please.'

'Aye aye, sir.'

'Mr. Crane, take charge of them.'

'Aye aye, sir.'

Peabody had noticed the difficulty the quartermasters had in holding the *Delaware* on her course with the following sea – it was partly to help them that he had had the jib set. Now the pressure of the big mizzen topsail would add to their difficulties, countering the steadying effect of the headsails. Six men below at the relieving tackles, applied direct to the tiller ropes, would not only be of assistance in turning the rudder, but would also damp down the rudder's sudden movements. And Mr. Crane, the sailing master, with his lifetime of experience – he had commanded in twenty voyages to the Levant out of Boston – would be the best man for the difficult task of correlating the work of wheel and relieving tackles; standing on the grating with his eyes on wheel and sails and sea, he would shout his warnings down to the tiller ropes.

Peabody watched warily as the mizzen topsail was sheeted home. The *Delaware* reacted to the added pressure instantly. There was nothing light or graceful about her movements now. She was crashing from wave to wave like a rock down a hillside. Even with the wind well abaft the beam as it was she was leaning over to it, the white foam creaming along her lee side to join her boiling wake.

'Mr. Murray, go aloft, and keep your eye on the strange sail.'

'Aye aye, sir.'

Peabody looked aft again, and at one of the *Delaware's* extravagant plunges he once more caught that fleeting glimpse of the British topsail above the horizon. He did not need Murray's hail from above.

'Deck, there! If you please, sir, I think she's nearer.'

Peabody's expression did not change. The *Delaware* was showing all the canvas she could possibly carry, and he had done all he could for the moment. If the wind would only drop a little, or the sea moderate, she would walk away from that tub of a two decker. If not, it would only be by the aid of special measures that she would be able to escape, and those measures, which involved considerable sacrifice, he would not take until the necessity was proved.

'Why don't we fight her, Jos?' asked Jonathan – when the crew were at quarters his station was on the quarterdeck at the captain's orders, so that he was in his right place, but Josiah wondered sadly how long it would take the boy to learn the other details of naval life.

'You must take your hat off when you speak to me, Jonathan,' he said, 'and you call me "sir," and you take your hand out of your pocket, too,' he repeated patiently – he had said it all before.

'Sorry, Jos – I mean sir,' said Jonathan, lifting his hat with the hand from his pocket. 'But why don't we fight her?'

He jerked his thumb over the taffrail to indicate the pursuing enemy.

'Because she's twice as strong as we are,' said Josiah. 'And with this sea running she's three times as strong – we could never open out maindeck ports. And besides—'

Josiah checked himself. Anxious though he was for Jonathan to learn, this was not the time for a long disquisition on tactics and strategy. The two decker had twice the guns the *Delaware* had, and some of them heavier than the *Delaware's* heaviest. She had scantlings twice as thick, too – half the *Delaware's* shot would never pierce her sides. However heavy a sea was running she would always be able to work her upper deck guns as well as her quarterdeck and forecastle carronades, and her clumsy bulk made her a far steadier gun platform, too. From a tactical point of view it would be madness to fight her; and from a strategical point of view it would be worse than that. Here he was on the point of escaping into the open sea. Once let him get free, and he would exhaust England's strength far more effectively than by any battle with a ship of the line. He could harass her fleet of merchantmen so that twenty frigates each as big as the *Delaware* would be engaged in convoy duty. He could be here to-day and there to-morrow, threatening a dozen places at once. The brigs and the sloops with which England guarded her convoys from privateers would be useless against a powerful frigate. If anything could force England into peace it would be the sort of pressure the *Delaware* could apply. There was nothing whatever to be gained by an immediate encounter with a superior force – such an encounter could only end in his having to put back for repairs and submitting once more to blockade.

Josiah felt all this strongly. To think strategically was as much part of his ordinary processes as breathing was; but he was not a man of words – it was not easy for him to put these ideas into phrases which could be readily understood, and he knew it, although he was not conscious of the other disadvantage under which he laboured; that of being a man of wildcat fighting blood forced to play a cautious part. But at the same time some explanation must be made to Jonathan, so that the boy would appreciate what was going on. He fell back on a more homely argument.

'That fellow there,' he said, with his thumb repeating Jonathan's gesture, 'wants us to fight him. Nothing would please him better than to see us heave to and wait for him to come up. Look how he's cracking on to overtake us. D'ye see any sense in doing what your enemy wants you to do?'

'P'raps not,' said Jonathan.

Josiah was glad to get even this grudging agreement, for Jonathan's good opinion meant much to him. He had grown fond of the youngest brother of his, whom he had never known before. His first action on his promotion to captain and appointment to the *Delaware* had been to use his one bit of patronage in the boy's favour, and nominate him as his clerk; to his mind it was a way of repaying Providence for Uncle Josiah's kindnesses to himself, and buying clothes for the boy and introducing him to naval life had somehow endeared the boy to him.

The *Delaware* was leaping and lurching under his feet,

and he could hear Crane beside the wheel shouting instructions through the grating to the men at the relieving tackles. He looked up at the straining rigging but the Navy Yard at Brooklyn had done its work well. He looked aft. It was not on rare occasions now, but every time that the *Delaware* heaved her stern over a wave, that he could see that ominous little square of white on the horizon. The two decker was still overtaking them, despite the aid of the mizzen topsail and the shaken out reefs. He could set no more canvas – the *Delaware* would not bear another stitch without driving bodily under. He thought about knocking out the wedges in the steps of the masts to give the masts more play; sluggish sailors often benefited by that, but the *Delaware* would not. During the four weeks she was lying in the East River he had seen to it personally that everything had been done to give her every inch of speed. She was trimmed exactly right, he knew.

But she was low in the water. He had crammed her with all the stores she would hold before setting out in his determination to make her as independent as possible. There were six months stores on board. There were fifty tons of shot, and twenty of powder. There were fifteen tons of water – he could relieve the *Delaware* of that fifteen tons in a few minutes by merely starting the hogsheads and setting the hands to work at the pumps. On the spar deck there were eighteen carronades weighing a ton and a half each, and it would not be difficult with tackles to heave them over the side. But powder and shot, guns and drinking water were what gave the *Delaware* her usefulness in war. Without them he would be forced into port as surely as if he had been crippled in action.

'Mr. Hubbard!'

'Sir!'

'Rig the tackles. I want the longboat and cutter hove overside.'

'Aye aye, sir.'

Longboat and cutter were on chocks amidships. Whips had to be rove at the fore and main yardarms at either side, and Peabody watched four hands running out along the yards to do so, bending to their work perched fifty feet up above the tormented sea. If any man of them lost his hold, that man was dead as surely as if he had been shot – the *Delaware* would not stop to pick him up even if he survived the fall into the icy sea. But the lines were passed without accident, and fifty men tailed on to them under the direction of Mr. Rodgers, the boatswain. Tackles and boats were his particular province; even when boats were being thrown away it was his duty to attend to the matter at the First Lieutenant's orders. At the last moment there was a hitch – young Midshipman Wallingford came running aft to his captain.

'What about the hogs, sir?' he asked breathlessly. 'And the chickens? Are they to go overside, too?'

'I'll give Mr. Rodgers one minute to get them out,' said Peabody harshly.

Hogs and chickens lived in the longboat and cutter; they were the only source of fresh meat on board, and important in consequence. Peabody was annoyed with himself for having forgotten about them, with having let his head get full of advanced warlike ideas to the exclusion of matters like hogs and chickens. He watched the livestock being herded aft to where a temporary pen was hurriedly designed among the spare spars. The longboat rose, cradled in its slings, and hung half a dozen feet above the deck. Then the men began to heave in on the leeside tackles, and let go on the weather side, and the longboat slowly swung towards the leeside bulwarks. The *Delaware* felt the very considerable transference of weight, listing in a manner which was a trifle dangerous in that gale. But the business was ticklish enough, for she still rolled and plunged, and the vast deadweight of the longboat swung about madly as far as the four suspensory ropes allowed. Peabody walked slowly forward; he had no intention of interfering with Rodgers' execution of his task – Rodgers' technical knowledge probably matched his own – but instinct drew him there.

Rodgers looked warily to windward, and studied the send of the sea, watching for his moment.

'Heave!' he shouted to the leeside men.

The longboat went out with a run, hanging from the lee

yardarms exclusively while the *Delaware* listed more sharply still.

'Let go,' shouted Rodgers to the men at the lee main yard-arm tackles. When they were let go the boat would hang vertically down in the slings until she slid down out of them, and the men obeyed promptly enough. But the line ran only for a second in the sheaves and then jammed. The longboat hung at too small an angle to slide out of the slings, and remained dangling from the yardarms, imperilling the very life of the ship.

'God damn the thing to hell,' said Rodgers.

A couple of hands sprang into the rigging with the idea of getting out to the block and clearing it.

'Let go, there, you men!' roared Peabody suddenly at the men holding the lee fore yardarm line. With a start of surprise they did so. The other end of the boat fell; she tipped up more and more, and then fell from the slings into the sea while the *Delaware* righted herself. Rodgers had been caught off his guard by the jammed line. He had been intending all along to drop the longboat stern first, and did not possess the flexibility of mind to reverse his plans instantly when the hitch came.

'Let's see that line!' he said irritably. 'Who made this long splice? God damn it, any soldier could make a better long splice than this. I'll find out if it takes me a month o' Sundays.'

'Get the cutter overside, Mr. Rodgers,' interrupted Peabody.

He walked aft again; the incident had made little impression on him save to confirm to him his already formed estimate of Rodgers' capacity. The gig which had been nested in the cutter was swayed out and deposited on the chocks of the longboat, and the cutter next rose in its slings from the *Delaware's* deck, traversed slowly across to leeward, and then fell into the sea. Peabody watched it as it went astern, broken backed and full of water, white among the grey of the waves, a depressing sight, and he turned back again to study the *Delaware's* behaviour now that she was relieved of six tons of deadweight. Peabody was not of the type to feel easy optimism. He approached the problem ready to see no appreciable difference, and yet, despite this discounting, he was forced to admit that the *Delaware* was moving a tiny bit more easily – the tiniest, tiniest bit. In that rough water it would give the *Delaware* no added speed, but it was the most he could do to ease her in her labours and still retain her efficiency. The deadweight had been taken from the point where it had most effect on the ship's behaviour – from the upper deck and forward. He glanced astern, and saw the fateful topsail on the horizon again.

The wind was still howling round his ears – it certainly ought to moderate soon, now that the glass had begun to move upward. But there was no sign of it at present. On the contrary – or was he mistaken – those topmasts were whipping badly. He was conscious as he stood that the wind had increased, and he felt in his bones that it was going to increase further. It was natural in a storm like this – he had seen the phenomenon a hundred times. The dying flurries of a storm were often more intense than anything that had preceded it. He felt a sudden wave of bitterness surge up within him. If he had to shorten sail the two decker would come romping up to him, and the voyage of the *Delaware* would come to an end. This was his first command, and he had been at sea less than twenty-four hours. The flurry of the gale might last no more than half an hour, and then the wind might die away to a gentle breeze, but that half hour would be enough to do his business for him. God – he was on the point of stupid blasphemy when he mastered himself sternly.

A big grey wave hit the *Delaware* a shuddering blow, and she lurched uncertainly as the water creamed over the spar deck. The high-pitched note of the wind in the rigging screamed a warning to him, and Hubbard was looking round at him anxiously for orders.

'Get the mizzen tops'l in, Mr. Hubbard,' said Peabody. 'And the jib.'

A dismasted ship would be of less use than a ship still under control, even if a two-decker were overhauling her. The hands raced aloft, shuffling along the footropes of the mizzen topsail yard, and bending forward over the yard to wrestle with the obstinate canvas. The wind shrieked down at them all the harder – it was in the very nick of time that they had shortened sail, and there was a grim satisfaction in that. The men poured down the shrouds again, and one of them after he had leaped to the deck paused for a moment to examine his right forefinger. The nail had been torn almost completely off, and was hanging by a shred from the bloody fingertip – some sudden jerk of the mad canvas aloft had done that for him. He took the dangling nail between his teeth and jerked it off, spat out the nail, and shook the blood from his hand and then ran forward after his fellows without a tremor. The crew was tough enough, thought Peabody grimly.

Murray was beside him, descended from his chilly post aloft.

'She's coming down on us fast, sir,' he said. He had a notable tendency to gesticulate with his hands when he spoke.

Hubbard was at his captain's other shoulder now, tall and saturnine, a master of his profession, and yet in this unhappy moment feeling the need for company and conversation.

'Those damned two deckers,' he said. 'They need a gale of wind to move 'em, and that one has it. Standing rigging like chain cable, sir, and canvas as thick as this pea-jacket of mine.'

The two of them looked sidelong at their captain, in need of reassurance. Hubbard was older than Peabody, Murray hardly younger, and yet he felt paternal towards them.

'D'you think he went through Plum Gut, sir?' asked Murray.

'No doubt about it,' said Hubbard, but Murray still looked to his captain for confirmation.

'Yes,' said Peabody.

The implications were manifold. A captain who had the nerve to take a two decker through Plum Gut had nerve enough for anything else whatever, and he had brains as well, and the ability to use them.

'They've had two years to learn in,' said Hubbard, his thin lips twisted into a bitter smile. For two years British ships had been studying American waters at first hand.

The wind shrieked down upon them with renewed force. The *Delaware* was labouring frightfully in the waves; even on deck, and despite the noise of the wind, they could hear the groans of the woodwork as she writhed in their grip.

'If you were down below, sir,' said Murray, 'and *he* wasn't behind us, I'd send down to you for permission to heave-to, sir.'

'And I'd give it,' said Peabody. He could smile at that, just as he could always smile in the midst of a struggle.

'Can we lighten the ship any more, sir?' asked Hubbard, with the extreme deference necessary at a moment when he might be suspected of offering advice to his captain.

'No,' said Peabody. Pitching the spar-deck carronades overside might ease her a little, but would give her no increase in speed in this rough water – only in smooth water with a faint wind would decrease in draft benefit them there, and he had already flung overboard the only weights which were not essential to the *Delaware's* efficiency as a fighting force. The nod which Hubbard gave indicated his argument with Peabody's unvoiced argument, and as if with one mind they turned to look back at the two decker. Something more than her topsails were in sight now – as the *Delaware* rose on a wave they could catch a glimpse of her black hull lifting menacingly above the horizon.

'She'll be within gunshot soon,' said Murray with despair in his voice, and Peabody looked at him searchingly. He wanted no cowards in his ship, nor men who would not fight a losing battle to the end. Yet Murray had come to him with the Commodore's enthusiastic recommendation, as the man who, in command of a gunboat flotilla in the Rappahannock had beaten off the boats of the British fleet in the Chesapeake.

'Yes,' said Peabody. 'And I want these two twelve pounders cleared for action. Rig double tackles on them, Mr. Murray, if you please, so that they won't come adrift.'

'Aye aye, sir,' said Murray. Peabody could see the change in him now that he had something to do – so that was the kind of man he was. Peabody had no definite labels for human beings, and no vocabulary with which to express his thoughts about them, but he could estimate a character pretty closely.

The *Delaware's* spar deck carried eighteen thirty-two pounder carronades, nine a side, but forward and aft at the end of each row was mounted a long twelve pounder. The Commodore at the Navy Yard had argued with Peabody about those long guns, pointing out how carronades instead would give the ship an additional forty pounds of broadside, but Peabody had been sure of what he wanted. On this raiding voyage he would either be running away or pursuing, and he wanted long guns on her upper deck to aid him in either of those tasks. He had even had the aftermost and foremost ports enlarged so as to allow these long guns to be trained fully round.

'By George, sir!' said Hubbard suddenly, as he watched the work. 'Do you remember what the Commodore said about these guns? You were right, sir. You were right.'

Peabody did not need Hubbard's approval; he needed no approval save his own.

Murray knew his business. He brought up a double crew – fourteen men – to each of the stern chasers. Cautious, they slacked away the breachings until the gun muzzles were free from the lintels of the ports, and even so, with the mad leaping of the *Delaware*, they careered up and down in the inch or two of slack in the breachings in a fashion which boded ill if they should take charge. Ten men tailed on to the tackles as the breachings were slacked away, keeping the guns steady against the breachings. As the ports were opened showers of spray came in through them, washing over the deck ankle deep. The gun captains took out the tompions, and tested with the rammers to see that the guns were loaded. One of them watched the spray bursting over the gun and shook his head. Despite its tarpaulin cover, the flintlock mechanism could not be expected to work in those conditions, at least, not until the gun was thoroughly hot with use. The powder boys sped forward and came running aft again each with a long coil of slow match in a tub, the ends smouldering and spluttering.

'Run 'em up, boys!' said Murray, and the men threw their weight on the tackles and ran the guns out.

'Ready to open fire, sir!' said Murray, lifting his hat to his captain.

'She's beyond cannon shot yet,' replied Peabody, looking over the grey-flecked sea, with the wind howling round his ears. The two decker was clearly in sight now, all the same, leaping and plunging over the mad sea. 'Mr. Hubbard, hoist the colours, if you please.'

The flag went up to the peak and streamed forward in the wind, its eighteen stripes rippling wildly. There had been a discussion about that, too, with the Commodore; an Act of Congress had given the flag fifteen stars and stripes, and yet – as Peabody had seen with his own eyes – the flag that flew over the Hall of Congress bore no more than thirteen, while the Commodore had maintained that there should be a star and a stripe for every state in the union, as Congress had also laid down. It was the Commodore who had decided upon eighteen stripes and stars in the end – Peabody would have preferred the fifteen under which he had sailed into Tripoli harbour. He wondered if the two decker would ever be able to get near enough to count them for herself.

'You can try a shot now, Mr. Murray,' said Peabody.

The gun captains already had their guns elevated to the last degree. Each snatched a priming quill from a powder boy, and thrust it in the vent of his gun. They took their matches in their hands, and peered once more along the sights. Then they stood back, watching the ship's motion, and each chose the same moment for firing. They waved their hands at the men at the train tackles to release their grip, and plunged the lighted matches into the quills. One gun hung fire for a moment, the quill sizzling and spluttering, and only exploded after the other gun had boomed out and recoiled to the limit of the breachings. The wind whirled the smoke forward in a flash, and that was all. There was nothing else to be seen; the sea was far too rough for the splash of a twelve-pounder ball to be seen at extreme range. The two decker came plunging along after them unhurt, as far as could be told, the spray still flying from her bluff bows.

The hands had crept aft to see the sport, and a sort of groan of disappointment went up from them, even though they were all experienced men who ought to have known better than to expect anything.

'Try again, Mr. Murray,' said Peabody – the guns were already being wiped and the powder charges rammed in.

He climbed up on the bulwark close behind the starboard, balancing with his hand on the mizzen rigging. The gun went off with a bang, while Peabody's keen eyes searched the line of flight. There it was! Like a momentary pencil mark – come and gone in a flash – upon the seascape, he could see the ball rise to the top of its trajectory, and drop again to the sea, where a minute white spot marked its fall.

'Half a mile short,' called Peabody. 'But the aim was good. Try again.'

The captain of the other gun had badly misjudged the roll of the ship – his shot plunged into the side of a wave not two cables' lengths away, in plain sight of everyone. Impatiently Murray thrust him on one side, and bent over the breach of the gun himself. Peabody watched the firing from his point of vantage; he was able to mark the fall of about half the shot fired, and nothing went nearer than a hundred yards from the target, as far as he could see, and he expected little else on that heaving sea, and with that gale blowing. But the firing was warming up the guns, so that they would soon be shooting with more power and so that the lock mechanisms would soon begin to function – no one could be expected to judge the roll of the ship accurately when firing with a match, so that at least two seconds elapsed between the intention to fire and the explosion.

The range was down to a mile – to less than that. Peabody suddenly saw the two decker's maintopsail emerge beside her foretopsail, and the mizzen beside that. Her bluff bows lengthened and her bowsprit showed in profile as she turned. She was yawing to present her broadside to the *Delaware* – Peabody could see her yellow streak and her checkered side as she rolled madly in the trough of the sea. Next came a brief wave of smoke, blown instantly to nothing by the gale, and next came – nothing at all. A hoot of derision went up from the watching sailors at Peabody's back.

'Missed! Clean missed!' said somebody, dancing with joy. 'A whole broadside, and we didn't see where a single shot fell!'

Probably the two decker had fired the long guns on her upper gun deck – sixteen or seventeen, if she were the seventy-four Peabody estimated her to be. To him there was nothing surprising about the broadside missing, considering the difficulties under which it was discharged. The *Delaware* had fired a dozen shots so far, under better conditions, and not one had gone near the target – the men did not stop to think about that.

The two decker had come before the wind again, and was plunging after them, her bowsprit pointed straight at the *Delaware.* But she had lost a good half mile by yawing to fire her broadside; Peabody doubted if her captain would waste valuable distance again in that fashion. Most probably he would reserve his fire until the two ships were yardarm to yardarm, and when that moment would come depended on the wind. He turned his attention once more to scanning first the sky and then the *Delaware's* behaviour under her storm canvas. He wanted most desperately for the wind to moderate, or to back, or to veer, for it to do anything rather than blow as it was doing, straight from the two decker to him. Perhaps his life, certainly the success of his voyage; possibly the good opinion of his brother captains, and certainly the good opinion of the American public, depended on that wind. The *Columbian Centinel* would have some scathing remarks in its columns if the *Delaware* were captured, even by a ship of the line – not that he cared, save for the depressing effect on the people. His whole power to do anything at all in this war depended on the wind; it was the wind which would settle whether he was to range the Atlantic a free man or rot as a prisoner, and the wind was still blowing its hardest. Peabody had the feeling that it was as well that it was the wind upon which all this depended. If it were some human agency he might be inclined to fret and chafe, possibly even to swear and blaspheme, but as it was he could await the decision of Providence calmly.

For some time he had been subconsciously noting the fall of the shot as the stern chasers banged away, and now suddenly his attention was called to the business with a jerk. The brief vision of the flying ball coincided with the two decker a mile astern, and terminated there.

'Good shot, Mr. Murray!' he called. 'You hit her fair!'

Murray turned a smiling face back to him, unconscious that the fumes from the vent of the gun had stained his face as black as a negro's. One of the hands was leaping about on the quarterdeck shaking his fists above his head. Peabody's hope that the hit might goad the two decker into yawing again to use her broadside proved ill-founded; the two decker held on her course inexorably, driven by the gale. In half an hour she had gained a quarter of a mile, and in an hour she was no more than half a mile astern. Peabody sent the crew by watches to have their dinners – he did not want the men to have empty stomachs while they fought, although he himself felt not the slightest need for food. He walked round the spar deck to see that every carronade was properly manned. With no chance of employing the main-deck guns he could have fifteen men at every carronade, quite enough to ensure that no carronade would get loose during the battle. And at every carronade there was a good gunlayer – most of them had learned their duty in the British Fleet – and still Hubbard had a hundred men under his orders to attend to the working of the ship.

It was a comforting sensation to have an ample crew, with every man an able seaman, and even the ship's boys seventeen years old and upward; there had been no difficulty whatever in enlisting a crew in New York when the *Delaware* commissioned. And yet the captain of the two decker, if he knew his business, would be able to nullify all these arrangements at his will. He could lie three cables' lengths from the *Delaware*, beyond the effective range of her carronades, and pound her to pieces with the long guns on his upper deck. Probably that English captain knew his business, too – he had proved it by bringing his big ship through Plum Gut in the night and guessing the *Delaware's* future course. Peabody allowed the hatred he felt for his implacable foe to well up freely within him.

He went back to where the stern chasers were still banging away. 'We've hit her eight times, sir,' said Murray, in a sort of ecstasy. Powder smoke and the din of the guns were like drink to him.

'Aim high and try to wing him,' said Peabody.

'Aye aye, sir,' said Murray, and then, respectfully, 'I've been trying to, sir.'

He bent to squint along the gun again, gave a couple of twirls to the elevating screw, and then stood aside and jerked the lanyard. The gun roared out and recoiled; it was so hot now that it leaped in its carriage at the discharge.

'That went close,' said Peabody. 'Try again.'

The sponge on its flexible handle was thrust up the gun, and the water with which it was soaked hissed against the hot metal. Someone whipped a paper cartridge of powder from out of the bucket which guarded it from spray, ripped it open and pushed it into the muzzle. The rammer thrust it further in, and then the big felt wad was thrust in in its turn, the rammer packing the charge hard up into the breach; slovenly packing might diminish the power of the shot by as much as a quarter. Then the ball went rolling down on top of the charge, and another wad was rammed down upon it to hold everything secure. Murray stood aside with the lanyard in his hand, watching the motion of the ship. Suddenly he jerked the lanyard and the gun came leaping back upon its breachings while the wind whisked the smoke round the gun-crew's faces for a second before heaving it forward.

Peabody looked for the flight of the ball, but this time he missed it. And then, as he stared, he saw the two decker's foretopsail suddenly shut down upon itself. From a clear cut oblong it changed into a vague strip cock-eyed across the foremast and shaking in the wind. Someone started to cheer, and the cheering spread along the deck, but it had not reached its full volume before the two decker, deprived of the balancing pressure of her foretopsail, came round abruptly into the wind.

'That's her foretopsail tie gone, sir,' said Hubbard, standing at his side. His lean face with its high arched nose showed more animation than usual.

'More likely the slings,' said Peabody. He had whipped his glass to his eye, and through it he saw the fore rigging of the two decker black with men struggling with the wreckage. 'That was a good shot, Mr. Murray.'

But Murray did not hear; he was already sighting his gun again, absorbed in the business of doing as much damage as possible. As Peabody put his glass to his eye again he saw the two decker's broadside momentarily shrouded in smoke, and directly afterwards he was conscious of a tremendous crash beside him. A shot from the two decker had smashed a hole in the bulwark and ploughed its way along the quarterdeck; splinters hummed round him and two men serving the other stern chaser lay mangled in pools of blood. There were other men staring stupidly at wounds inflicted by the splinters, and when he looked forward he saw other men lying dead on the deck, while two severed mainmast shrouds on the starboard side showed where the ball had found its way out of the ship again.

'Get those shrouds spliced and set up again, Mr. Hubbard,' said Peabody.

Crippled the two decker might be, but she was determined on inflicting the utmost possible damage before her antagonist escaped out of range. The two stern chasers roared out their defiance; the surgeon's crew were already carrying the wounded below in their canvas chairs and dragging the dead out of the way. Again the two decker was wreathed in smoke, and Peabody found time to feel a momentary misgiving lest this broadside should do more damage than merely parting a couple of shrouds. But even as the thought came into his head he saw two jets of water rise from a wave top a cable's length astern – the danger was past, and although two guns had been well pointed they had not been given sufficient elevation.

'She's out of range, sir,' said Murray, turning back to him from his gun.

'Yes, Mr. Murray, thanks to you,' said Peabody.

Murray showed a gleam of white teeth in his smoke-blackened face.

'Thank you, sir,' he said.

Peabody remembered Stephen Decatur's words of thanks to him when they met, sword in hand, on the deck of the captured *Khaid-ed-Din* in Tripoli harbour, and how he himself had stood flushed and tongue-tied and unable to reply.

'I'll remember this in my report to the Commodore,' said Peabody. 'Now get those guns secured.'

He realised now that he and everyone else on the quarter-deck were soaked to the skin by the spray which had come in through the gunports, and he was shuddering with cold and lack of exercise. His heavy pea-jacket was wet as a soaked sponge and hung like lead from his shoulders. Looking through his glass he could see men still hard at work on the two decker's foretopsail yard; they looked like ants on a twig. It would be fully ten minutes before the two decker got before the wind again; in ten minutes they would be a mile farther away; to regain that mile would take the two decker at least two hours, if not more; and in less than four hours it would be dark. They were almost safe – as safe as any United States ship could be on a sea whose length and breadth was searched and scanned by the British fleet.

Hubbard had the hands at the braces trimming the sails, and Peabody looked sharply up at the commission pennant fluttering from the maintopmast. The wind had backed noticeably, and, just as important, it was moderating.

'Set the mizzen tops'l and jib again, Mr. Hubbard,' said Peabody.

'Aye aye, sir.'

Hubbard stood beside his captain with his eyes on the men casting off the gaskets and a wry smile on his long face.

'We can just walk away from that old tub now, sir,' he said. 'It would ha' saved us a bit of trouble if the wind had made up its mind sooner.'

Peabody stared at him. The dead men were lying by the spars, forward; their lives would have been saved, undoubtedly, but apart from that – Providence helps those who help themselves. Peabody's philosophy was such – illogical though he would have admitted it to be if he had happened to analyse his feelings – that to him it was the most natural thing in the world for the wind to shift and moderate after his own efforts had made the change almost unnecessary. To grumble at the whims of uncontrolled natural forces – at the dictates of Providence – was a little absurd to him, like a heathen beating his god for not responding to prayer. He was growing a little set in his ways of thought.

CHAPTER THREE

The *Delaware* had crossed the blue water of the Gulf Stream. She had caught the north-east trades by now, and was thrashing along with the wind over her port quarter and with all sail set, driving so hard that Mr. Hubbard was keeping an eye on the studding sails lest there should be a trifle too much strain on the booms. The blue water – so blue that it might have been a painted surface – turned to a dazzling white as the *Delaware* broke through it, and in the waves thrown off from her sharp bow a dozen dolphins tumbled and somersaulted.

The lookouts were at their dizzy posts at the fore and main topgallant mastheads, swinging in vast circles against the blue sky as the *Delaware* soared superbly over the waves. They were on duty; so were Mr. Hubbard and Midshipman Quincy, walking the deck with their telescopes under their arms, and so were the men at the wheel. So were the two carpenter's mates at work on the deck planking aft by the taffrail – there was a bloodstain there which no amount of scrubbing during the past few days had been able to remove, and by Mr. Hubbard's orders a section of planking was being replaced. Mr. Hubbard would not on any account have bloodstains marring the spotless white of his decks.

Otherwise, in this dog watch, the ship's company was free. Forward the deck was covered with little groups of men, chattering, sewing their clothes, or merely lounging in idleness; aft the ship's officers were taking air and exercise, lieutenants, the master, the surgeon and his mate, walking solemnly up and down their little bits of deck, and turning inwards towards each other at each end of their beats without a break in their conversation, while up in the mizzen rigging half a dozen midshipmen were valorously emulating the athletic feats of young master's mate Hayward who was leading a game of follow-my-leader.

On a day like this all troubles could be forgotten. The memory of the bitter cold of the blizzard in which they had started had vanished as completely as the ice which had festooned the ship, and already the memory of the dead whom they had left behind them was beginning to fade along with it. The sun was warm and not too warm; the ship had her studding sails set slow and aloft; there were sparkling rainbows in the spray tossed from the bows, and sail drill and gun drill had ceased for the day. There was nothing more that a sailor's heart could desire.

Peabody came on deck, a cigar all ready for smoking between his teeth, and the officers herded away respectfully from his side of the deck. He lit his cigar from the smouldering bit of punk which during the dog watches was left in a tub aft for the convenience of the officers, and inhaled deeply as he glanced round the ship as every captain since the world began has done on his arrival on deck. All sail set and drawing well – the cut of that main course was a perfect masterpiece. She must be going all of the eleven knots which he had noted on the traverse board on his way on deck. And tobacco was good on a sunny evening like this – he drew again deeply on his cigar. It was several hours since he last smoked, for Peabody had a strict rule against smoking below deck, and he had been confined below for several hours dealing with the ship's papers. Most of what he had been doing was the clerk's work, but Peabody was fully conscious of his own competence to deal with it, and guiltily conscious of the clerk's inability. And he had not wanted to bother the boy; he looked sharply across the deck and saw him leaning, gloomy and solitary, against the taffrail with his back to all the merriment and lightheartedness of the ship.

That was a pity. Peabody would have preferred to see

Jonathan skylarking up in the rigging along with the midshipmen, and he sighed a little. The boy was a little too old to adapt himself readily to a life at sea. Peabody blamed himself for not having obtained his captaincy earlier so that he could have rescued the boy from the plough – from his mother and father – a little younger, before he got so set in his gloomy habits, when it would have been easy to initiate him into the pleasant delights of algebra and spherical trigonometry and gradually make him into a midshipman, a lieutenant, and in the end a captain. He himself was profoundly grateful to Providence for what he had received. He was captain of this superb ship. He had work to do which he felt competent to perform – that was a most gratifying feeling. And he was already wealthy. As captain he was paid the enormous salary of one hundred dollars a month – a stupendous amount. The Connecticut farm did not produce one hundred dollars a year in real money; the terrible father who had beaten him as a child had never in his whole life held in his hands the sum which his son received monthly. There was a grim, unpleasing pleasure in the thought.

But he should have reached this eminence five years ago, for Jonathan's sake, saving his five years of frightening tyranny, five years of a maudlin mother's insane antics. There was every excuse in the world for the boy; but tobacco did not taste so good now. He walked across the deck to pitch his half-smoked cigar overboard to leeward, and Hubbard took off his hat to his captain with the formal courtesy which characterised him – the formality of the Navy combined with the graces of the South.

Here came the marine band, all six of them marching stiffly behind their sergeant, two side drums and four fifes, the sergeant saluting captain and quarterdeck with a single gesture. He swung his brass-mounted cane, and the drums gave their triple roll before beginning their exhilarating rhythm while the fifes squeaked bravely away at 'Yankee Doodle.' Up and down, up and down, marched the marines; the fifers in their tall stocks were purple in the face with the effort of blowing. It was all very gay and lighthearted; even Peabody caught the infection. To be at sea again, to have broken the close blockade, was stimulating and exhilarating. The prospect of action cheered everyone on board. The sail drill and the gun drill during those tedious weeks in the East River had been dull and pointless, but now there was a chance of putting them to use. And every man on board, except for Jonathan Peabody and some of the midshipmen, was an experienced sailor, with the sea in his blood. The joys of home, of life in port, were not exaggerated, but were liable to cause surfeit, and some of the men on board had not been to sea for two years now. They felt as if they were free of chains.

On the starboard beam the sun was setting in a glory of red. Three bars of cloud, as straight as if drawn by parallel rulers, hung over the western horizon above the dying sun; typical trade wind clouds bearing the promise of unchanged weather, thought Peabody, noting them. He watched the red disc sink slowly into the sea while the light faded from the sky – in the east it was already dark. The young moon was just in sight in the western sky now that its light was not submerged in that of the sun.

'Deck there!' from the maintopgallant masthead. A pause.

'What is it?' hailed Hubbard.

'I thought I saw a sail. Yes, there she is, on the starboard bow, sir! Right to leeward, sir!'

All Peabody's instincts exploded into action. He did not stop to calculate that with night coming down so fast every second was of value, and he did not consciously allow for the waste of time if a junior had to report to him; his reactions were quicker than his thoughts. He snatched the glass and threw himself into the main rigging. Up the ratlines he went, up the futtock shrouds back downwards without pausing for breath, up to the maintopmast crosstrees, hand over hand to the topgallant masthead. He was hard and lean despite his heavy shoulders, and his pumping heart and quickened respiration did nothing to unsteady him.

Up at this height there was perceptibly more light than on deck. Eastward all was black, with a star or two beginning to show, but to the westward the sky still showed a gleam of red.

The awed lookout on his narrow perch pointed over the starboard bow, momentarily too impressed by the sudden appearance of his captain to speak. Peabody saw what he was pointing to. At the very edge of the colour in the sky, silhouetted sharply in black against the red, were two minute geometrical shapes close together. Peabody fixed them in his glass, swinging the instrument in accordance with the roll of the ship, but in that light the glass was not of any help to his own keen eyesight. The upper sails of a brig, royals and topgallants, decided Peabody, standing to the north close hauled on the opposite tack to the *Delaware.*

'Has she changed course since you saw her?' he demanded of the lookout.

'No, sir, not as far as I can tell.'

Peabody glanced back over his shoulder again; the eastward sky was quite black. The *Delaware's* upper sails, viewed from the brig, would not stand out in the fashion hers did, and there was not enough light from the westward to illuminate them, either. The chances were that the brig had not seen her, and moreover if she had she would probably have put up her helm and hurried over the horizon as a precautionary measure. His eyes sought her again unavailingly, for the red patch had dwindled almost to nothing and the brig had disappeared into the darkness.

'Mr. Hubbard!' he bellowed down to the deck.

'Sir!'

'Put the helm up. Bring her round on the other tack.'

'Aye aye, sir.'

Far below him he could hear the orders called, and he could just hear the bustle of the men hurrying to the braces. The *Delaware* rose momentarily to an even keel beneath him, and then heeled again. The darkness round him was filled with the creaking of ropes as the yards came round. As he looked forward he saw the starboard foretopmast studding sail blot out the last of the red patch of sky. The foretopsail followed round.

'Keep her at that!' he roared.

'Aye aye, sir!'

Now the *Delaware* had the wind nearly abeam, while the

brig to leeward had been close hauled. The courses of the two ships were sharply convergent. Two hours, two hours and a half, perhaps, before they met – always provided, that is, that the brig did not alter course. But although Peabody strained his eyes peering into the night he could see nothing of her at all. He was about to descend, when he remembered the good services of the lookout.

'A tot of rum for you to-morrow,' he said.

'Thank'ee, sir. Please, sir—'

'Well?'

'Beg your pardon, sir, but could you make it 'baccy? A plug o' chawing, sir—'

'Yes. What's your name?'

'Gaines, sir.'

A seaman who preferred tobacco to rum was quite a rarity. Perhaps he had been through the same desperate struggle that Peabody had, when every nerve in his body shrieked for the drink he denied it. Peabody had won his victory over the monster as a lieutenant of twenty, after he realised that in the wardroom mess his behaviour, which he had thought so clever, was like that of his mother when she was wearing her stupid grin. There had been three months of torment, three years of temptation. Now even the temptation was gone, and Peabody could trust himself to have one drink, two drinks, when the occasion demanded, but perhaps this man Gaines was still in the period of temptation. He looked over the starboard sky, somehow oddly moved, and then he realised that he was in danger of having a favourite on board, which would not do at all. He grunted something inarticulate, swung himself into the rigging, and began his slow descent. Murray was officer of the watch now, but Hubbard was still on deck with him awaiting his captain.

'Send the hands to quarters, Mr. Murray, and clear for action.'

The drums which had beaten so merry a tune an hour ago now went roaring through the ship calling the men to quarters. The *Delaware* was filled with the clatter and bustle of it all as the men rushed to begin their allotted tasks, and the weeks of drill during those grim days in the East River were justified now as even in the darkness the men did their work without confusion. The marines climbed to the tops with elephantine clumsiness; the powder boys came running to the guns with their buckets of cartridges. Down below the bulkheads were coming down, the guns were being cast loose, the sand was being scattered over the deck. Rodgers the boatswain formed up his two fire-fighting parties with the head pumps fore and aft and the canvas hoses coiled in the scuppers. Two boys hurried along the deck with their arms full of lanterns, hanging them on the giant lines which Rodgers had set up.

'I don't want a light in the ship until I give the word.'

'Very good, sir.'

The main-deck guns were being run out with a threatening rumble – the distant thunder of the approaching storm – while on the spar deck the crews of the carronades adjusted their pieces for elevation and primed the vents. The *Delaware* was singing through the sea; running thus, two points free, was perhaps her best point of sailing, and there was most decidedly a chance that she would pass ahead of the quarry.

'Get the stuns'l in, Mr. Hubbard.'

'Aye aye, sir.'

There was not much chance of danger. A brig-rigged vessel even if she were a man-of-war, was bound to be smaller than a big frigate like the *Delaware*; if she were part of a convoy the escort would have been to windward of her and in plain sight. She must be sailing alone, and in that case she might be perhaps an American privateer or one of those footy little British Post Office packets. Peabody called up before his mind's eye the memory of those topsails silhouetted against the sky. Yes. The chances were that she was a Post Office packet, and in that case she must be overwhelmed before she could throw her mail bags overside. Yet at the same time he must be quite certain that she was not an American privateer; it would be disastrous if she were and he fired into her.

Peabody remembered the British naval officers whom he had encountered often enough in the cafés of Valetta. Many of them spoke in a curious throaty manner which he had been given to understand was looked upon nowadays as the newest fashion in England, with the vowels broadened and the consonants disregarded. He thought for a moment of Hubbard, but Hubbard's South Carolinian speech had nothing British about it. He turned upon Jonathan.

'Go and find O'Brien for me. Master's mate – he'll be at the headsail sheets.'

It was five long minutes before O'Brien came looming up on the quarterdeck; it was a pity that Jonathan had not yet familiarised himself with every part of the ship and every man on board.

'O'Brien, sir. Come to report.'

O'Brien's voice had not lost the Irish in it, even though it was twenty years since he had sailed from Cork.

'Stay by me. I want you to hail for me when the time comes.'

The night was clear although dark; the crescent moon, right down on the horizon, contributed almost no light, but the stars were bright. A ship could be seen at a couple of miles, certainly.

'Cover that binnacle light,' said Peabody.

The *Delaware* surged along through the darkness; it was fortunate that he had been able to spare the studding sails, because the reduction in speed would make a considerable difference to the visibility of her bow wave. There came a low hail from the foretop – the sergeant of marines there must be an intelligent man as well as having keen eyes.

'Deck, there! She's in sight, sir. On the larboard bow.'

Peabody put down his night glass – the thing was not of much use. There she was, most certainly, a black outline faintly showing against the slightly lighter surface of the sea, holding the same course as when he had seen her last, and the two vessels were closing fast. In five minutes – but she was wearing round on the instant.

'Loose the stuns'ls, Mr. Hubbard, if you please. Put your helm up a point, quartermaster.'

Peabody had caught sight of the first movement of the brig's sails as she wore. The fact that her foretopsail came round before the mainsails proved that she had a small crew and was no man-of-war, and it also gave the *Delaware* two full minutes in which to cut the corner. She was tearing down upon the brig now.

'Pass the word to the starboard guns to stand by.'

A faint hail came from the brig.

'Ship ahoy! What ship's that?'

Peabody nudged O'Brien, but there was no need. The Irishman's tongue was ready enough.

'His Britannic Majesty's frigate *Calypso*. Heave to!'

There was a moment delay, while the *Delaware* still fore reached upon the brig. If the chase were American, she would open fire.

'Heave to, and wait for my boat!' hailed O'Brien.

These seconds were precious. There was no chance of escape for the brig now; in a few more seconds they could overwhelm her perhaps without firing a shot. The brig had not opened fire, and it was clear she was not American. Peabody was certain, as it was, that she was a Post Office packet; he recognised the cut of those sails. But at any second she would recognise in her turn the *Delaware* for what she was, by her clipper bows and raking masts and spar deck. There were no other ships at sea like the big American frigates. Peabody nudged O'Brien again.

'Heave to, damn your eyes!' yelled O'Brien into the speaking trumpet.

Five more seconds elapsed before the answer came – four bright orange flashes from the brig's side. A ball sang over Peabody's head, and at the same time there was a crash below as another struck home.

'Mr. Murray!' shouted Peabody, and the words had hardly left his lips before the *Delaware's* broadside replied – a little ragged, but just passable. The enormous orange flames from the quarterdeck carronades left Peabody momentarily blinded. All was dark around him and he could see nothing. But overside he could hear the results of what he had done – a clatter of falling blocks and a man shrieking in agony. He had not wanted to do this; he had wanted to overwhelm the brig without effusion of blood, but once he had opened fire it was necessary to crush her before the mails could be thrown overboard.

He blinked his eyes until he could see again. The brig had come up into the wind a helpless wreck, braces and halliards shot away; the smashing broadside had almost torn her to pieces. He heard the *Delaware's* guns rumble loudly as they were run out again.

'Back the mizzen tops'l, Mr Hubbard, if you please. Brig ahoy! Have you struck?'

'Yes, God rot you,' said a voice in the darkness.

'Take the quarter boat and take possession, O'Brien. Send the captain over to me.'

'Aye aye, sir.'

The wounded man on board the brig had stopped screaming as the quarterboat dropped into the water. Peabody took a restless turn or two about the deck – the two vessels were close enough together by now for him to hear voices on board the brig, and the sound of the oars being laid down in the boat as she went alongside.

'Mr. Hubbard, take charge. I want a boatswain's chair to hoist the brig's captain in.'

Lights gleamed at the entry port, the sound of oars proclaimed the return of the quarterboat, and the tackles squealed as the brig's captain was hoisted on board. Someone led him aft to where Peabody stood in the faint light of the uncovered binnacle; he was short and square and stocky, with a stiff rheumatic gait. Peabody took off his hat. 'Your servant, sir.'

Truxtun in the *Constellation* had drilled his young officers in the manners expected of them, and Peabody's graces dated from that time. The British captain touched his hat in the new manner of the British service.

'Perhaps you would be so good as to come below with me, sir?' asked Peabody.

Down below they were just replacing the bulkheads of the main cabin; they had a glimpse of the long gun deck where, in the dim light of the lanterns, the men were securing their guns again. Washington, the negro servant, was trying to set the cabin to rights, bustling about with chairs, lighting the big cabin lamp, putting cushions on the lockers. He was flustered by the fact that his master was receiving company in a cabin which had been cleared for action. The British captain sat down in the chair which Washington dragged forward for him, while Peabody took his seat on the starboard-side locker.

'What was your ship, sir?' asked Peabody. He knew how bitter the use of that word 'was' would be for his prisoner but there was no way round the difficulty.

'Brig *Princess Augusta*, seven days out from Kingston. My name's Stanton.'

'Post Office packet, Captain Stanton?'

'Yes.'

'Whither bound?'

'Halifax.'

Letters for the British troops in Canada, then. The capture was doubly important.

'And what ship is this?' asked the British captain in his turn.

'United States ship *Delaware*.'

There was no need to say whence or whither – this prisoner might be recaptured.

'I didn't guess you were a Yankee until it was too late,' said the British captain bitterly. 'There aren't so many Yankee frigates at sea nowadays.'

The *Delaware* was the only one, as far as Peabody knew, unless Decatur had managed to escape from New London.

'I hope my broadside did not do too much damage,' said Peabody.

'Four killed and seven wounded – two of 'em mortal, I think.'

Washington came back into the cabin and spread a cloth on the table. He had brought an appetising-looking tray, but the British captain waved away the food which Peabody offered.

'No thank you,' he said. 'I've no appetite for food.'

'I shall send my surgeon on board the *Princess Augusta*,' said Peabody. 'I hope he will be able to relieve the wounded.'

'Thank you, sir,' said the captain.

There came a knock at the cabin door, and Washington opened it.

'It's Mistah O'Brien, sir.'

'Tell him to come in.'

O'Brien was carrying two small but heavy leather bags, on the fastenings of which dangled leaden seals.

'I brought these over myself, sir. I didn't want to trust 'em to anyone else.'

The bags as he set them on the deck gave out the clink of gold; Peabody glanced at the British captain and saw the look of mortification which passed over his face. But now that the discovery had been made the captain took it with the best grace he could.

'Two thousand guineas,' he said. 'I was hoping you wouldn't find it before we were retaken.'

'That's pay for the British army in Canada,' said Peabody. 'You were quite right to bring it to me, O'Brien. Are the mail bags still on board?'

'Yes, sir.'

Stanton's hint about the chance of the *Princess Augusta* being retaken no more than echoed what was already in Peabody's mind. It was hard for the United States Navy to take prizes, but it was harder still to profit by them. The rigid blockade off every American port made it extraordinarily difficult to send in captured ships. Peabody's instructions from the Secretary of the Navy, locked in the desk at his elbow, expressly authorised him to destroy prizes – even neutral vessels with contraband – at his discretion. The gold would be far safer on board the *Delaware* than in charge of a prize crew. But the mails were a different matter. At Washington they might be able to extract valuable information from them. It was worth while trying to send the brig in with the mail bags, even though it meant exposing a prize crew to the risk of capture. He sent O'Brien away with instructions before he turned back to Captain Stanton.

'If you will give me your parole on behalf of yourself and your crew,' he said, 'not to attempt escape before you reach an American port, it will make your voyage far more comfortable.'

Stanton shook his head.

'You know as well as I do that I can't do that, sir,' he said.

'More's the pity,' said Peabody. Stanton and his men would be left battened down below, at that rate, until the *Princess Augusta* reached Charleston. 'You are sure you will have no refreshment before you leave, sir?'

'You're very kind, sir. Perhaps I will – only a small one, sir. Just four fingers. Thank'ee, sir.'

Stanton looked at Peabody over the top of his glass; he forbore to comment – wisely enough, perhaps, seeing that he was only a prisoner – on the smallness of his host's drink.

'Confusion to the French,' he said.

Peabody was a little startled. The French were at war with England; America was at war with England, but France and America were not allies. He wondered if he could drink such a toast, all the same, even in the privacy of his cabin. Stanton's homely wrinkled face broke into a smile at his confusion.

'Let's say "a speedy peace," then,' said Stanton.

'A speedy peace,' said Peabody, solemnly.

Stanton took a pull at his glass before speaking again.

'You've heard the latest from the Continent, sir?'

'What is it?' asked Peabody, with native caution.

'The news came in the day before we cleared from Kingston. Wellington's over the Pyrenees. The Russians are over the Rhine, and Boney's licked. Licked as sure as a gun.'

Peabody stared at him, but there was no doubt the man was speaking the truth. In Peabody's throat the weak rum that he had sipped burned with the fierce pleasure which he had always to disregard, and for a moment it distracted him from making any deductions from what he was being told.

'Come midsummer,' said Stanton, 'and France'll be neutral. Aye, or before that.'

Then the British Navy would be free to turn its whole strength against the American coast, the British Army would be free to strike at exposed points, and what hope would there be then of an honourable peace?

'And then we'll have nothing to fight over,' went on Stanton. 'We won't want to press your men, and we won't care how much wheat you sell to the French. I'm no naval officer, sir. England was at war when I took my first command to sea in '94, and we're still at war twenty years after. I'd like to make a voyage – just one voyage – without wondering whether I'd be in prison before I reached the end of it.'

He drank off his glass without winking an eyelid, and stood up, submissive to any orders which Peabody might give him. On deck in the darkness he shook hands with his captor before hobbling stiffly off to the ship's side. Peabody lingered on deck; Mason, his youngest lieutenant, had fifty men and all the skilled hands of the *Delaware* repairing the tattered rigging of the *Princess Augusta*, and when the work was finished Mason would retain six of them and make an attempt to reach Charleston – or Georgetown or Wilmington, or any other port where he could slip past the British cruisers.

Peabody suddenly became aware of Jonathan at his side, whispering urgently in the darkness.

'Jos,' he was saying, 'Jos, is it true that ship's going back to America?'

'Yes, I'm sending the brig in with a prize crew.'

'Jos, send me back in it, too.'

'What's that?' said Peabody, quite unable to believe his ears.

'Send me back in that ship – brig, I mean. Please, Jos. Let me.'

'What in God's name are you saying?'

'I want to go back on that ship. I want to get out of here. I hate all this. I know they're going to the South, but I'll be able to get back to Connecticut somehow, Jos.'

'Call me "sir,"' snapped Peabody. He was still too astonished to attempt to deal with the matter of what Jonathan was saying, and temporised by finding fault with the manner.

'"Sir," then. Won't you let me go?'

The boy was frantic now, plucking at his captain's sleeve. He had at least the grace to whisper his ridiculous request, but that was little enough in his favour – on the contrary, rather, for it showed he knew he ought to be ashamed of it.

'No, I will not,' said Peabody, coming to a decision. 'Get

below, and don't let me see you again to-night. Get below, I said.'

The boy went off into the darkness with something like a sob, leaving Peabody tapping angrily with his foot on the deck as he debated this extraordinary happening. There must be something seriously the matter with Jonathan if he wanted to exchange this ideal life on board ship again for the hardships of home, the orderly discipline for the madness of his parents. Peabody went back in his mind to his first days at sea. Yes, he had been homesick, too, homesick for the green valleys and the rocky hills, even homesick for his chaff mattress in the corner of the room. But he had been only twelve, and Jonathan was twenty. Now he came to think of it, it was strange that Jonathan had endured the Connecticut farm up to that age; he could have escaped from it long ago into the West, into Ohio, where the farming was so good, or even into the Federal army during the past two years.

Peabody was conscious of a feeling of disillusionment, or of disappointment – in either case, it was something which he was always prepared for.

CHAPTER FOUR

Peabody wiped his mouth with his napkin and looked down the table, the largest that could be rigged in the mess cabin. The afternoon sunlight was streaming in through the skylight, and the cabin was sweltering hot – there were trickles of sweat down his lean cheeks, while fat little Purser Styles beside him was mopping his face unashamedly.

'Dammee, sir,' said Styles, 'but those beans were good. The weevils haven't got at 'em yet. Here, Washington, I'll have another cut o' that pork.'

Only skeletons remained of the four scrawny hens which had been sacrificed for dinner, but there was plenty of fat meat left on the two legs of fresh pork which had been served. Everyone had eaten well, and before Washington brought in the dessert it was time for a toast. Peabody was uneasily conscious that it was time for a speech, too, but that he would not be able to give. The toast would have to suffice – he could remember by heart well enough the formula he had heard repeated in past years. He got to his feet, glass in hand, and conversation died away as all eyes turned to him.

'To the memory of the immortal man whose birthday we are celebrating to-day,' he said. 'To the memory of George Washington.'

Everyone rose with inarticulate murmurs while the toast was drunk, and sat down again a trifle self-consciously.

Purser Styles, with his red face, took it for granted now that he could unbuckle the stock which was putting him in danger of apoplexy. Lieutenant Murray took wine across the table with his *vis-à-vis*, Acting Lieutenant Howard; Mr. Crane, the master, beamed quite genially at the three lads at the end of the table – Midshipman Wallingford, Midshipman Shepherd, and Acting Midshipman Peabody.

The captain, at the head of the table, experienced a feeling of relief; he had proposed the toast without stumbling, and this formal dinner party was bidding fair to be a success – Peabody always felt qualms of doubt when responsible for a social occasion. He frowned a little as he noticed Jonathan refilling his glass. The boy was a little flushed as it was – although that might merely be the heat – and he did not like to see it. Jonathan had so obviously benefited by his appointment as acting midshipman. It really had been fortunate that they had captured the *Princess Augusta*, and that Mason had gone off in her as prize master; the acting promotion of Howard had left a vacancy which Peabody was entitled to fill. Now Jonathan was acting midshipman, with his foot on the ladder leading to executive rank, and with the discipline of Hubbard and Murray and Crane to drive out from his mind the fantastic troubles which had been worrying him. Peabody was well content, or would have been if Jonathan were not quite so flushed.

A knocking at the cabin door heralded the admission of Quincy, out of breath with hurrying.

'A message from Mr. Hubbard, sir,' he panted. 'Cutter in sight, and bearing up for us.'

'My compliments to Mr. Hubbard, and I'll come on deck.'

Peabody turned to his guests.

'I beg your pardon, gentlemen. I hope you will excuse me for a moment.'

They rose in reply – it was a continual mild surprise to Peabody that the conventional manners which he found it so hard to employ always worked so well.

Peabody ran up on deck; Hubbard was looking through his glass at the jaunty cutter which was running towards them – a typical island boat with patched brown sails.

'Heave to, Mr. Hubbard, if you please.'

The cutter was bowling along briskly under a light air which had hardly been moving the *Delaware*, but then the latter had had no more than topsails set. The cutter, as Peabody saw through the glass, had a coloured hand in the bows and two more in the waist; aft, at the tiller, there sat a man in dazzling white clothes. He put up his tiller, and the cutter came neatly into the wind and took in her head sail; a moment later, the dinghy, which had been towing astern, came sculling briskly across the glittering water with the white-clad man in the stern sheets, and a half-naked negro at the sculls. Peabody met the visitor as he came dexterously up the side.

'Mr. Hunningford?'

'Captain Hunningford, sir. And I have the honour to address—?'

'Josiah Peabody.'

'Of the United States frigate *Delaware*,' supplemented Hunningford, looking round the ship with a keen professional eye.

'I have been beating about waiting for you for the last week,' said Peabody irritably.

'And I, sir,' said Hunningford, with sublime insouciance, 'have been waiting for you for two months.'

He was a man as tall as Peabody, and even thinner, and without Peabody's heavy shoulders. He had a lean, mobile face and a twinkle in his eye – it was the face of a young man in strange contrast with his snow-white hair.

'What news have you for me?' demanded Peabody.

Hunningford looked round the deck.

'I would prefer,' he said gently, 'to tell you that in conditions a little more private.'

'Come below,' said Peabody curtly.

He led the visitor down the companion, pausing outside the door of the main cabin he heard Styles' voice lifted in song, and directly afterwards the rest of the company joined in the chorus.

'This way,' said Peabody, opening the door of the sleeping cabin.

Hunningford sat down on the locker and left the cot to Peabody.

'You are comfortable enough here,' he said, glancing about him. 'But I would prefer to have that skylight closed.'

Peabody followed his gaze, and reopened the door to give the order to the sentry outside. Then they waited in silence until the skylight closed over their heads.

'Well?' said Peabody.

'The Jamaica convoy sails in nine days' time,' said Hunningford. 'The escort will be the *Calypso*, 36, corvette *Racer*, 20, if she's back in time, which I expect, and the brig *Bulldog*, 14. They will sail by the Windward passage, and will rendezvous with the Leeward Islands convoy in Latitude 25 North, Longitude 65 West.'

This was precise enough information, if it were correct.

'How do you know this?' asked Peabody.

Hunningford shrugged his shoulders.

'I am paid no commission for revealing that,' he said. 'But if you imagine that a convoy of a hundred sail can be assembled without certain facts leaking out you have a higher opinion of human nature than I have. My commercial connections give me certain opportunities and privileges.'

Peabody felt a certain surly hostility towards this elegant spy, partly because of his elaborate manner, and partly because of the way he lived, associating with honest merchants, and selling them to their enemies.

'Are you sure of what you say?' he asked.

'My dear sir,' said Hunningford, crossing his knees, 'you are treating me with a suspicion which is quite unwarranted.

If I wished to betray you, you can be quite sure that it would not be my cutter which kept our appointment, but a squadron of British frigates.'

That was perfectly true, and it ought to have lessened Peabody's instinctive dislike for the man, but it did not. But he did not allow his dislike to interfere with his questioning.

'What news of the privateers?' he asked.

'Ah!' replied Hunningford archly. 'Now we approach the crux of the matter. I am in touch with the schooners *Emulation*, Captain Daniel Gooding, and *Oliver*, Captain James Curtis, both out of Baltimore. I have already passed on to them some valuable pieces of information, but the Jamaica convoy is rather more important, as both you and they agree. They are anxious to receive instructions from you. With your assistance, Captain, they hope to make themselves both wealthy for life. To me, it is more important that my commission on their captures will make me wealthier still.'

'I'll give you a letter to them.'

Hunningford put his fingers to his lean throat, and made a realistic choking noise.

'You must dislike me very much, Captain, if you are so anxious to see me cut off in my respected old age. I will carry any verbal message you like, but nothing in writing.'

Peabody looked his puzzlement, and Hunningford condescended to further explanation.

'I come and I go,' he said. 'My manifold business interests take me from island to island. As far as I know, no suspicion attaches to me. No one, save my negroes, knows that to-day I encounter you just out of sight of land, and to-morrow Captain Gooding. I could be arrested and examined at any moment, and I should welcome the examination, which could only clear my fair name. But if I carried a letter from a United States captain—'

He repeated his former gesture, putting his head on one side, and rolling up his eyes with hideous added realism.

'What do you want done, then?'

'You must tell me your plans, Captain, and I'll pass them on.'

Peabody rubbed his chin, and stared at Hunningford; the

latter's malicious grey eyes met his own hard blue ones without flinching.

'What's the force of these two schooners?' he demanded.

'They're both big enough to take care of themselves. The *Emulation's* two hundred and fifty tons, the *Oliver's* over two hundred. *Oliver* has four long nine and ten twelve-pounder carronades. *Emulation* threw half her guns overboard last December, when the *Fox* chased her in a calm, but she's rearmed herself from prizes – sixes, nines, and a couple of twelves.'

Peabody's mind began to analyse the tactical problem presented.

'Neither Gooding nor Curtis,' said Hunningford, 'will fight a King's ship if they can help it.'

Peabody knew that; no privateer captain who knew his trade would risk his ship and face certain crippling damage in action with a man o' war. If he were to lock yardarms with the *Calypso* there was still the rest of the escort to consider – the *Bulldog* alone could probably beat off the privateers, and the *Racer*, if she were present, could outfight them both. But the disparity of force was not so great as to be insuperable; the West Indian convoy was a prize, indeed, and any serious loss to it would raise a storm among the merchants of London. It was most unlikely that, for some time to come, there would be any equally attractive objective for an attack at smaller risk.

'Tell them,' said Peabody, 'to meet me behind Tortuga on the second of next month.'

Hunningford nodded.

'They wouldn't come,' he said, 'unless I told them that there was a capable captain in command. I'll tell them that, too.'

Peabody shot a surprised glance at him, but Hunningford reverted instantly to his former tone of light cynicism as he rose to his feet.

'This has been a stimulating interview, Captain,' he said. 'I'm glad to see a ship of force in these islands again. And I expect the prizes taken will return me a very handsome commission.'

Peabody watched the cutter go racing off again, wing-and-wing, to the southward. He wondered, as he saw her sink over the horizon, whether her captain was a mere venal person who took tainted money, or a very brave man who was cheerfully risking the gallows in his country's cause. He strongly suspected Hunningford to be the latter. When he reached his cabin again he found that his dinner party had progressed perfectly satisfactorily in his absence.

CHAPTER FIVE

Captain Gooding was bluff and hospitable, but Captain Curtis was young and eager – quite half a dozen years Peabody's junior. They were both waiting at the side when Peabody came on board the *Emulation* to return their call, both in their best clothes, with swords at their sides and cocked hats on their heads. The *Emulation* copied man o' war's ways; the boatswain's mates twittered on their pipes, and there were sideboys in white gloves ready to assist him, and twenty landsmen – the privateer's equivalent of marines – in green coats making a workmanlike job of presenting arms as Peabody stepped on the deck. The hands were uniformly dressed in red check shirts and white trousers, and the deck was as white as Captain Gooding's cravat.

'Honoured to receive you, sir,' said Gooding. 'Please be so good as to step this way. The coaming's high – *Emulation's* a wet ship on a bowline – and the cabin's not as lofty as you've been accustomed to, I'm afraid. Mr. Merton! Take Captain Peabody's hat and sword. Sit here, sir. I've a nice drop of Jamaica, sir, which I took out of the *Blandford*. No? There's some Madeira and a fair Marsala. Merton! The Madeira for Captain Peabody. Please take your ease, sir. There's no reason for worry as long as the wind's nor'-easterly. Merton! How's the wind?'

'Nor'-east by east, sir,' said Merton, in a tone of infinite patience.

He was a tall, spare negro, who got his information, after a glance at the tell-tale compass over Gooding's head, by craning his neck up to the chink in the cabin skylight and looking up at the pennant at the maintopmast truck.

'Serve the dinner, then, you black pole mast.'

The ludicrous simile made Peabody grin; there was a strange likeness between the lean negro and a skysail mast without the skysail set.

'I would be glad to hear your suggestions again for the attack, sir,' said Curtis, the moment the flow of Gooding's talk was checked.

'Anyone would think Curtis and I hadn't spent the last two hours discussing 'em,' said Gooding promptly. 'This is dinner-time. How's the wind, Merton?'

'Nor'-east by east, sir.'

'The British don't know your ship's in these waters?' persisted Curtis.

'They can't know yet,' said Peabody, 'not unless Hunningford has told them.'

'Hunningford wouldn't say a word,' said Gooding. 'He has too keen an eye for business.'

The three captains exchanged glances, Peabody keenly observing the other two.

'Three fat commissions has he screwed out of me,' admitted Curtis.

Peabody had a flash of insight. The fact that these hard-headed Baltimore captains had to pay Hunningford good hard cash for his information made them far more ready to respect his suggestions. His heart warmed to the memory of the man.

'Try some of this alligator pear, sir,' said Gooding. 'I can't ever stomach it myself, but the natives of these parts don't think they've dined unless alligator pear has been served. Take plenty of the pepper sauce, sir. That'll help it down. How's the wind, Merton?'

'Nor'-east by east, sir. Mebbe east nor'-east.'

'Veering southerly a bit. The British know we're here, at least. That convoy'll sail in order of battle, just as it always does.'

'I followed the last convoy eleven days,' said Curtis, 'and

ne'er a straggler was I able to pick up.'

'So you told us before, my lad. But I don't think your owners have much to complain about, so far,' said Gooding. 'May I carve you some of this cold brisket, sir? You're making a poor dinner. And look at your glass! Drink fair, sir.'

'*Calypso* has twelve pounders on her main deck,' said Curtis thoughtfully.

'Yes,' said Peabody. He thought of his own long eighteens, and the good use he could put them to if he dared risk crippling the *Delaware*.

''Scuse me, sir,' said Merton, 'but the wind's east by south now, and still veering.'

'That interrupts our dinner,' said Gooding. 'If you're wrong, you black fathom o' pump water, I'll go a thousand miles out o' my course to sell you at Charleston under the hammer.'

'Yes, sir,' said Merton, quite unmoved. He craned his neck up to the skylight opening again and announced: 'Mr. Chase says east by south. I should say east sou'-east, sir.'

'Would you, by God!' said Gooding.

They were all of them on their feet now, and Merton produced, as though it were a conjuring trick, Peabody's cocked hat and sword from nowhere.

'The black heathen'll be telling me what sail to set next,' protested Gooding, while Merton buckled the belt round Peabody's waist. 'Have you called Captain Peabody's gig?'

'Yes, sir,' said Merton.

Before Peabody went down the side Gooding held out his hand.

'When we meet again we'll be half a million dollars richer,' he said.

'Good luck, sir,' said Curtis, with a young man's enthusiasm in his eyes.

The gig took Peabody rapidly across the dancing water to where the *Delaware* lay hove-to, a beautiful sight. As she swung towards him he could see her lovely bows and round, sweet run. The rake of the bowsprit and of the masts was as beautiful as a quadratic equation – masts and bowsprit exactly complementary. The proportion between topsails and courses was ideal, and the painted gunports threw in the right note of menace, so that she was not merely a beautiful thing, but a beautiful fighting thing. He looked back at the schooners, with their heavy spars and long sharp bows. They were like birds of prey, ready for a sudden swoop upon the defenceless, but incapable of the smashing blow which the *Delaware* could deal. And yet it was only by schooners like these – save for his own ship – that the American flag was displayed anywhere through the wide Atlantic.

If only they had decided ten years ago in Washington to build a dozen seventy-fours! Gouverneur Morris had advocated it a score of times, but Mr. Jefferson had decided against it. In this world only a display of force could exact respect. A battle fleet would have prevented the coming of this war, and would have saved the people of the United States a thousand times its cost. In normal times a hundred ships a day cleared from American ports, and a hundred entered them, but now two thousand American ships rotted at their moorings – flour in Boston was just twice the price it was at Baltimore, while Baltimore had to pay three times as much for sugar as the price demanded on the quay at New Orleans. The United States were dying of a slow gangrene. Unemployed sailors crowded the waterfronts of every seaport; for every hand in a privateer there were a hundred looking for work, and all because Mr. Jefferson had not thought himself justified in spending money, and was obsessed with that quaint fear that a powerful navy would make an autocracy out of America.

And Mr. Madison had proposed to establish a neutral zone in the Atlantic, as far as the Gulf Stream, and to bar foreign ships of war from it; Peabody had helped Commodore Rodgers to write a professional opinion of this proposal only a year before British ships of war dropped anchor at Sandy Hook and slammed the door of New York in Mr. Madison's face. It was because of this kind of muddled logic that the *Delaware* was faced with a task for which a dozen ships of the line would not have been too powerful, and that he himself was prowling furtively like a jackal instead of challenging battle like a man.

The bowman hooked on to the chains as the gig came alongside, and Peabody climbed to the deck and raised his hat in acknowledgement of the salutes paid him. The schooners were still nodding and dipping across the water, awaiting the time when he would move; southward the mountains of Haiti rose from the horizon, and northward lay the rounded outline of Tortuga. The wind was veering more and more southerly, and close hauled the Jamaica convoy would be able to make the Windward Passage.

'Dip the colours and fire a gun to leeward as soon as the gig is hoisted in, Mr. Hubbard,' said Peabody.

A flight of pelicans was flapping solemnly over the water, dark against the bright western sky, keeping their steady line ahead as they passed close to the *Delaware's* side. The sudden bang of the gun and the jet of smoke threw them all aback in confusion, and they turned and flapped away in a disorderly line abreast.

'Square away, Mr. Hubbard. Course west by south.'

'West by south, sir.'

Under easy sail the *Delaware* crept slowly along westward, with the mountains of Haiti towering up in the south, the white cliffs just visible at their foot. The two privateers were five miles off to windward, blotted out every now and then by the sudden rainstorms which passed over them on their way down to the *Delaware*. The storms were heavy while they lasted, and they kept busy Mr. Hollins, the cooper, and his mates and working party. Hollins had a sail stretched after from the knightheads to catch the rain water, the aftermost edge pulled down to form a lip from which, when it rained, the water poured in a cataract into the hogsheads which Hollins had his men trundle beneath it. Peabody watched the operation with a grim satisfaction; as long as his water butts were full he was independent of the shore for three months at least – if the *Delaware's* career should last so long.

Cape St. Nicholas was close under their larboard bow, and night was coming down fast.

'Heave to, Mr. Hubbard, if you please. And I'll have two lights hoisted at the peak.'

The Windward Passage was under the direct observation of his ship now, there was a beautiful three-quarter moon, and no convoy of a hundred sail could get by without his knowledge. He turned and went below to his cabin, where Washington was making up his cot.

'I 'spect your coat's wet, sir,' said Washington.

It was, of course – Peabody had stood out through half a dozen tropical showers – and so were his breeches.

'Now here's your nightshirt, and you get right into it, sir,' said Washington, fussing round the cabin.

Peabody had not been able to grow accustomed to having a body servant. Washington had thrown himself into his duties when he was first engaged with all the abandon of his race; perhaps with generations of dependence preceding him he was merely seeking to make himself quite indispensable as quickly as possible. Peabody had thrown cold water on some of his enthusiasms; Washington no longer crouched to him, holding out his breeches for him to step into, as he got out of bed, but Peabody had not yet been able to break him of his habit of touching him to see if he were wet, and of trying to dictate to him what he should wear and when he should sleep. Peabody could recognise each of his shirts individually, and during his years as a poor lieutenant had devised a satisfactory system of rotation of duties for them, and he still bore unconsciously some slight resentment against Washington for breaking into his orderly habits.

'I don't want my nightshirt,' he said curtly. 'Get me out a dry shirt – one of the plain ones, and take it from the top of the pile – and a pair of the white ducks. Hang my old coat on the hook there where I can find it.'

'You ain't goin' to turn in all standing, sir,' said Washington resentfully.

'I am,' snapped Peabody.

He threw off his wet gala clothes – there was a queer uncontrollable uneasiness at being naked when he was not alone, but he fought against that because he felt it was not quite justifiable – and pulled on the shirt which Washington handed him. He put his feet into his trousers, balancing against the roll of the ship first on one leg and then on the other with a habitual facility of which he was unconscious, and stood tucking in his shirt.

'Put my shoes against the bulkhead and take that lamp away,' he ordered.

'Yes, sir. Good night, sir,' said Washington.

Alone in the darkness Peabody lay down on his cot, 'all standing' – with his clothes on – as Washington had protestingly said. He could lay his hands instantly on his shoes and coat, and could be on deck within forty seconds of an alarm; Peabody had no self-consciousness about appearing on deck with his nightshirt-tails flapping round him, but the picture did not coincide with his idea of a well-ordered ship. He bent his long length and turned on to his side, his hands clasped before his chest in the attitude of sleep he had habitually employed from babyhood, and he closed his eyes. There was a momentary temptation to lie awake and brood over the dangers before him, but he put it aside like the temptation to drink. There was a time for everything, and this was the time to sleep.

At midnight he was awake again; twenty years of watch-and-watch – four hours waking and four hours sleep – had formed a habit even he could not control. He went on deck and prowled round, although he had complete confidence in his officers' ability to carry out routine orders. The lights burned brightly at the peak, and the moon shone clearly from beyond the Windward Passage, while the *Delaware* rose and fell rhythmically over the long swell as she lay hove-to before the gentle wind. The atmosphere was warm and sticky, and on the side on which he had been lying his clothes were wet with sweat which hardly evaporated in the hot night. There was nothing to do except sleep, and he went below again to his stuffy cabin, lay down on his other side, emptied his mind of all thought for the second time, and went to sleep in the accustomed stuffiness, lulled by the *Delaware's* easy motion over the waves.

Dawn brought him on deck again, and there was still no sign of the convoy, although the wind had stayed to the south of east all night. Five miles away to windward the schooners lay hove-to under their mainsails alone, and there was no need to signal to them, for privateer captains had as much need for patience as for dash in their work. All day long the *Delaware* lay-to off Cape St. Nicolas – an easy day in the hot tropical sunshine, while the rainstorms came up to windward and burst over the ship and passed away to leeward in rainbows. The decks were washed down; the forenoon watch was spent in drill – gun drill, boarding drill, sail drill, and when the men's dinner-time arrived there was still no sign of the convoy. Last night had been the earliest possible moment it could appear, but Peabody was wise to the ways of convoys and knew quite well that he might have to wait a week.

In the afternoon Hubbard found work for the crew. He had the anchors and the ironwork tarred, while Rodgers the boatswain, kept a select party doing neat work on the rigging – knots and flemish-eyes and pointings. The ship's boys were making sinnet, and the sailmaker had a party at work with needle and palm on a new foretopsail, while the spun yarn winch buzzed cheerfully away spinning yarns with which a few fortunate men – for some odd reason it was the most popular work in the ship – walked solemnly forward and aft. The rain squalls came up; sails and yarns were bundled under cover, and the helmsman had a moment's activity keeping the ship from being taken aback. Then in an instant, as it were, the rain was past, the deck steamed in the hot sun, and the wind began its cheerful note again.

The first watch was called, and work on the ship was suspended. Peabody gave permission for clothes to be washed, taking advantage of all the unwanted fresh water on board, and soon the lines which had been rigged were gay with all the red and white shirts and white trousers of four hundred men.. The sun was dipping to the west. Two bells were struck, and then three, and then came the hail which Peabody had been waiting for.

'Deck there! Sail to leeward! Two sails, sir! A whole fleet, sir!'

'Clear for action, Mr. Hubbard, if you please. Hoist the colours, and dip them twice.'

The drums went roaring through the ship. Like magic the

lines and the clothes vanished from forward. Boys went racing along the deck strewing sand. Groups of men came running to every gun, casting off the breachings, taking out the tompions, pulling rammers and sponges from their racks. The marines came pouring up into the quarterdeck, falling into stiff military line in their blue and white uniforms and jaunty shakoes, while the sergeants inspected them before taking their parties up into the tops.

'The schooners have hoisted their colours and dipped them twice, sir,' said Midshipman Wallingford.

'Yes,' said Peabody.

That was the acknowledgement of his prearranged signal for the convoy in sight to leeward – if the convoy had by some chance appeared to windward the colours could have been dipped once. Peabody took his glass and ran up the mizzen rigging. Halfway to the top was as far as he needed to go; with his feet astride and his back leaning against the shrouds he could see the convoy coming down upon him, close hauled on the starboard tack. There was only one ship-rigged vessel in sight although there were two barquentines and four brigs. None of the brigs was a man o' war, for he could recognise their familiar outlines as typical West India traders. But the ship – he looked at her more closely. She was flush-decked, and she showed a line of gun ports, checkered black against yellow. Fore and main topmasts were about equal, and her canvas was faintly grey instead of a lively white. She was a British ship-of-war, then, and presumably the twenty-gun corvette *Racer* whose presence Hunningford had been doubtful about.

'Ship cleared for action, sir,' hailed Hubbard from the quarterdeck.

There were more sails crowding up over the horizon now, and as Peabody turned his glass upon them he checked himself in instant certainty. There was no mistaking those topsails, that silhouette – a British frigate, or he had never seen one before in his life. He scanned the other sails closely, and then traversed his glass back again over the fleet. No, there was no sign whatever so far of the brig *Bulldog* which Hunningford had mentioned, and Peabody would have been surprised if there had been, yet. The senior officer of the British squadron, if he knew his business, would have the corvette to windward of the van – as she was, the frigate to windward of the main body when she could most easily cope with trouble – and she was there; and the brig in rear to keep her eye on the stragglers, where presumably she was. He closed his glass and descended to the deck.

Murray was positively dancing with excitement and anxiety, and even Hubbard was walking up and down the quarterdeck with quick, rapid strides.

'Set all plain sail to the royal, Mr Hubbard, if you please, and put her before the wind.'

'Aye aye, sir. Before the wind, sir.'

'Mr. Murray!'

'Sir!'

'I want the round shot drawn from the guns. Load with two rounds of dismantling shot.'

'Aye aye, sir. And I'll point the guns high, sir.'

Murray was quick to grasp a plan. The *Delaware* had three ships-of-war to deal with, and must put all three out of action so as to leave a free hand for the privateers. Peabody watched the men at work on the quarterdeck carronades. With corkscrew rammers they drew the wads from their pieces. They twisted the elevating screws, forcing in the wedges under the breeches, until the carronades were pointing sharply downwards. With the roll of the ship the round shot came tumbling from the muzzles, falling with a thump on the deck, to be snatched up and replaced in the garlands against the bulwark. Next the dismantling shot was rammed in – cylindrical canvas bags, which concealed the missiles within. For these big thirty-two pounders each bag contained a dozen six-foot lengths of iron chain, each joined to a single ring in the centre. On discharge they would fly like a hurtling star, effective to a range of five hundred feet, cutting ropes and tearing canvas to shreds. Sawyer, of the Boston Navy Yard, had long advocated the use of dismantling shot, but Peabody had yet to see it employed in action. Peabody was aware that the British thought its use unfair, but for the life of him he could not see why; he supposed it was because they had not thought of it for themselves.

Peabody looked ahead. The frigate had tacked about, and was heading towards the *Delaware*, to inspect this strange ship-of-war which had so suddenly appeared. The corvette had backed her mizzen topsail, and was allowing the convoy to catch up with her while she took the frigate's place; the British had been guarding convoys for twenty years continuously now, and understood their business. There was a string of flags rising to the frigate's main yardarm.

'M W P' read off Wallingford. 'It doesn't make sense, sir.'

The private recognition signal, of course. There would be a code reply of which he was ignorant, but there was a reply he could make which would be quite sufficient.

'Bring her to the wind on the port tack, Mr. Hubbard.'

As the ship came round the ensign at the peak became visible to the British frigate. Peabody smiled grimly as he saw the effect it produced – more signals soared up the frigate's halliards, and a white puff of smoke from her bows showed that she was firing a gun to demand the instant attention of her consorts and the convoy. This was the moment of surprise. No king's ship in the West Indies could know until that moment that a big American frigate was loose on the high seas. He watched his enemies warily to see what they would do.

The frigate was holding her course, parallel to the *Delaware's*, both of them lying close hauled. Now the corvette was coming round, too; Peabody could only see her topsails, and she was six miles farther to leeward of the frigate. And dead to leeward of the frigate, and far beyond her, Peabody saw another pair of topsails on the horizon wink as they came round, differentiating themselves sharply from the others beyond. That was the brig, then. They were all three heading towards him, as he had hoped; the privateers, far astern of him and on a course diametrically opposite, were out of their sight and would soon have a free hand with the convoy.

Vigilant, he watched his enemies. If they were wise, they could close up together to meet his attack. The *Calypso* by herself was of slightly inferior force to the *Delaware*, and in a ship to ship duel he would fight with confidence in victory, even with his knowledge of the chanciness of war at sea. But the *Calypso* and the *Racer* together would be grave odds against him, and even the *Bulldog* could cause him serious annoyance if the *Delaware* were involved in a hot action. By bringing his ship to the wind he had made a pretence of refusing battle – they might chase him in heedless pursuit, as they were doing at this moment, widening their distance from the convoy, confident that there could not possibly be two United States ships at sea simultaneously and forgetting the lurking privateers.

It was a complex series of factors, and Peabody turned his attention to another complication – the setting of the sun. Red and angry it was setting, beyond the convoy. There was not much more than an hour's daylight left, and he needed daylight to do his work well. He glanced to windward; there was the familiar black cloud coming down with the wind, as might have been expected, for it was two hours at least since the last rainstorm. He held doggedly on his course, aware that Hubbard was looking at him with faint surprise and that even the men at the guns were glancing over their shoulders, wondering why their captain was running like this from the enemy. The enemy to leeward, the squall to windward; Peabody transferred his attention first to the one and then to the other. Now the squall was close upon them. There was a warning flap from the sails and Peabody heard Crane cautioning the men at the wheel. Now it was here, heavy fluky gusts of wind and torrential warm rain, heavy as if from a shower-bath, drumming on the decks and streaming like a cataract in the scuppers.

'Wear ship, Mr. Hubbard, if you please. I'll have her before the wind again.'

Round she came, the heavy gusts of the squall thrusting her forward perceptibly. She was in the heart of the little storm, travelling down wind with it for several minutes before it drew ahead of her. As Peabody turned his head a little cascade of water poured out of the brim of his cocked hat, but the rain was already lessening. Yet even when it had ceased entirely, and the decks were beginning to steam in the hot evening, it was still ahead of blotting the *Calypso* from Peabody's sight, and presumably concealing the *Delaware* from the *Calypso.*

'Stand to your guns, men!' called Peabody. He was glad to see Murray attending to the distribution of lighted slow-match round the ship – he wanted nothing to go wrong with that first broadside.

Only a scant mile ahead of the *Delaware* a grey shape emerged from the rainstorm – grey one moment, sharply defined the next; the *Calypso* still holding her course and beyond the immediate help of her consorts. Certainly there was no time now for the British ships to close together, not with the *Delaware* rushing down upon them at eight knots. There was a chance of raking the *Calypso*, of crossing her bows and sweeping her from end to end, but her captain was too wary. As the two ships closed he put up his helm – Peabody saw her broadside lengthen and her masts separate.

'Larboard a point,' snapped Peabody to the helmsman. He wanted that broadside delivered at the closest possible range.

The *Calypso* was just steadying on her new course as the *Delaware* forged up alongside her. The forecastle twelve pounder went off with a bang; Peabody took note of that, for the captain of that gun must be punished for opening fire without orders. Peabody could see the white deck and gleaming hammocks of the British frigate, the gold lace of the officers, and the bright red coats of the marines on the quarterdeck. Where he stood by the mizzen rigging he was just opposite the frigate's taffrail; it was almost time for the broadside – it was interesting to see how Murray down on the main deck came through this test of nerves. At last it came – a crashing simultaneous roar from the main-deck guns, followed instantly by the spar-deck carronades. The *Delaware* heaved to the recoil of the guns, and the smoke poured upwards in a cloud, enshrouding Peabody so thickly that for a moment the *Calypso* was blotted from his sight. Something struck the bulwark beside him a tremendous blow which shook him as he stood. There was a gaping hole there; something else struck the mizzen mast bits and sprayed all the deck around with fragments. Peabody watched death flitting past him; and in the sublime knowledge that he had done all his duty he felt neither awe nor fear.

The carronades beside him, speedily reloaded, roared out again. The ship trembled to the recoil of the guns, while Peabody could feel, through the deck beneath his feet, the heavy blows which the *Calypso's* guns were dealing in return. The British frigate was firing fast, accurately, and low; the earlier defeats of British single ships had shaken up the service into renewed attention to gunnery, as the action between the *Shannon* and the *Chesapeake* showed. Peabody peered through the smoke to see what damage was being done to the enemy, but with the wind directly abaft it was hard to see anything. There was the *Calypso's* main mast standing out through the smoke, mistily visible from the main yard upward. Yet everything there was in such confusion that Peabody actually found it hard to recognise what he saw. The maintopsail was in ribbons, with strips of canvas blowing out from the yard, which was canted wildly sideways and precariously supported the topgallant yard, which, slings, ties, and braces all shot away, was lying balanced upon it in a wild tangle of canvas and rigging. As Peabody watched, half the main shrouds parted as though a gigantic knife had been drawn across them, the mast lurched, and the whole mass of stuff came tumbling down into the smoke.

The *Delaware* was drawing ahead fast; the chance of crossing the *Calypso's* bows and raking her was obvious. Peabody leaned forward to the man at the wheel.

'Larboard your helm,' he said.

Hubbard had seen the chance too, had heard his words, and was bellowing his orders into the smoke. Over went the helm, round came the yards, and Peabody turned back to watch the *Calypso*. But she was coming round too – the distance between her vague main mast and mizzen mast was slowly widening. Peabody saw a red-coated marine come running out towards him along the *Calypso's* mizzen topsail yard, musket in hand; the man must have been mad with the lust of battle to have attempted such a feat. He reached the yardarm, but as he was bringing his weapon to his shoulder something invisible struck him and he was tossed off the yard.

With the wind abeam they were passing out of the smoke, and the *Calypso's* outlines became more distinct. From the deck upward she was more of a wreck than Peabody would ever have thought possible, her canvas in shreds and her running and standing rigging cut to pieces. Her headsails were trailing under her forefoot; her spanker gaff hung drunkenly with the upper half of the spanker blowing out from it like a sheet on a clothesline, and although the main-topgallant was the only yard which had fallen all her spars sagged and drooped as if a breath would bring them down. There could be no doubt whatever as to the efficacy of dismantling shot, Peabody decided.

Midshipman Shepherd was beside him. His cheek had been laid open over the bone, so that half his face was masked in blood which dripped down on to his torn coat.

'Number seven gun has burst, sir,' said Shepherd. His chest was heaving with his exertions as he tried to hold himself steady. 'Mr. Atwell sent me to report. The ship caught fire on the main deck, but the fire's out now, sir.'

'Thank you, Mr. Shepherd. Get that cut bandaged before you return to duty.'

Peabody made his reply steadily enough, but he had felt a wave of bitterness at the news. These cursed iron guns! The *Belvidera* had escaped from Rodgers in the *President* because of just such an accident. The Pennsylvania foundries had not learned yet to cast iron without flaws. Shepherd's report explained the slackening of the main-deck fire which Peabody had detected just before. Another shot hit the deck beside him at that instant, sending a ringbolt flying through the air with a menacing whirr – the *Calypso* was still firing rapidly and well; a wreck from the deck upwards, her gun power was not in the least impaired. Through the roar of the carronades beside him he could hear the smashing blows which the *Calypso's* guns were still dealing out, but the main-deck guns were firing back again as fast as ever now. The *Calypso's* tottering foretopmast came down, falling nearly vertically – she was dropping astern fast again. Peabody wanted to hurl his ship close alongside of her, to pound her in a mad flurry of mutual destruction, to sink her, to burn her, to cover her deck with corpses. Mad lust for battle wrapped his mind like a cloak.

'Shall I back the mizzen topsail, sir?' asked Hubbard, crossing the deck towards him.

'No,' said Peabody.

Battle-madness passed and common sense returned at Hubbard's question. The level-headed Yankee temperament took charge when Peabody saw the swarthy Carolinian's blazing eyes. There was the *Racer* to think of, and the brig, and the convoy, and the approach of night. He looked away to leeward, and there was the *Racer* clawing gallantly up to windward to join in the fight. Aft, and there was the brig doing the same, while against the red western sunset were silhouetted the countless sails of the convoy. Another broadside from the *Calypso* crashed into the *Delaware* and shook him as he stood talking to Hubbard.

'Up helm, if you please, Mr. Hubbard. We'll go down to the corvette.'

The *Delaware's* sails filled as she bore away, and the infernal din of the battle died away magically. Borne on the wind came a wild cheer from the British ship – the fools thought they had made the *Delaware* seek safety in flight. There was a moment's temptation to tack about and show them that they were wrong, but Peabody put it aside.

Peabody looked round the ship. On the larboard side – the disengaged side – a carronade slide had been smashed and the carronade's crew was at work securing the clumsy lump of metal which lay on the deck. There were big holes in the bulwark and the deck was torn up in several places. Aloft someone was reeving fresh maintopsail halliards, and there were a few big holes in the sails. There were dead men here and there, but the *Delaware* was still an efficient fighting unit. Someone came running up to him – a carpenter's mate whose name Peabody could not instantly remember, Smith or Jones, perhaps.

'Mr. MacKenzie sent me, sir. We've been holed twice below the bends, sir, on the starboard side for'rard. We've plugged one hole, but the other's beside the beef an' we've got to move the hogsheads, sir. But there's only a foot of water in the well and Mr. MacKenzie's gotten the pumps to work.'

'Right. Get below again.'

They were coming down fast on the *Racer*; Peabody waved the man away as he peered keenly forward to watch her movements. A glance astern assured him again that the *Calypso* was out of the action for good – she was wallowing quite helpless in the trough of the sea. But the *Racer* was not going to falter, all the same. She was holding her course steadily, the white ensign flying bravely from her peak. It was her duty to protect the convoy, even at the cost of her own destruction. Peabody swung round upon Shepherd.

'Go find Mr. Murray,' he snapped. 'Tell him to load with dismantling shot again.'

The sun was completely below the horizon; there was not much daylight left and the moon would not be of much help for accurate gun fire. Peabody saw the *Racer's* maintopsail swing round until it reflected the pink of the sunset in sharp contrast with the dark silhouettes of the other sails. She was laying it to the mast, heaving to for a steadier shot at the big frigate plunging down upon her. Her best chance of saving the convoy was to cripple the enemy while she still had the opportunity. Peabody felt a grim approval of the British captain's tactics as he waited for the broadside to come.

A neat row of white puffs of smoke appeared along the corvette's side, and Peabody's mathematical mind leaped into a calculation.

'One, two, three, four—' he counted.

The air was full of the sound of the balls overhead. A fresh hole appeared in the foretopsail, and the maintopsail halliards, just replaced, parted again, the loose ends tumbling to the deck. The *Delaware* was going six knots; there would be two more broadsides – three, if the corvette's guns were specially well served – before she was at close quarters. Peabody wondered what was the maximum damage the corvette's long nine pounders could inflict. He might actually lose a mast, although the chances were that he would not lose even a spar. The ship was deadly quiet now. There was only the clanking of the pumps forward to be heard beside the eternal note of the wind in the rigging and the sound of the sea under the bows. The men were standing quietly to their guns awaiting their orders; the rush and bustle of the powder boys had ceased now that each gun had its reserve cartridge beside it.

Again the puffs of smoke from the corvette's side.

'One, two, three—'

Elevation was bad this time, or the corvette's gunnery officer had mistimed the roll of his ship. One ball tore through the air close to Peabody's side, the wind of it making him stagger, but the others struck the *Delaware's* hull, to judge from the splintering crash forward. The sound reminded Peabody suddenly of something he was astonished at having forgotten. The two guns of Jonathan's section were numbers seven and eight, main-deck starboard side – and number seven had burst. Jonathan might be dead; probably was. Peabody forced his mind to leave off thinking about Jonathan. The corvette was within easy cannon shot now – the shots came as soon as he saw the smoke.

There was a crash overhead; the spanker gaff was smashed, close to the vangs. The foretopsail lee braces were gone – no other damage; and the corvette's maintopsail was coming round again as she got under weigh ready to manouvre.

'Starboard a point,' snapped Peabody to the helmsman. There was a chance of crossing the corvette's bow, but she was well handled and parried the thrust.

'Let her have it, boys!' shouted Peabody as the ships came together, and the two broadsides roared out together.

Through the smoke Peabody saw a chance of crossing the corvette's stern, but she hove in stays and went about like clockwork, baulking him. The corvette was a handy craft, quicker in stays than the big frigate. Peabody followed her round, bellowing his orders to the helmsman through the maddening din of the guns; it was dark enough now for the big flames to be visible shooting from the muzzles of the guns. Peabody could see the corvette's rigging melting away under the hail of dismantling shot, although the corvette was hitting back as hard as she could with her nine pounders against the *Delaware's* eighteens, contending fiercely against odds of five to one. The *Racer's* main topmast fell suddenly, and along with it the mizzen topmast, just at the moment when the air round Peabody was filled with flying splinters from a shot which struck close by. As he rallied himself he found the *Delaware* flying round into the wind. There was a thunderous flap from the sails as she was taken all aback, and the guns fell abruptly silent as they ceased to bear. Peabody swung round upon the clumsy helmsman, and then shut his mouth with a snap upon the angry words he was intending to use. For the helmsman was dead, and so was the second helmsman, and so was Mr. Crane the master, and where the wheel and binnacle had once stood was now a mere splintered mass of wreckage in the darkness.

'Man the relieving tackles, Mr. Hubbard. Jib sheet, there! Haul out to starboard.'

The *Delaware* was rapidly gathering stern-way; Peabody could hear the bubble of water under the counter in the eerie silence which had settled on the ship. It seemed to take a strangely long time to work the ship's head round and get her under control again.

'Jib sheets, there! Are you asleep?'

'Tiller rope's jammed with the helm a bit to starboard, sir,' reported Hubbard.

'Clear it, then. Jib sheets! Haul out to port!'

That was better; the *Delaware* was coming round again into control, but she was circling away from the *Racer*, which was barely visible as a dark mass a full half mile away. It would take some time to work to windward and close with her again.

'Tiller rope's cleared, sir.'

'Keep her on the wind on his tack, then.'

The *Racer* was a disabled wreck, as helpless as the *Calypso*. She would be able to do nothing to-night to protect the convoy. Peabody searched the darkness to leeward. There was the brig! She had given up the attempt to join the battle, and was heading away with the wind on her quarter to evade the *Delaware* and rejoin the convoy. He might have guessed that she would.

'Hard up, the helm!' said Peabody.

There was not time to destroy the *Racer* and still be able to head off the *Bulldog*; he put the *Delaware* before the wind again and went charging down upon the brig in the darkness. The stars were already out, gleaming over the dark sea, and the moon was lighting a wide path over the waves, and two battered wrecks were being left far behind. Five minutes later Peabody saw the brig abruptly alter course to avoid being intercepted, and he brought the *Delaware* round in pursuit, staring after her amid the clatter and racket of the working party who were busy rigging a jury wheel. An hour later there came a hail from aloft.

'Deck there! There's a light way off on the starboard beam. Might be a burning ship, sir.'

It must have been a burning ship – two minutes after the hail the light was visible from the deck, reflected in a yellow glow from the clouds in the sky, lighting a quarter of the heavens. Evidently Gooding and Curtis were in among the convoy – that blaze meant that they were destroying a worthless capture. So the brig could go on holding that course until she ran aground in Cuba, if she wanted to. The *Delaware* had achieved what she set out to do. All that remained to be done was to lay on such a course as would be likely to keep the escort ships from rejoining the convoy, and give a chance of picking up stragglers. Then to go round the ship and give what orders were necessary to make her as efficient a fighting unit as possible, and after that there would be a chance of finding out what had happened to Jonathan.

CHAPTER SIX

Captain Peabody looked over the side of the *Delaware* as she crawled along in the hot sunshine with bare steerage-way.

'Mr. Atwell,' he said, harshly.

The young third lieutenant came running across to him.

'You're not attending to your duty, Mr. Atwell. What is *that* floating there?'

Atwell followed with his gaze Peabody's gnarled forefinger.

'An orange, sir,' he said, haltingly. The orange rose on a little wave against the ship's quarter and drifted astern.

'Did you see anything about that orange which interested you?' asked Peabody.

'N-no, sir,' said Atwell.

'Then either your eyesight or your wits aren't as good as they should be,' said Peabody. 'That orange had a piece bitten out of it. And its sides were hollow instead of rounded. What does that tell you?'

'Someone has been sucking it, sir,' said Atwell, a little bewildered at all this fuss over a mere orange already a hundred yards back in the ship's wake.

'Yes,' said Peabody, and he was about to continue with his Socratic questioning when his expression changed and he pointed again to something floating past the ship.

'And what's *that*?' he snapped.

'Coco-nut shell, sir,' said Atwell, and a light dawned upon him. 'Some ship's emptied her slush bucket overside.'

'And not merely that, Mr. Atwell. Oranges and coco-nuts – where does that ship hail from?'

'The West Indies, sir!' said Atwell.

'Yes,' said Peabody. 'That means we're in the track of some part of the convoy. Now do you understand why you should have seen it?'

'Yes, sir.'

'Don't neglect your duty again, Mr. Atwell,' said Peabody, turning away.

Atwell was a 'good officer,' thought Peabody. There was never any slackness about the men when he had charge of the deck, and the sails were always properly set, and the helmsman was always on his course. But there was another side of the picture. Officers of that sort were so engrossed in the details of their routine duties that they had no thought to spare for anything else. And not merely that; years of routine duties had a stunting effect upon their imaginations and logical faculties. Atwell ought to have made deductions from the sight of that floating rubbish instantly. Peabody was afraid that Atwell would never develop into a great commander, into a Truxtun or a Decatur.

But the sight of that rubbish confirmed Peabody in his conclusions as to the movements of the convoy. He had acted correctly in taking the *Delaware* through the Caicos Passage. The convoy, scattering like sheep before the wolves of privateers, must have headed for the Atlantic by the first route open to them. A dozen rich prizes probably lay only just over the horizon ahead. He looked keenly aloft to make sure that the *Delaware* was getting every possible yard out of the feeble three-knot breeze which was wafting her lazily along. He would maintain the pursuit for eleven days – or until he had taken ten prizes – before he put his ship about again to see what further trouble he could make in the West Indies. He and the *Delaware* were like a farmer and his money on market day. He had to find the best value he could for her, lay her out to the best advantage in the sure and certain knowledge that sooner or later she would be expended. Lawrence in the *Chesapeake* had chosen badly; even if he had captured the *Shannon* a captured British frigate would have been a poor exchange for the cutting up and crippling of an American one. Porter had the better notion when he headed for the Pacific instead of making a dash for home – Peabody wondered how the cruise of the *Essex* in the Pacific was succeeding.

A sorry procession was coming on deck. The wounded and sick were returning from their morning visit to the surgeon. Jonathan was leading them, his left arm in a sling – a flying fragment of iron from the burst cannon had gone through the muscles above the elbow – and behind him followed men with bandaged heads, with bandaged legs, and after them came the sick-bay attendants carrying in canvas slings the men who were too injured to walk. Downing, the Surgeon, and Hoyle, the Surgeon's mate, followed, and supervised the laying of the wounded against the spars in the shadow of the mainsail. They were a couple of surgeons from New York, obsessed with fantastic ideas; they had the notion that sick men should not be kept in a comfortably dark 'tween decks. They were perfectly convinced that sunshine did sick men good, and they even declared that there was no danger for them in night air at sea. Downing was most emphatic on the point that air once breathed had a deleterious effect upon the system, in defiance of the common knowledge that air thoroughly warmed and humanised was far better than raw fresh stuff. Peabody himself could not sleep if there was a suspicion of a draught in his cabin, and as a New Englander born he was innately suspicious of Yorkers, but he had not been able to enforce his ideas upon the two mad doctors. By virtue of their warrants from the Secretary of the Navy they were independent of him in the matter of the sick, and they traded upon the fact quite shamelessly, littering the neat deck with sick men, and always willing to argue with their captain.

Peabody strolled forward.

'Good morning, Jonathan.'

'Good morning,' and then after an interval, 'sir.'

Jonathan was sick with his wound; otherwise he would not have spoken in such a surly fashion.

'How's the arm to-day?'

'Hurting like hell,' said Jonathan.

Peabody turned to the others.

'Doing well, sir,' said one of them.

'Stumps as clean as a whistle, sir,' said the one whose leg had been shattered below the knee. He was grey with loss of blood and weakness, but he made himself smile as he lay there.

'Cross and Huntley died during the night, sir,' said Downing, in a quiet aside to Peabody. 'I'm sorry about Huntley – I thought he'd pull through. But I never had any hope for Cross.'

'So I remember,' said Peabody.

This would be the third successive day in which they had buried dead men overside, and he contemplated the approaching ceremony with distaste. Murray had come up, and was talking earnestly to Jonathan, and trying to catch his captain's eye at the same moment.

'Damn it, man,' Murray was saying, 'you *must* remember something about it.'

'I don't,' said Jonathan, doggedly.

'I was asking about that burst gun, sir,' explained Murray to Peabody. 'I was thinking, it might have been double-loaded, and it was in Mr. Peabody's charge.'

'What makes you think it was double-loaded?'

'I'd just given the order for round shot, sir, because the range was drawing out. If the gun was already loaded with dismantling shot the men might be excited and put in another charge and a round shot on top. That'd burst any gun.'

'So it would,' agreed Peabody, and he looked at his brother.

'He's trying to blame something on me, the same as always,' said Jonathan.

'It's important, sir,' explained Murray. 'If the men don't trust the guns they're serving—'

He left the sentence unfinished but adequate to the occasion.

'You're quite right, Mr. Murray,' said Peabody, looking at his brother again; but Jonathan only shook his head.

'I don't know anything about any double-loading. Mr. Murray wants me to say that's how it happened, of course – anybody can see why. And then he'd have me in trouble, which is what he wants just as much, too.'

'Don't speak so insolently,' snapped Murray.

'Mr. Peabody cannot be asked questions which might incriminate him,' said Peabody, gently.

If it could be proved that Jonathan had allowed a gun under his immediate charge to be double-loaded, Murray might easily charge him with inattention to duty, and Jonathan was clearly aware of the danger, so that he was justified in being cautious in his replies, although not in his manner of making them – only the pain of his wound could excuse that. Murray must have seen all this, for he opened his mouth, shut it again, and turned away after raising his hat to his captain.

'You must be more respectful another time,' said Peabody, a little testily. He was annoyed that his capable second lieutenant should be annoyed.

'All right, all right,' said Jonathan.

Peabody left him to doze in the sun, and walked aft again to see that Atwell got every inch of speed out of the *Delaware.* The word had got round the crew that there were prizes ahead, and everyone was keyed up in anticipation. The hands worked with a will as the sails were trimmed to the fitful wind, and half the watch below spent their time aloft eagerly scanning the horizon for sails. When the wind backed northerly there were more frequent calls for the watch, because Peabody would not allow the *Delaware* to tack far off the direct course which he had mentally allotted to the flying convoy, but drove her along in a succession of short boards, tacking every half hour. But nobody minded the extra work; everyone realised that a weatherly ship like the *Delaware* had her best chance of overtaking dull-sailing merchant ships with a foul wind.

The first sail they sighted proved a disappointment. She showed up to windward on the opposite tack to the *Delaware,* and the latter intercepted her with ease because she made no attempt to escape. Midshipman Howard's sharp eyes first detected the fact that she was flying two flags, and a moment later a score of telescopes identified them as the Stars and Stripes flying above the Red Ensign. When they closed within hailing distance she announced herself for what she was – the ship *Dalhousie*, Kingston to London, prize to the *Emulation*, Daniel Stevens, prizemaster, heading for Charleston with prisoners.

'We've gotten together two hundred of 'em under hatches, sir,' yelled Stevens. 'Rum, sugar, an' coffee.'

She would be a nice prize if she could be taken through the British blockade into an American port; the prisoners themselves represented a fortune, with the Federal Government paying a hundred dollars a head for British seamen placed in the hands of a United States sheriff. Gooding had destroyed some of his smaller prizes, after stripping them of everything valuable, and had sent the *Dalhousie* in, with the hope that she might make an American port. She had nothing better than an even chance, Peabody decided, watching her sail over the horizon.

Six hours later the lookouts reported more sails, dead to windward, close hauled on the port tack.

'Two brigs an' two barquentines, sir,' reported master's mate O'Brien, all breathless, having run to the masthead with his glass and descended, all within two minutes. 'Merchantmen for sure, sir, an' sailing in company.'

That meant without a doubt that they were part of the disrupted convoy. There was small chance for them, with the *Delaware* to leeward of them, so that it was impossible for them to scatter far. The barquentines held on their course, and the brigs went about on the other tack, as soon as the *Delaware's* dread topsails had climbed up over the horizon sufficiently far to be clearly identified.

'Keep her steady as she goes, Mr. Hubbard,' said Peabody, 'We'll have the barquentine first.'

The *Delaware* could lie nearly a point closer to the wind than the clumsy merchant ships, and could sail almost two feet to their one – she was like a pike among minnows. Remorselessly she ran them down, Peabody watching grimly as the distance shortened.

'Try a shot from one of the bow guns, Mr. Murray, if you please.'

The shot crashed out, and Peabody saw a black speck rise to the peak of the nearer barquentine, flutter a moment, and then descend. Apparently all on board were careless of what should happen to their ship now she was taken. She was allowed to fly up into the wind, and lay there all aback in a flurry of disordered canvas.

'Back the mizzen topsail, Mr. Hubbard. Mr. Sampson! Take the quarter boat and take possession. Mr. Kidd! Take six men and go with Mr. Sampson. Pull to the other barquentine and take possession as soon as she strikes. Square away, if you please, Mr. Hubbard. Mr. Murray, put a shot across that other barquentine's bows.'

The flag of the leading barquentine rose and fell again, and she hove-to. Peabody watched for a moment until he saw the *Delaware's* boat pulling towards her.

'Tack after the brigs, please, Mr. Hubbard.'

The brigs had won for themselves no more than an extra two hours of freedom; the *Delaware* caught up to them hot-foot. It was a little pitiful to see their flags come fluttering down – Peabody felt an odd twinge as he stood in the hot sunlight and watched his prizes come clustering together, obedient to his orders. He listened a little gloomily to the reports sent over by his prizemasters – Barquentine *Richmond*, three hundred and twenty tons, Kingston to London, cargo of sugar, twenty-nine of a crew; Barquentine *Faithful Wife*, three hundred and forty tons, Kingston to Liverpool, and so on. They were all bulk cargoes – no valuable specie for him to take under his special charge. Murray and Hubbard were eagerly turning over the pages of the prizes' logs, in search of possible hints as to the whereabouts of any other survivors of the convoy.

'Twenty-five sail took the Caicos Passage, sir,' announced Murray. 'The others must still be ahead.'

A laughing working party were swaying up a miscellaneous collection of livestock from the longboat of one of the barquentines, chickens and pigs and a score of big turtles; the city of London aldermen would go short of their favourite dish this coming winter, and the crew of the *Delaware* would have a brief taste of fresh food again. The four captured captains stood in a sullen group on the other side of the deck, saying nothing to each other, and trying to display no emotion while their captor decided on their fate; they might as well have been Mohegans awaiting the stake.

'Mr. Hubbard!'

'Sir!'

'I'll have those two longboats hoisted on board. They'll serve instead of the boats we lost.'

'Aye aye, sir.'

'Which of you gentlemen is captain of the *Laura Troughton*?'

'I am.'

The captain of the smaller of the two brigs came with a rolling gait across to Peabody, to listen sullenly to what Peabody had to say.

'I'm setting your brig free after my prize crew has thrown those guns of yours overboard. You will take on board the officers and crews of the other three vessels.'

'But Holy Peter! That'll make a hundred souls on board or more.'

'Yes.'

'The water won't last, sir. I've only ten tons on board.'

'You've a fair wind for the Cuban coast. Four days and you'll be in Havana.' Peabody turned to the other three captains. 'I'll give you twenty minutes to get your property transferred to the *Laura Troughton*. At four bells I shall set fire to your ship.'

It was the best thing to do. Releasing the prisoners meant a loss of ten thousand dollars in prize money; burning the ships meant a loss of ten times as much, but the *Delaware* had few men to spare for prize crews, and they must be reserved to take in really valuable captures – if there was any chance of evading the blockade. And sending the *Laura Troughton* in to Havana – the water shortage would ensure that she went nowhere else – would deprive England of her services and those of her crew for some time to come.

Peabody looked aft as the *Delaware* bore up to the northward again. The *Laura Troughton* was heading south with all the sail she could set, and the hot sun glared down on the other three vessels drifting aimlessly on the blue water. Each of the three was enshrouded in a faint mist, rendering their outlines vague and shimmering. As he watched, he saw the sails of the *Richmond* suddenly whisk away into nothing as the flames, invisible in the bright sun, ran up her masts. The *Faithful Wife's* main mast suddenly lurched drunkenly to one side, and a dense volume of black smoke poured out from her gaping decks, drifting to leeward in an ugly cloud. Sugar and rum made a fine blaze. A sudden hard explosion from the *Richmond* told how the flames had reached her small powder store – only a hundredweight or two, but enough to send a column of smoke shooting upwards. He could see that the whole of her stern had been blown away, and as the misshapen wreck drifted on the surface the billows of smoke told how the invading sea was battling with the roaring flames. The *Faithful Wife's* masts had fallen now, and so had the brig's, and the two blazing hulks had drifted together and were wrapped, side by side, in the clouds of murky smoke. It was a horrible sight, and Peabody could hardly bear to look at it. But he made himself do so, for a strange mixture of reasons which he himself made no attempt to analyse. Under the influence of the New England conscience he was mortifying himself, making himself pay in person for his country's weakness, rubbing his own nose in the dirty fact that he was here as a skulking commerce destroyer and not as the fighting man which all his instincts guided him to be.

CHAPTER SEVEN

By the time that Peabody decided to turn back from the pursuit of the convoy the *Delaware* had overtaken and destroyed fourteen sail of merchant shipping. Another small brig had been released laden with the crews, and the ship *Three Sisters* had been despatched with a prize crew in the attempt to run the blockade into an American port. The *Three Sisters'* cargo of mahogany and log wood was not specially valuable, but she was armed with no less than twelve beautiful long brass nine pounders, and it was for this reason that Peabody had sent her in. There was a terrible shortage of cannons in the United States, as he well knew; there were privateers waiting in harbour fully equipped save for their guns. America was still laughing over the story of the privateer captain – a Connecticut man at that – who sold one of his prizes, as she lay at the quay, for a greatly enhanced price because she carried guns, and it was only later that the purchaser discovered that the guns for which he had paid so dearly were merely wooden 'Quaker' guns. It was an amusing story – especially amusing in the Wooden Nutmeg State – but it abundantly illustrated the shortage of weapons which was hampering the United States. Those twelve guns would serve to arm another *Emulation* or *Oliver*, while if the British retook them before they reached American shores it would be small gain to Britain, glutted as she was with the guns taken from a hundred thousand prizes.

Three of the ships overhauled were Spaniards, and Peabody had to let them go. Spain was an ally of England against France, and those cargoes, consigned to Passages, were almost certainly destined for the use of Wellington's army, but still, the United States were neither at war with Spain nor in alliance with France. Peabody's instructions were explicit – he read them through carefully again – and he had to let them go, sadly realising, for by no means the first time, that Mr. Madison had not the least idea of how to fight a war. There was the comforting thought that perhaps, now that he had crippled the convoy escort, some French privateer or other might snap those Spaniards up when they reached European waters. It was a ridiculous political situation; Mr. Madison's polished hair splitting might make it sound logical, but Peabody, the man who had to implement the policy at the risk of his life and liberty, was acutely aware of its practical fallacies.

And now he knew the convoy was scattered over the breadth of the Atlantic, with each ship laying its own course for home – what ships were left of it – and it would be an unprofitable use of the *Delaware* to proceed farther into that waste of waters in the hope of further captures. It was at focal points that he wished to strike; he thought for the moment of crossing the ocean and appearing in the mouth of the Channel, but decided against it. Those waters would be thick with British ships of war, and the arguments which had in the first place directed the *Delaware* to the West Indies still held good. The day they let the last of the Spaniards go Peabody gave the order which turned the *Delaware's* bow to the southward again. Presumably the *Emulation* and the *Oliver* had taken every prize they could find a crew for, and had headed for Savannah days ago, so that there would be need of the *Delaware's* presence.

It was comforting to think of the outcry which would

arise in London when the news arrived there that two privateers and a frigate had got in among the West Indian convoy. There were Lloyd's underwriters who would drive home in their coaches broken men; there were shipowners who would lapse into bankruptcy. Perhaps it was only a pin prick in an elephant's hide, but it was Peabody's duty to go on pricking, until either his career should end in an ocean grave – or in Dartmoor prison – or until the enemy was pestered into asking for peace. It was not a very dignified part to play in a world convulsed in the titanic struggle which was going on at present, but it was the part which Providence had allotted him, along with other seemingly trivial and yet solidly satisfactory duties like keeping track of the consumption of ship's stores.

Peabody was at work on this very matter when the next break in his routine duties came. He was sitting at his desk with a plan of the *Delaware's* hull in front of him. Every week his crew consumed a ton of salt meat, and a ton of hard bread and other stores. Since they left Long Island Sound they had fired away nine tons of shot and six tons of powder, and the bursting of the long eighteen pounder on the main deck had relieved her of a further two tons of metal. He shaded in upon the outline the parts of the ship which had been relieved of weight, the tiers where only empty beef barrels stood and the bilges which had been emptied of shot. He sat back and looked at the result, and then narrowed his eyes as he visualised the *Delaware* afloat. She would be down by the stern a little – but then on the other hand he had the feeling that she would be a trifle handier and faster if she were. He was willing to give it a trial, even with the knowledge that the continued success of his voyage might depend at any moment on his being able to get every foot of speed out of his ship. He made a mental note to tell Fry, the gunner, to draw ammunition until further orders from the after magazine.

He had become aware a second or two before of a bustle on the deck above his head, of a hoarse voice hailing from the masthead, and he was not surprised when Midshipman Kidd came into his cabin after knocking at the door.

'Mr. Murray's respects, sir. There's a sail in sight to the east'ard, sir.'

Peabody's eyes went up to the tell-tale compass over his head as Kidd went on speaking.

'She's on nearly the same course as us, sir, and she looks like a sloop of war.'

'Thank you,' said Peabody. 'My compliments to Mr. Murray, and ask him to send the hands to quarters.'

He put his papers neatly away into the three upper right-hand pigeon-holes of his desk, each paper into its appropriate place, and he shut and locked the desk with unhurried movements. The roar of the drums sending the crew to quarters was already echoing through the ship, and when he stepped out of his cabin the main deck was swarming with men running madly to their posts, with the petty officers snapping out sharp orders at the laggards. He put on his hat and moved towards the companion; the after guard came pouring past him and threw themselves into their task of pulling down the cabin bulkheads. He had been intending to put the crew through this exercise to-morrow, but it was better as it was. Even with a first-class crew drill was more effective when there was a definite goal in sight. On deck Hubbard and Murray uncovered to him; Hubbard had his watch in hand and was noting how long it took to clear for action.

'I'll give the order for the guns to be run out myself, Mr. Murray.'

'Aye aye, sir.'

Hubbard pointed to windward to where a tiny triangle of white showed over the horizon.

'She looks like a man o' war, sir, but I can't make her out fully.'

'Bear up for her, if you please, Mr. Hubbard.'

On converging courses the two ships neared rapidly.

'Masthead, there!' yelled Hubbard. 'Is there any other sail in sight?'

'No, sir. Ne'er a thing, sir.'

The strange sail was a ship of war without a doubt. There was a man o' war pennant at her masthead, and a row of gun ports along her side, but she came sailing securely along as though with a perfectly clear conscience, strange for a ship of war in sight of another much larger. But there could hardly be any sort of ambush planned with nothing else in sight from the masthead.

'I reckon she's French, sir, to judge by the cut o' that foresail,' said Hubbard, squinting through his glass. 'A Frenchie'd run from us until he knew who we were.'

'Hoist the colours, Mr. Hubbard, if you please,' said Peabody, looking at her through his own glass.

The odds were at least ten to one that any ship of war at sea was British – this might be a British prize, which would account for her French appearance, and if she were thinking the *Delaware* were British a careless captain might perhaps come down as confidently as that. But if she were a British ship her doom was sealed by now, for she would never be able to escape to windward from the *Delaware*. A victory over her, petty though it would be, would be a stimulus for the American people. It was over a year since the last King's ship had struck her flag to the Stars and Stripes.

The colours were at the peak now, and Peabody saw a dull ball run up to the sloop's peak in reply, and break into a flutter of white. The white ensign? Peabody looked through his glass again. No. It was a plain white flag, unrelieved by any red cross or Union in the hoist.

'What in hell—?' said Hubbard beside him, peering at the flag. 'Maybe she's a cartel, sir.'

Hubbard meant that the white flag was a flag of truce, and that the ship was on her way to exchange prisoners or to deliver a message. But a cartel would fly the national colours above the white flag, and Peabody would hardly believe that any naval officer could be ignorant of that convention.

'Fire a gun to leeward,' he said.

That was the politest way of stressing his demand for further information. The sloop's course and position were sufficient proof that she was not bound for anywhere in the United States. If as a cartel she were a British vessel negotiating with France he would not recognise the white flag, he decided. France was no ally of America, and any temporary suspension of hostilities between France and England meant nothing to his country.

The gun went off, and every eye on deck watched the strange sloop. She did nothing whatever except to hold steadily on her course with the white flag at her peak, blandly ignoring the *Delaware* altogether.

'God-damned impertinence!' said Hubbard.

''Bout ship, Mr. Hubbard. Mr. Murray! Run out the guns and put a shot across her bows!'

Amid the bustle and hurry of going about came the dull thunder of the wooden gun trucks rumbling across the deck seams as the *Delaware* showed her teeth. As she steadied on her new course the other bow-chaser went off with a crash. Peabody saw the sloop's starboard jib-guy part like a cracked whip – Murray had put a liberal interpretation upon his orders. Immediately afterwards the sloop showed signs of life. She threw her topsails abruptly aback, and came up into the wind like a horse reined up from full gallop, her canvas slatting violently. Apparently the shot and the threatened broadside had had their effect.

The *Delaware* forged up alongside her, the gun captains looking along their sights, not a sound in the ship save for her sharp bows cleaving the water.

'Heave-to, if you please, Mr. Hubbard,' said Peabody, taking up his speaking trumpet.

'Sloop ahoy! What sloop's that?'

A high-pitched voice sent a reply back to him down wind, but the words were unintelligible.

'French, maybe. Or Eyetalian,' said Hubbard.

'What sloop's that?' asked Peabody again, irascibly.

There was a second's pause before the reply came, in English this time, with a marked foreign accent.

'Say it again!' roared Peabody.

One of the gold-laced officers on the sloop's quarterdeck raised his speaking trumpet again. When he spoke his intonation betrayed quite as much exasperation as did Peabody's.

'His Most Christian Majesty's Ship—'

What the name was they could not be sure.

'Sounded like "negress," sir,' said Hubbard. 'Queer name for a ship. But she's a Dago, or mebbe a Portugee.'

'Neither of those,' said Peabody.

The King of Spain was His Most Catholic Majesty, and the King of Portugal was His Most Faithful Majesty – he had heard the pompous expressions used time and again when he was with Preble in the Mediterranean. He had never heard of His Most Christian Majesty.

'I'll send a boat,' he roared into the wind, and instantly decided that this was a business which he himself had better attend to; if an international incident were to grow out of this he wanted full responsibility.

'Pass the word for my servant to bring my sword,' he said. 'I'll go in the quarter boat, Mr. Hubbard – and pass the word for Mr. Peabody to come with me.'

Washington came running with sword and belt and boat cloak; Jonathan came up from his post below. There was a fair sea running, but they made a neat job of dropping the quarter boat into the lee which the ship afforded, with Jonathan sitting nursing his wounded arm in the stern sheets. Peabody swung himself down the fall, timed the rise of the boat as a wave lifted her, and dropped in a moment before she fell away again. With the spray that was flying he was glad of his boat cloak to preserve his uniform from salt.

'Give way,' he said to the boat's crew, and they thrust against the Delaware's side and took up the stroke, the boat bobbing up and down over the big Atlantic waves.

'She's surely French enough in looks,' he said, examining the smart little ship towards which they were heading.

'Is she?' said Jonathan.

'Oars!' said Peabody to the crew, and the slow rhythmic pulling stopped while the boat ran alongside the sloop. The bowman got to his feet with a boathook. A boatswain's chair came dangling down to them, and Peabody threw off his cloak and swung himself on to it.

'Follow me,' he called to Jonathan, as the swell took the boat from under him.

A dozen curious faces looked up at him as he swung over the rail and dropped to the deck; he stepped down, removed his hat, and eyed the waiting group. With a little surprise he noticed two women standing aft by the taffrail, but he did not have time for more than a brief glance. A stout officer with massive epaulettes stepped forward.

'Captain Nicolas Dupont,' he said – his English was stilted and he pronounced the French names in French fashion, unintelligibly to Peabody, 'of His Most Christian Majesty's sloop *Tigresse*.'

'Captain Josiah Peabody, United States Ship *Delaware*,' said Peabody.

Malta had accustomed him to encounters with officers of foreign services, but there was for him still a vague sort of unreality about stiff formality.

'You wore your – your coat in the boat, Captain,' said Dupont. 'We could not see your rank. Please pardon me for not receiving you with the appropriate compliments.'

'Of course,' said Peabody.

All this was the preliminary salute before crossing swords, he felt. He and Dupont eyed each other so keenly that neither paid any attention to Jonathan swaying down in the boatswain's chair behind Peabody.

'And now, sir,' said Dupont. 'Would you have the goodness to explain why your ship fired upon me?'

'Why didn't you show your colours?' riposted Peabody. He was in no mood for a passive defensive.

Dupont's bushy brows came together angrily.

'We showed them, sir. We still show them.'

He gesticulated towards the peak, where the white flag fluttered. Peabody noticed for the first time a gleam of gold on the white, and felt a moment's misgiving which he was determined not to show.

'Where are your national colours?' he asked.

'Those are they. The flag of His Most Christian Majesty.'

'His Most Christian Majesty?'

'His Most Christian Majesty Louis, by the grace of God King of France and Navarre.'

Dupont's rage was joined to genuine and obvious distress,

like a man facing approaching humiliation.

'King of France!' said Peabody.

'King of France and Navarre,' insisted Dupont.

Peabody began to see the light, and at the same time worse misgivings than ever began to assail him.

'Napoleon has fallen?' he said.

'The usurper Bonaparte has fallen,' said Dupont solemnly. 'Louis Eighteen sits on his rightful throne.' It was the most tremendous news for twenty years. The shadow which had lain across the whole world for twenty years had lifted. They were emerging into the sunshine of a new era.

Dupont's distress was evaporating as he guessed at Peabody's astonishment, and Peabody began to feel sympathy for Dupont in the quandary in which he had found himself. A simple hoisting of the tricolour flag which the world knew so well would have saved all this misunderstanding, but Dupont had not been able to bring himself to hoist it – it would have been a horrible humiliation to have received protection from the colours of the Revolution against which he had struggled for a lifetime. It must have been a humiliation, too, to discover that the world had forgotten that title of Most Christian Majesty which had at one time overawed Europe. And he knew immediate qualms at the thought that he had fired upon the flag of what was presumably a neutral country now. He saw the need for prompt apology, unreserved apology.

Mr. Madison would be furiously angry if he heard of the incident, but that was not the point. The United States could not afford to antagonise anyone else, not while she was locked in a death struggle with the greatest antagonist of all. He had thought for the moment of laughing at the whole affair, turning on his heel and quitting the *Tigresse*, leaving the politicians to disentangle the business as best they could, but he put aside the insidious temptation to reckless arrogance. It was his duty to humble himself. He swallowed twice as he collected the words together in his mind.

'Sir,' he said slowly, 'I hope you will allow me to apologise, to apologise for this – this unfortunate thing that has happened. I am very sorry, sir.'

It was not the words of the apology which mollified Dupont as much as the tremendous reluctance with which the words came. A lion could hardly have given back a lamb to its mother more unreadily. An apology from a man so totally unaccustomed to apologising was doubly sweet to the fat little captain, and his face cleared.

'Let us say no more about it, sir,' said Dupont. He creased himself across his fat middle in a profound bow which Peabody tried to imitate, and then they looked at each other, Peabody at a loss as to what to say next. Polite small talk, always difficult to him, was more difficult than ever after the strain of the last few minutes, but Dupont was equal to the occasion. He glanced across at Jonathan.

'And this gentleman is—?' he asked.

'My brother, Midshipman Peabody,' said Peabody, gratefully.

'Your servant, sir,' said Dupont. He turned to the group of officers behind him, and the two brothers were engulfed in a wave of introductions. Everyone was bowing and scraping and making legs on the instant, and there was an immense amount of broken English being spoken. Peabody had yet to meet the naval officer of any nation who did not possess at least a few words of English, but these officers all had more than that, even though their syntax was doubtful and their accents marked. As the flurry died down Dupont said:

'Would you please come and be presented to my passengers?'

The whole business of bowings and scrapings began again the moment Dupont began to lead them away; it left Peabody a trifle dazed – as a young man he had always been a little amused during Captain Truxtun's careful lessons in the deportment of a gentleman and a naval officer, finding it hard to believe that grown men really did these things.

Across the deck, beside the taffrail, stood a little group of three people, including the two women whom Peabody had noticed some time back. The third member of the group was a man.

'Your Excellency,' said Dupont. 'May I present Captain

Josiah Peabody of the United States Navy? – His Excellency the Marquis de St. Amant de Boixe, Governor of His Most Christian Majesty's possessions in the Lesser Antilles.'

Peabody put his hand with his hat on his heart and moved his feet into the first position, but his bow was cut short by the Marquis stepping forward and offering his hand. His grip was hearty and firm. Peabody, a little more dazed still, had the impression of a strong face, extraordinarily handsome, with piercing blue eyes. The Marquis was a man in his early forties, with his hair clubbed at the back in a fashion a trifle old-fashioned; across his gold-laced blue coat he wore the broad ribbon of some order of nobility, of a vivid blue which complemented the blue of his eyes.

'It is a pleasure to meet you, Captain,' he said, without a trace of accent, 'and you, too, Mr. Peabody. It would be a further pleasure to present you to my sister, Madame la Comtesse d'Ernée, and my daughter, Mademoiselle de Breuil.'

Everything contributed to Peabody's bedazement; perhaps the fact that he had just shaken hands when he was preparing to bow had thrown him off his balance at the start. The two women had put back their veils, and revealed faces which strongly resembled the Marquis's. The sister was the older, and there was a line or two on her face and something in the set of her features which made for hardness and supplemented the widow's black which she wore. But the daughter – Peabody's wits drowned in those blue eyes. He had already bowed to the Countess and was preparing to bow again when he met their glance, but the bow was cut short while he stared. He was conscious of no other details about her; the Countess was speaking to him, but Peabody's ears registered the words as a flat series of meaningless sounds. She was going down in a curtsey to him, her eyes still on him, and it was only with an effort that he managed to push his foot forward and complete his bow. He tore his glance away to make himself listen to the Countess.

'Confess, Captain,' she was saying, 'you did not recognise our flag when you saw it.'

Peabody, until he could find words, looked up to where the golden lilies – visible enough from here – flapped on the white flag at the peak.

'I have been at sea twenty years, ma'am,' he said, 'but this is the first time I have seen it.'

'Fie,' said the Countess. 'The flag of Lafayette, of de Grasse, which freed you from King George, and yet you fire on it!'

'Louise,' said the Marquis. 'The captain did no such thing. I have Captain Dupont's word for it that not a shot has been fired this morning.'

Peabody looked at him gratefully, and caught at his cue.

'No indeed, sir,' he said, and then tried to correct himself: 'Your Excellency.'

These cursed titles of honour! He looked away and met those blue eyes again. There was a friendly twinkle in them which made his heart miss a beat. He wanted to wipe his face with his handkerchief, but he knew that would be inelegant. He was hot under the skin, and the burning sun was calling forth the sweat on his forehead. It may have been on account of his embarrassment that the Marquis brought the conversation round to business, so as to give him a chance to recover.

'The incident is forgotten,' he said. 'It is my intention, as soon as I reach Martinique, to maintain the strictest neutrality.'

'It will be a strange experience,' said the Countess, 'for French people to be neutral while there is a war on.'

'Yes,' said Peabody. His mind was already at work upon the problems set him by the defeat of France. 'Martinique is to be French again?'

'Martinique, Guadeloupe, and their dependencies.'

This was of lively interest. Up to this moment the British had conquered and ruled all the West Indies save for Haiti and the Spanish possessions; the former was not strong enough to defend her neutrality, and Spain, as an ally of Great Britain, although not at war with the United States, would hardly be likely to afford a safe refuge in her colonies to the *Delaware* should she need it. Until now there had been no neutrals worth mentioning in this war which had involved the whole world, and he was already wondering how he could put the new situation to use. A fresh consideration struck him, and he turned to include Dupont as well as the Marquis in his inquiry.

'You won't inform the British of my position of course, sir?' he said.

'That would be un-neutral,' said the Marquis, quickly, before the captain could reply.

'Thank you,' said Peabody, and then, remembering again : 'Your Excellency.'

Once again there was that twinkle in the girl's blue eyes.

'I hope you are planning to visit us at Fort-de-France, Captain Peabody,' she said.

'Anne!' exclaimed the Countess, a little scandalised.

'My daughter has said exactly what was in my mind,' interposed the Marquis. 'It would give me the greatest pleasure to be able to return some of the hospitality which my daughter and I owe to America.'

Peabody looked his inquiries.

'I was born in your country, Captain Peabody,' said the girl – Anne was her name, apparently.

'How's that again?' asked Peabody.

'Anne was born in Philadelphia,' explained the Marquis, and then, after a moment's hesitation, 'my wife is buried there. We were in America during the Terror. Anne was born the day they guillotined Robespierre.'

'We all thought then,' said the Countess, sadly, 'when the news came, that the world would soon be at peace again. And that is twenty years ago, and some of us are still at war.'

'But you haven't been living in America for the last twenty years?' said Peabody to Anne. As far as he was concerned there was practically no one else on deck.

Anne shook her head and twinkled again.

'I left when I was four,' she said. 'I have no memory of it, and I am sure that is a pity.'

'I acted as envoy from my King to your President,' explained the Marquis. 'After four years I was transferred to Europe. For the last five we have been living in London.'

Conversation died away at that. Peabody had too much to

think about to be able to say anything while he digested the two remarkable facts that Napoleon had fallen and that Anne was American born. He shook himself back into politeness.

'This has been a delightful visit,' he said, racking his mind for the right words. 'I must thank you very much.'

The ladies went down in curtseys as he bowed; the Marquis shook hands, and Dupont prepared to accompany him to the ship's side.

'Don't forget you've promised to visit us!' said the Countess.

This time there were formalities, pipes twittering, and marines presenting arms as his boatswain's chair swung him off the deck, and then the boat danced back to the *Delaware*.

'A couple of peaches, they were,' said Jonathan.

'Good God!' said Peabody, turning on him.

He was simply amazed that anyone could possibly think of Anne as a peach; the two notions were so far removed from each other.

'The old 'un's getting long in the tooth,' said Jonathan, 'but I reckon she could still give a bit of sport. And the young 'un—!'

'Shut your mouth!' snapped Peabody.

They ran under the *Delaware's* counter and grabbed the falls; Peabody swung himself up, hat, sword, and all, on to the quarterdeck, hand over hand, where Hubbard called all hands to attention. Peabody blinked about him at the familiar surroundings. It was odd to be among these familiar things and yet to feel so strange, to have commonplace details to attend to during this moment of unusual exaltation.

'Mr. Murray!' he yelled. 'A salute of nineteen guns, if you please! Mr. Hubbard, dip the colours at the salute. Dismiss the watch below, and square away.'

The ensign ran slowly down and up again as the saluting gun barked out. The yards came round, and the *Delaware's* idle pitching over the waves changed to a more purposeful rise and swoop. The sloop's sails were filling, too, and repeated puffs of smoke broke from her bows as she answered the *Delaware's* salute. Peabody stood staring back at her while the two ships diverged; there was – he was almost sure – a speck of white waving from her quarterdeck, and he snatched off his hat and stood bareheaded.

CHAPTER EIGHT

Peabody sat pen in hand bending over the ship's log. 'Encountered French Government sloop *Tigresse*, Captain Dupon, having on board—'

This was hard work. The name *Tigresse* came easily, because Peabody had read it cut into the ship's bell. He was fairly sure about the 'Dupon,' too, having heard the captain enunciate it clearly enough although with his odd French accent. But it was not so easy to describe the *Tigresse*. He was not at all anxious to write 'His Most Christian Majesty's,' or 'The French King's,' because he was by no means sure whether the American Government had recognised that potentate, and it had called for a little thought to devise a way round the difficulty. And now that he had come to the point of saying who else was on board he was quite at a loss. There was a Marquis, he knew – he had caught the word during the introductions – but what he was Marquis of Peabody had not the least recollection, even if he had ever really heard the cumbrous title. Somehow he had formed an accurate idea as to what were to be the Marquis's official duties, but the actual words used by Dupont in his presentation quite escaped him. Peabody scratched his nose with the end of the quill, pondered, and went on writing – 'Having on board the new Governor of Martinique and his family.'

That solved the difficulty. She had blue eyes (Peabody's thoughts went off at an abrupt tangent) and very black hair whose curls were in the most vivid contrast with her white forehead. Her given name was Anne, but what the rest of it was he could not tell, not for the life of him. Anne de Something-or-other. That did not describe her in the least – she was somebody much more definite than that. Into those blue eyes there sometimes came a twinkle which was one of the most exciting things he had ever seen. But for the rest of her— Peabody tried methodically to piece his memories of her together. Tall? Short? Peabody forced himself, with rigid self-control, to remember what he had noticed about her before he had met her eyes; he tried to call up before his mental vision his glimpse of her on the quarterdeck when his only reaction to the sight of her had been surprise at the presence of females. The carronade beside her had been a twelve pounder, and that came up as far as – yes, of course, she was short. The Marquis was not a tall man, and she had appeared small beside him. She had been wearing some sort of veil which she had put back to twinkle at him. What else she was wearing he could not remember at all, not at all. But the black curls and the blue eyes and the pink-and-white skin he could remember more vividly than he had ever remembered anything. Jonathan had called her 'the young 'un,' and spoke of her as a peach. Jonathan was a young fool who was not fit to approach any young woman.

Peabody put the log on one side, rose from his desk, and walked up on deck; before his eyes, in the dark alley way, there floated the vision of Anne, which only faded – just as a ghost would – as he entered the strong sunshine of the deck. Atwell uncovered to him, and he paced rapidly up and down the quarterdeck for a few turns while he looked over the ship. Everything there was just as it should be; the sails were drawing well, the ship was exactly on her course, the watch was at work in a quiet and orderly fashion. Peabody contrasted his own happy lot with that of the British captains. The maintenance of American ships of war – what few of them there were – was a mere flea-bite compared with the enormous resources available; there had been no need for niggardliness in any respect whatever, while the British, maintaining the largest fleet possible, during twenty continuous years of war, were compelled to skimp and scrape to make the supplies go round. When he had commissioned the *Delaware* he had been able to pick his crew from a number of applicants three times as great as he needed – every man on board was a seasoned seaman, every specialist had spent a lifetime in his trade, while the British officers had to man their ships by force and train their crews while actually on service. He was a fortunate man.

His eye caught sight of a midshipman forward in charge of a party setting up the lee foremast shrouds. He was lounging against a gun in a manner which no young officer should use when supervising hard work done by older men. It was Jonathan.

'Mr. Peabody!' roared Peabody.

A little stir ran round the ship, unnoticed by him alone; Jonathan looked up.

'Mr. Peabody!' roared Peabody again.

Jonathan came walking aft, a faint look of surprise on his face.

'Move quicker than that when I call you!' snapped Peabody. 'Pull yourself up straight and stand at attention!'

The look of faint surprise on Jonathan's face changed to one of deep, pained surprise.

'Take that look off your face!' said Peabody, but the surprise merely became genuine.

'I don't like to see you squatting about, Mr. Peabody, when your division is at work.'

'But my arm—' said Jonathan.

'Damn your arm!' said Peabody; not so much because Downing had declared Jonathan fit for duty yesterday as because he was irritated that a member of his ship's company should plead bodily weakness when there was work to be done.

'I'm not feeling good,' said Jonathan, 'and you wouldn't either.'

It may have been surprise which had deprived Jonathan of his usual tact; he ought to have guessed that his brother was in an unusual mood, and he ought to have modelled his bearing for the moment on the slavish deference of the other officers which so excited his derision. Peabody for a couple of seconds could only gobble at him before he was able to find words for his indignation.

'Call me "sir"!' he roared. 'I don't like your damned impertinence, Mr. Peabody.'

Jonathan, still amazingly obtuse, pushed out his lower lip,

hunched his shoulders, and sulked.

'Fore top-gallant masthead! Wait there for further orders,' snapped Peabody. 'Run, you – you whippersnapper.'

He was in a towering passion, and Jonathan, looking at him for the first time with seeing eyes, suddenly realised it and was afraid. He turned and ran, with every eye in the ship following him. Halfway up the foremast shrouds he paused for a moment and looked down, saw Peabody take an impatient step, and pelted up again. Peabody watched him to the masthead, and turned abruptly to continue pacing the deck while his fury subsided. He was actually trembling a little with emotion. He had been over-indulgent to the boy, and he knew it now. The realisation that he had actually had a favourite on board since the voyage began was a shock to him.

He was by no means self-analytical enough to know that he had been indulgent to Jonathan merely because he had already been indulgent to him – that he felt the natural fondness for him which was only to be expected after his kindness to him. And fortunately for the sake of his own peace of mind, he most certainly was unaware of the reason for his new perspicacity, which was Jonathan's ill-advised remark about the two women on board the *Tigresse*. He was angry with himself, not with Jonathan, although no one save himself knew it. Atwell turned and looked away to leeward, over the blue water, so as to hide a smile; the hands at work on deck were grinning secretly to each other; below deck already the excited whisper was going round that the captain had parted brass rags with that cub of a young brother of his. and at the fore top-gallant masthead, on his uncomfortable perch, with his arm linked through the fore royal halliards, Jonathan sat and shed tears as he bemoaned the fate which had dragged him into this unsympathetic service with its unyielding discipline and soulless self-centredness, which denied to his personality any play at all. Jonathan did not accept gladly the function of being a cog in a machine. He did not even bother to look up when the lookout began bellowing 'land-ho!'

In his present mood he cared for no land that was not his

native Connecticut, where he could find sport in dodging the ire of his terrible father, who was at least a known hazard with human foibles as compared with this hard unknown brother of his. The romantic blue outline, dark against the bright sky and the silvered surface of the distant sea, had no appeal at all for him.

Down on deck Hubbard, whom the cry of land had brought up from below, was exhibiting the modest complacency natural after an exact landfall following thirty days at sea.

'Antigua, sir,' he said to his captain, fingering his telescope.

'Yes,' said Peabody, without much expression.

Now they were putting their heads into the lion's mouth. The chain of islands was one of the richest possessions of England – in sterling value hardly smaller than the whole extent of India. It was the most sensitive of all the spots in which he could deliver a pin prick. From the Virgins down to Trinidad wealth came seeping towards London. A myriad small island boats crept from island to island with the products that made England rich, accumulating them in the major ports until the time should come for a convoy to start for Europe. For several years the British had been undisputed masters here, conquering island after island – the Danish Virgins, the Dutch St. Martin, the French Martinique – in their determination to allow no enemy to imperil their possessions.

The American privateers had effected little enough in this region; the small island vessels were not tempting as prizes, for they called for a disproportionate number of men as prize crews in relation to their size, while the distances between protected harbours were so short as to give them a fair chance of evading capture. Privateers fought for money; there were shareholders in Baltimore who demanded dividends, and mere destruction – especially when that destruction was bound, sooner or later, to call down upon them the undesirable attention of British ships of war – made no appeal to them. Peabody could foresee a rich harvest awaiting the *Delaware's* reaping for a while, and perhaps ruin and perhaps death at the end of it. No one was expecting him here, for he had last been reported in the Windward Passage six hundred miles away. It was his business to wring every drop of advantage out of the surprise of his arrival, to ravage and destroy to the utmost before counter-measures could be taken against him. He looked through his glass at the steep outline of Antigua. His thin mobile lips were compressed, and the two lines which ran from the sides of his nose to the corners of his mouth showed deep in his face.

CHAPTER NINE

The cutter was only a small vessel – the mulatto captain had only two coloured hands to help him handle her – but she was all he owned. He squatted on the deck of the *Delaware* with his face in his hands, sobbing, while she burned; and Peabody and the other officers whose business brought them past him cast sympathetic glances at his unconscious back. They liked this callous destruction no better than he did, and she was the thirtieth vessel which had burned since the *Delaware* had come bursting into the Lesser Antilles. Sloops and cutters, and the little island schooners; the *Delaware* had intercepted and burned every one she had been able to catch from Antigua to Santa Cruz. The Leeward Islands must be in an uproar of consternation. Peabody walked the deck as the *Delaware* bore away from the scene; in these narrow waters where instant decision had to be taken he did not care to be even a few seconds removed from the position of control.

To windward lay St. Kitts, green and lovely, towering out of the sea with its jagged outline climbing up to the summit of Mount Misery, and on the port bow lay Nevis, sharply triangular, the narrow channel between its base and St. Kitts not yet opened up by the *Delaware's* progress along the land. Over there in Basse-Terre people must be wringing their hands and shaking their fists in helpless anger at the sight of the American frigate sailing insolently past, Stars and Stripes flying. The soldiers in the batteries there must be impotently looking along their guns, measuring the impossible range, and praying without hope for some chance which might bring the enemy within range. There were strange feelings in Peabody's heart as he gazed. It was here, in this identical bit of sea, that the *Constellation* had fought the *Vengeance*. Peabody had been a lieutenant then, in charge of eight spar-deck guns. He remembered the battle in the wild sea, then destruction and ruin, and Truxtun on the quarterdeck with his long hair blowing.

Out here to-day in the lee of St. Kitts the wind was uncertain and fluky. Every now and again the sails would flap thunderously as a puff came from an unexpected quarter, for it was at this time of day that the sea breeze might be counted upon to spring up and overmaster the perpetual breath of the trades.

'There's shipping there, sir,' said Hubbard, stabbing the air with a long forefinger. Against the white of the surf could be seen three or four small cutters creeping along on the opposite course to the *Delaware's*, hoping to reach the shelter of the batteries of Basse-Terre.

'I see them,' said Peabody.

'They'll catch the sea breeze before we do out here, sir,' went on Hubbard warningly.

'That's likely,' said Peabody. He swept his glass in a minute search of the shore line beyond Basse-Terre; there was no recent information at his disposal regarding the coastal defence of these islands, and he had no wish to incur a bloody repulse. But the most painstaking examination failed to reveal any battery hidden among the lush green of the island's steep sides.

'I'll have the boats ready to put over the side, Mr. Hubbard, if you please,' said Peabody with the glass still at his side. 'Arm the boats' crews.'

'Aye aye, sir.'

The orders were briefly given, and the boats' crews bustled into their stations, excitedly buckling cutlasses about them and thrusting pistols into their belts.

'Uncock that pistol, damn you,' bawled Hubbard suddenly.

In the privateer in which Hubbard had served before joining the *Delaware* a landsman had once let off a pistol by accident, and the bullet, flying into the arms chest, had discharged a loaded musket which in turn had set off every weapon in the chest and caused a dozen casualties.

'Starboard a little,' said Peabody to the helmsman. 'Keep her at that!'

'Keep her at that, sir!' echoed the helmsman.

The *Delaware* edged in towards the shore, skirting the extreme range of the Basse-Terre batteries, so as to give the boats the shortest pull necessary. The tiny airs of wind sent her through the water with hardly a ripple. She crept along over the matt blue amid a breathless silence.

'Boats away, Mr. Hubbard, if you please.'

'Boats away! Boats away-ay!'

Hubbard began to shout the order as soon as the first two words had left Peabody's lips; the polite remaining five were drowned in his yell. A hundred hands who had been awaiting the order went away on the run with the hoists. The two big boats rose and fell simultaneously into the water and their crews tumbled down into them, Murray commanding one and Atwell the other. They thrust clear and then flung their weight upon the oars, making the stout ash bend as they drove the big craft through the water, dashing for the shore.

'We might be a whaler, sir,' grinned Hubbard to Peabody, as he watched their progress.

The cutters saw their doom hurtling at them. The leading one manned four sweeps in a desperate effort to gain the shelter of the batteries; Peabody saw the long black blades begin their slow pulling, but the other three incontinently went about and headed for the shore. Atwell's longboat altered course for the cutter under sweeps, Peabody following her with his glass. A white pillar of water emerged suddenly from the surface of the blue sea a cable's length ahead of the longboat; the big guns at Basse-Terre were chancing their aim. But a minute later Atwell was alongside, and not long after that he was pulling away again. A crowded dinghy was taking the cutter's crew to the land, and a black cloud of smoke was slowly rising from the cutter and spreading over the surface of the sea.

Peabody swung his glass towards the other vessels. They had reached the shore, and their crews tumbled out into the surf in a wild rush for safety. Peabody watched Murray steady his boat on the edge of the surf for a moment and then dash in after them; it was interesting to see if Murray kept his head during his tenure of independent command. A little group of white-shirted man ran up the narrow beach as a guard against surprise, and another group moved along to the beached boats, while the longboat waited in the surf with oars out ready for instant departure. Murray was acting with perfect correctness, decided Peabody. His glass caught a glint of steel in the sunshine – someone was wielding an axe to stove in the cutters. Directly afterwards came the smoke as first one boat and then another was set afire; by the time Atwell's boat reached the scene all the cutters were on fire and blazing fiercely.

Something impelled Peabody to traverse his glass along the shore towards Basse-Terre. He saw a big red dot, the twinkle of steel – a detachment of the garrison was pelting hot foot along the coastal path to try to save the boats. But Murray still had ten minutes in hand, and he coolly made the most of them. Probably all three of the cutters had stove their bottoms running ashore, and certainly ten minutes' axe work upon them damaged them beyond repair, while the fire had time to take a good hold and sweep the upper works. The infantry detachment was a quarter of a mile away when Murray recalled his picket, and by the time the sweating soldiers had reached the scene of action the longboat had shoved off and was just out of musket range beside Atwell. It was a neat piece of work, as Peabody ungrudgingly told Murray when he reached the ship again.

'Thank'ee, sir,' said Murray. His eyes were still bright with excitement and his chest was still heaving in sympathy with his quickened pulse. 'Those sogers were black. Their facings were blue an' they had a white officer. West India Regiment, I reckon, sir.'

Another good mark for Murray, seeing that during the excitement of the retreat he had kept his head clear enough to identify his pursuers. The information was of trifling importance, but all information was of some potential value. Murray looked back at the beach, where the red-coated soldiers and white-clad inhabitants were trying to salve something of the wrecks.

'We didn't leave much for 'em, sir,' said Murray, grinning, but Peabody was no longer paying him attention. He was a-looking at Nevis, which was slowly growing more defined as the *Delaware* made her leisurely way along the coast. Already the two-mile wide channel between Nevis and St. Kitts was fully opened up from where he stood.

'Bring in the captain of the cutter we've got on board,' he said.

They brought him the mulatto, who stood sullenly in front of him in his ragged shirt and trousers. His bare feet were seemingly too hard to feel the hot planking under them.

'John O'Hara,' said Peabody, and the mulatto nodded. 'Your boat was registered at Charlestown, Nevis.'

Another nod.

'What soldiers are there?'

O'Hara said nothing.

'Did you hear me speak to you?'

'Yessir. I don't know nothin', sir.'

The mulatto's speech was accented like no other on earth. It was only with difficulty that Peabody could understand him.

'You know the answer to that question,' said Peabody.

'No, sir.'

Even if patriotism did not motivate him, O'Hara owed a grudge against this captain who had just destroyed his all. Peabody looked at the sullen face, and then away, at the blue sky and the blue sea, and the steep green slopes of Nevis. War was a merciless business.

'Listen to me, O'Hara,' he said. 'Tell me what I want to know, and I'll set you free. I'll give you fifty golden guineas as well.' He kept his hard blue eyes on O'Hara's face, but he could detect no sign of weakening at the offer of the reward. So it was time for threats.

'If you don't tell me, I'll sell you at New Orleans. I promise you that, and you know what it means.'

Peabody saw the expression of the mulatto's face change, he saw the melancholy black eyes with the yellow whites wander round the horizon, just as his own had done a moment before. The wretched man was thinking of his present life, free, in this blue and green paradise, and comparing it with the prospect offered him – the canebrake and the cotton field and the taskmaster's lash.

'I'll get eight hundred dollars for you,' said Peabody. 'Somebody'll get eight hundred dollars' worth out of you, and a profit beside.'

The mulatto shuddered as he emerged from his bad dream.

'I'll tell you,' he said.

Bit by bit Peabody drew the facts from him, halting every now and then to make sure he understood O'Hara's patois. No, there were no red-coated soldiers in Nevis, although there were plenty in St. Kitts. There was a white militia, perhaps a thousand in the whole island, perhaps two hundred in Charlestown itself. They drilled once a month on Sunday afternoons. The coloured people, even the free ones, were not allowed arms except for the men enlisted in the West India Regiment. Yes, there were some guns mounted at Charlestown – two big ones, in a battery at the north end of the bay. There were two old white soldiers who looked after them all the time, and some of the white militia were supposed to be trained by them. Yes, that was the battery, there. Yes, those warehouses round the jetty were full. Sugar and molasses and coffee.

'Right,' said Peabody. 'If this is the truth, I'll set you free to-night. Take him away, and bring me the other two.'

The two negroes who had constituted the crew of the burned cutter were more easily frightened, though their speech was even more unintelligible than their captain's. Peabody did not have to use threats towards them; it sufficed for him merely to repeat his question once, with his eyes narrowed, for them to pour out their answers in their gobbling speech. They were silly with fright, and they knew little enough, but all they said went to confirm the information wrung from O'Hara. It was worth while to take the risk.

'I shall want the two quarter boats manned as well as the longboats,' said Peabody to his officers, and they stood in a semicircle before him as he gave them his orders.

They looked at each other as they listened, exchanging glances, and then looked back at him. His hard blue eyes had a light in them, and the firm compression of his lips seemed to make his thin nose more pronounced than ever in the frame of the deep lines beside it.

Two leadsmen in the chains chanted the depth as the *Delaware* glided round; steep-to as these West India islands all were there were soundings and a dangerous shoal in the shallow channel between these two islands. Peabody looked over at Nevis, at the white houses of Charlestown broadcast over the green slopes like cubes of sugar, at the shallow crescent of the bay with its gleaming beach, and then back at St. Kitts. The guns rumbled out as the ports were opened, and with a scampering of feet the men at the weatherbraces backed the maintopsail.

'You can go now, Mr. Hubbard,' said Peabody.

There was a cheer from the crew as the four boats dropped into the sea, and the men at the oars needed no urging as they drove the blades foaming through the water. This was an expedition whose daring was obvious to everyone, and which appealed to everyone. It was paying back in her own coin the thousand mortifying insults which Britain had dealt out to American shores. British squadrons might lord it in the Chesapeake and in Long Island Sound, but they could not guard the West Indies against reprisals. Peabody walked slowly back and forth across the quarterdeck, keeping wary watch upon all the three points of stress, on Nevis and on the battery and upon the mole at Charlestown. Murray was leading the two fast gigs against the battery, the most vital point; Atwell with the two longboats was heading straight for the mole. There were a hundred and fifty men in those boats, every single one which the *Delaware* could spare and still remain a fighting entity; Peabody watched their progress with an anxiety which he found it hard to conceal.

A movement over on the St. Kitts shore caught his attention.

'Mr. Shepherd,' he said to the midshipman commanding the port-side quarterdeck guns. 'Try a shot with that twelve pounder at those boats.'

The gun roared out and a spout of water in the smooth shallow sea showed where it had pitched; the row boats which had crept out from shore manned by redcoated West Indians promptly turned back. There was no hope of crossing in row boats two miles of open water swept by the guns of the *Delaware.* The garrison of St. Kitts would have to stand by impotently and watch the attack upon Nevis. Over in the battery appeared first one jet of smoke and then another; it was not until a quarter of a minute later that the sound of the shots, flat in the heated air, reached Peabody's ears. Peabody could see no sign of the fall of the shot; perhaps the gunners were using grape – at twice the effective range of grape shot – or perhaps they had utterly misjudged the range, or perhaps they had forgotten to put in any shot at all. Militia gunners were capable of anything, especially when taken by surprise, and there could hardly be a greater surprise for them than the arrival of a powerful enemy in the same week that everyone was drawing a long breath at the conclusion of a war twenty years old.

Murray's men were running up the beach; at three miles the flash of the sun on the cutlass blades was still reflected clearly back. There was no need to worry then any more, and Peabody turned his attention to the mole. He could see the longboats coming alongside, but he had to guess at the sequence of events – the blue marines marching methodically forward while the white-clad sailors set about the work of destruction. Even through his glass the drowsy town still seemed eminently peaceful.

A sudden tremendous roar startled him a little. It came from the battery, which was concealed in a cloud of smoke. Murray must have blown it up, battery, magazine, guns and all. Peabody hoped that none of the *Delaware's* men had been hurt, for blowing up magazines was a tricky, chancy business. But there were the gigs pushing off from the beach, so that presumably all was well. They were heading along the arc of the bay towards the mole to act as a reserve to Atwell if necessary. Over in St. Kitts row boats were making their appearance again, far away on the further side of the channel.

'Shall I try another shot at 'em, sir?' asked Shepherd, looking round at him.

'They're out of range,' said Peabody, shaking his head. The St. Kitts' garrison was welcome to try and interfere as long as they circled round beyond the range of the *Delaware's* guns – their course would land them on the far side of Nevis. After a four-mile row and a four-mile march they could do what they liked in Charlestown, seeing that the raid would be over long before their arrival.

Shepherd's wound had robbed him of his good looks; his scarred left cheek gave to his sunburned face a lop-sided appearance which was utterly sinister, as he stood there beside his guns. Peabody looked back at Charlestown. There was still no sign of war in the drowsy town; the only things moving were Murray's gigs, creeping beetle-like over the blue water towards the mole, and he took the glass from his aching eye and walked slowly back and forth across the quarterdeck. Providence had decreed that he should be subjected to these long and dreary waits; it was that which robbed them of their sting. There was no break until the sound of another loud report came from the town, sending his glass to his eye again on the instant. It was a cannon shot without doubt, but search as he would with his glass he could see nothing whatever of the source of the sound. Murray had reached the mole and was landing his men. There were fifty marines and a hundred seamen there now, and Murray ought to be safe enough.

Yes, that was what he had been looking for. A wisp of black smoke was drifting slowly over the town, coming from the general direction of the warehouses grouped round the mole. It thickened even as he watched. There would be a maximum of twenty minutes or thereabouts to wait, and he resumed his pacing. The *Delaware* with her maintopsail aback, swung idly round in response to a fortuitous puff of wind – apparently the sea breeze was beginning to win its daily victory over the Trades. The black smoke was growing all the time in volume and intensity, and the sea breeze was spreading it like a fog over the slopes of Charlestown. Once those warehouses with their inflammable contents were well alight, no effort whatever on the part of the British could extinguish them.

Here came a little block of white down the mole to the boats, the first party of retiring seamen. First one longboat and then the other detached itself from the mole and began to crawl out into the bay, and then the swifter gigs followed.

'Square away, Mr. Hubbard, if you please. We'll run down to the boats.'

On the quarterdeck Murray made his second report of the day.

'We blew the battery up, sir. Dismounted the guns and sent the whole place to glory. They only had time to fire two rounds at us – I guess you saw that, sir. There weren't more than twenty men serving the guns, an' they ran when we arrived. I had two men hurt, sir – Able Seaman Clarke and Seaman Hayes, both badly. They were hit by rocks when the magazine went up.'

Atwell took up the tale, with a side glance to where the wounded were being swayed up to the deck.

'I had two men killed, sir – Robinson and Krauss. Some of their militia got an old gun – a six pounder, sir – hidden in a lane an' fired it slap into my picket. Herbert lost his leg. But we burned everything there – boats, warehouses, everything.'

Atwell looked back again to Peabody, and his expression hardened.

'And I have two men under arrest, sir – those two.' He pointed to a couple of helpless figures, one of them a marine, hanging in the slings before they reached the deck. Atwell swallowed for a moment; what he was about to say was going to put those two men in peril of their lives, and he went on with the grimmest formality.

'They are charged with looting and being drunk on duty, sir. They swilled neat rum from the casks we were setting on fire.'

The two accused men were dumped roughly on the deck, and Peabody looked down on them. The marine was conscious enough to wave his arms slowly across his face while gurgling some drunken nonsense; the seaman was as motionless and helpless as if he had been stunned with a club, and pale under the mahogany skin. He must have filled his stomach with neat rum at a single draft. Peabody knew that passionate yearning for liquor, that wild desire for oblivion.

'Put them in irons in the peak,' he said harshly. 'I'll deal with them to-morrow. Ask the surgeon to look at this man after he has attended to the wounded.'

He turned away; the setting sun was gleaming across the bay at Charlestown, but it could not penetrate the vast cloud of smoke which engulfed the town, where a million dollars' worth of property was burning.

CHAPTER TEN

A court-martial had not been possible. Not until her voyage was completed – not until the war should be over – could the *Delaware* hope to be in a place where it would be possible to assemble the imposing array of officers who could try such an offence. But three lieutenants were able to compose a Court of Inquiry who could listen to Lieutenant Atwell's evidence and make recommendations to the Captain. Seaman and marine had no defence to offer, and could only throw themselves on the Captain's mercy. They stood white-faced while they listened to Lieutenant Hubbard's formal report to the Captain, studying the lean features and hard eyes of the man who could send them to their deaths in the next five minutes. Punishment in this little speck of a ship, encompassed by enemies and friendless through the oceans of the world, could be terrible and must be swift. Death, or such less penalty—

It was torment for Peabody. Far within him the devil was tempting him. He had two drunkards in his power, and he could repay on their persons the misery he had endured from a drunken father, the agonising distress caused him by a drunken mother, the torture he himself had gone through in his battle with the enemy. Deep down inside him a little well of blood-thirsty lust brought up into his mind the prospect of repayment. He submerged the hideous temptation and turned an expressionless face to the two wretched men.

This was a happy ship which he commanded; there had been punishments when she was lying at Brooklyn, but not a single one since she had escaped to sea. He felt a dull resentment towards these two who had imperilled the frail structure of happiness. If he should pardon them, he would be running the risk of unsettling the crew; there were some members – he knew it so well! – who would resent the pardoning of a crime which they had been tempted to commit. Yet punishment would not reform drunkards, would not make better men of them. But they had disobeyed orders, that was their worst crime. On this desperate venture every man on board must be shown that disobedience was instantly visited with punishment, and for men steeped in the tradition of the sea there was only one form of punishment besides death. Peabody passed sentence with a face set like stone.

The marine was bovine, phlegmatic, and suffered his flogging in stolid silence, but the seaman screamed under the lash. It was a horrible sound, which rent the fair beauty of the multi-coloured morning.

Montserrat lay in the distance, its jagged peaks purple and green against the sky; from the Soufriere at its southern end a cloud of white steam merged with the clouds which hung over it. In the opposite direction the low sun had waked a rainbow from the rainstorm which had just driven by. Its brilliant arch dipped to the sea at either end, and above it the reverse rainbow was visible, not as brilliant, but still beautiful. The sea was of such a vivid blue that it was hard to think of it as a lively liquid; with that deep colour it was more logical to think of it as of a creamy consistency through which the *Delaware* was cutting her way, leaving behind her a white wake lovely on the blue. It was Peabody's plan to spread desolation and misery and lamentation throughout this peaceful scene, to burn and harry and destroy, to sweep through the Lesser Antilles like a hurricane of destruction from end to end.

Here lay Montserrat; beyond lay Guadeloupe, French again now, but worth investigation on the chance of finding British shipping; beyond that Dominica, and then, after the French Martinique, a whole series of British possessions, St. Vincent, Barbados, Grenada, Trinidad, Guiana, stretching nearly to the Line. There might be convoys with which he would be unable to interfere, ships of war from which he might have to run, but there would be plenty of weak points – joints in the British armour – at which he could thrust. The *Delaware* was capable of keeping the sea for three months more at least – much longer if he could find the opportunity to reprovision from his prizes – and during that time he would do damage costing a hundred, a thousand, times as much as the Federal Government had expended on the ship. He refused to let his mind dwell again on what might have been the result if only Mr. Jefferson had decided to build a squadron of ships of the line. With his glass levelled at Montserrat he gave the orders which set the *Delaware* to work again on the task she had begun.

The days that followed were monotonous only in their sameness – ships destroyed and anchorages raided, West India planters ruined, and West Indian merchants bankrupted. The smoke of the fires which the *Delaware* lighted drifted over the blue sea and up the green hillsides, while Peabody could only guess at the terror and the uncertainty he was spreading, at the paralysing of commerce and at the shocked outcry in London. And through it all there was the constant dribble-dribble of casualties; two men killed by a round shot from the battery at Plymouth, three wounded by the single desperate broadside fired by the trading brig intercepted off Basse-Terre, one drowned when the *Delaware* was caught under full canvas by a sudden squall near the Saintes. It was not want of food and water which was likely to put a period to the *Delaware's* career, nor even shortage of powder and shot, but the loss of mortal men. Of every six men who had come aboard in the East River one man was now dead or useless. When the hands were at divisions, Peabody used to find himself looking along the lines of sunburned faces and wondering who would be the next to go. Britishs ships of war could find recruits whenever they met a British merchant ship, but the *Delaware* was alone.

It was off Roseau that they saw the big schooner. Hubbard himself announced the sighting of her to Peabody.

'Right to windward, sir, but she's bearing down on us fast.'

So fast, indeed, that when Peabody came on deck she was already nearly hull-up. The enormous extent of her fore and aft sails, the pronounced rake of her masts, her beautifully cut square topsails, were obvious at a glance, and as she came nearer Peabody could see the sharp lines of her bows and the beauty of her hull. Peabody took the glass from his eye and looked at Hubbard.

'Baltimore privateer,' said Hubbard, and then, slowly: 'Well, I don't know.'

Peabody had the same doubts. At first glance those bows and that canvas seemed eloquent of Baltimore, and yet at second glance they seemed nothing of the kind. If ever a ship had a foreign appearance it was this one.

'What d'you make of her, Mr. Murray?'

'Baltimore schooner, re-rigged in some foreign port, I reckon, sir.'

Murray's home was in Baltimore; his earliest recollections were of the white wings of the schooners on the Patapsco; his judgment ought to be correct if any was.

'Privateer dismasted in action and refitted at Port-au-Prince, most likely,' said Hubbard.

That was by far the most probable explanation.

'She's carrying heavy metal, sir,' commented Murray.

So much the better. Peabody had been hoping that chance would bring him in contact with a privateer; not only did he need news and information, but he wanted to concoct fresh plans of attack. There ought to be a convoy due soon from Port of Spain, and Peabody would be glad to deal with the escort if only there were a privateer at hand to snap up prizes.

'Hoist the colours, Mr. Hubbard.'

'She's rounding-to,' exclaimed Murray.

Much more than that. She had spun round on her heel, hauled in her sheets, and was beating her way back to windward as hard as she could go.

'Thought we were a merchantman until she saw our teeth,' chuckled Murray. 'Now she's having the fright of her life. I guess she'll be glad to see the Stars and Stripes.'

If the sight of the American flag brought any comfort to the schooner, she showed no sign of it, for she went on clawing up to windward in a desperate hurry.

'Fire a gun to leeward,' said Peabody testily.

But the gun brought no reply from the schooner.

'Nobody'd think we're trying to make the damned fools' fortune for 'em,' grumbled Hubbard, watching her go.

'Stand by to go about,' snapped Peabody. 'We'll look into this.'

The Delaware went on the other tack, and, hauled as close as she would lie, started in pursuit. The schooner was right to windward, two gun shots away, and heading for the open Atlantic with Dominica on her larboard beam. Far away to starboard the stark bald peak of Mont Pele showed above the horizon.

'Queer,' said Hubbard.

The schooner was heading neither for the active assistance of the British Dominica, nor for the neutral protection of French Martinique.

'If she was British you'd expect her to run for Roseau,' said Murray.

'And if she were anything else she wouldn't run at all,' said Hubbard.

'Maybe she's a Yankee with a British licence,' suggested Murray sagely.

The same thought had already passed through Peabody's mind. The New England merchants had not taken very seriously this war which Mr. Madison had decided upon, and they had certainly resented the loss of their profitable trade with Britain. Massachusetts had come within an ace of declaring herself neutral, and a good many Yankee ships had continued in British service, supplying the British forces, under licence issued by British admirals. If this schooner were one of those, Peabody had every intention of making her a prize of war, and the schooner probably knew it.

Peabody looked up aloft. Every stitch that the *Delaware* could carry was set, and every sail was drawing its best. He looked through his telescope at the schooner.

'She's fore-reaching on us, damn her,' said Hubbard.

'I guess she's weathering on us, too,' supplemented Murray.

The schooner was going through the water a trifle faster than the *Delaware*; she was lying a trifle – half a point, perhaps – nearer the wind; and, as Murray had suggested, she probably was not sagging off bodily to leeward quite as much as the *Delaware*, although Heaven knew that the *Delaware* on a bowline was better than most.

'Call all hands,' said Peabody. 'Put the watch below in the weather shrouds. And I'll have the watch on deck carry the shot up to windward. Keep her up, quartermaster!'

'Keep her up, sir!'

Two hundred men in the weather shrouds, thicker than apples in a tree, meant over ten tons of human ballast, and the mere area of their bodies, exposed to the wind on the weather side, was a help to the *Delaware* in keeping closer to the wind. The rapid transference of shot from the garlands and lockers on the leeside to the weather side helped to stiffen her as well. The weather braces were hauled in taut, and every sail was as flat as a board and drawing to the utmost; the cast log gave them nearly eight knots.

'Eight knots!' said Murray surprised.

'She's still fore-reaching on us, all the same,' said Hubbard bitterly.

'Get those men out of the foremost shrouds,' said Peabody. 'Bring 'em aft. Run out the larboard side guns, and then bring the watch on deck aft as well.'

Running out the guns on the weather side would stiffen her enormously. Bringing the men aft would set her a little by the stern, and Peabody, his mind conjuring up diagrams of the *Delaware's* underwater form, thought it just possible that she might give a few more yards of speed in that case – possible, but not probable. The guns rumbled out; the foremast men came running aft and scrambled up the mizzen rigging, packing themselves in among the men already there. The watch on deck came and clustered aft in an eager crowd, herded by the sharp orders of the petty officers.

'Heave the log again!' said Peabody to O'Brien.

O'Brien performed the duty with the utmost care. The seaman with him forced the peg into the log-ship and stood holding the reel of line above his head. O'Brien made a level base on the slide of the after carronade for the sand-glass. He did not intend to trust to the transmission of orders; he took the log himself and cast it, and as the fluttering marker of bunting passed his left hand, with his right he neatly inverted the glass. The spool rattled as the line ran out, so that the sailors' uplifted hands shook as if with the wind. O'Brien kept his eye on the glass during the twenty-eight seconds it took the sand to run out, and as the last grain fell he nipped the line.

'How much?' said Peabody.

'Seven, sir, an' a half. Nearer eight than seven, sir.'

No better than before, then, and perhaps a little worse; the wind had kept steady during those twenty-eight seconds. The tension on the seaman's hands ended as the peg was jerked out, and the log towed unresistingly. He began to reel in the line.

'She's still fore-reaching on us, sir,' said Murray gently.

Even a glance showed that; the distance between the schooner and the *Delaware* had grown perceptibly.

'We'll keep after her, though,' said Peabody. 'She may carry something away.'

That was always the last hope, pursuing or pursued, that the other ship would damage herself in some fashion. It was not a very dignified thing to hope for, and in this case the hope was to bear no fruit. The strange schooner steadily increased her distance. By noon she was hull down before the first dog watch was called; Peabody gave the order to wear ship, and laid a course for St. Lucia.

'But all the same, I'd like to know who the devil she is,' said Hubbard with a jerk of his head back to the vanishing topsails of the schooner.

For Peabody it was sufficient to be aware that there was a fast schooner in the vicinity which was not anxious for inspection; after that there was no use in regretting the hours wasted in pursuit of her. The next job to be done was to continue to exploit the surprise of the *Delaware's* arrival among the Lesser Antilles, to continue to burn and destroy, even though his heart sickened of the wasteful business. Even though the towering peaks of Martinique looked down upon his exploits, so that Anne on some country picnic may have seen the sails of the *Delaware* as she passed her career of destruction. Peabody looked over at the mountains of Martinique; he was not proud at the thought that Anne might be watching him carefully striking down those powerless to strike back at him. And Martinique was now at peace; in that island the open wounds of war were beginning now to close. As a sensible man, Peabody was fully aware of the blessings of peace; the task which lay to his hand made him more aware still. They were very mixed feelings with which he looked over at Martinique.

CHAPTER ELEVEN

During the hot night Peabody awoke to a knocking on his cabin door; and he had called 'Come in' before he was fully conscious. He sat up in his cot as someone came stumbling into the stuffy darkness. It was Midshipman Kidd, and he had hardly entered before Washington appeared with a candle lantern, his shirt outside his trousers, but ready for duty. Peabody suspected him of sleeping on the locker of the main cabin.

'Mr. Atwell sent me, sir,' said Kidd. 'There's a strange sail to leeward he'd be glad to have you see, sir.'

'I'll come,' said Peabody, and swung his legs off his cot. In that instant of time Washington had snatched up his trousers and was crouching for Peabody to put his legs in them – Washington was always alert for opportunities to perform the most menial duties. He continued on his knees while Peabody buttoned his flaps, holding the shoes ready for his master's feet.

On deck the brilliant tropic moon illuminated everything, showing up the familiar shipboard objects in a strange new light, and illuminating a broad path all the way down to the western horizon. It was down this path that Atwell pointed, after lifting his hat to his captain.

'There she is, sir,' he said.

Certainly there was something there, an outline brighter than the sky behind it, darker than the sea below it. Peabody's eyes accustomed themselves to the light, and he could see more clearly. There were the upper sails of a ship, from the royals down to mainyard, reaching with the wind abeam on the opposite course to the *Delaware's*. Peabody looked again, struck by the memory of something hauntingly familiar about the ship. He took the proffered night-glass and focused on the vessel, took the glass from his eye again, having once more convinced himself that at night his eyes saw no better with artificial assistance, and looked again with narrowed eyes. The distance between those fore-and-main-topmasts, and the odd proportion between them, meant something to him, without his figuring it out, as he might remember an acquaintance's face without thinking whether one eye was bigger than the other or the nose a little out of the straight.

'I know her,' he said decisively.

'I thought you would, sir,' said Atwell.

'She's the *Racer*,' said Peabody. 'The corvette we dismantled in the Wind'ard Passage.'

'Yes, sir,' said Atwell.

'Turn up the hands, Mr. Atwell. I want the ship cleared for action without noise.'

'Aye aye, sir.'

'No lights are to be shown without my orders.'

'No, sir.'

'Put up the helm and go down to her.'

'Aye aye, sir.'

On that still night, with a favouring wind and over such a kindly medium as water, the sound of the drums calling the men to quarters might easily reach acute ears on board the corvette, and there was always the possibility of surprise – faint, but in war no possible chance must ever be neglected. In all the bustle of clearing for action Peabody stood looking over the dark sea at the *Racer*. As the *Delaware* wore he watched closely. For several minutes she showed no sign of having seen her, and then suddenly her masts blended into one. She had turned tail, and Peabody nodded to himself as he did at the solution of a mathematical problem. It would have been suspicious if she had not acted in that way – he could not imagine a King's ship not sighting an enemy at that distance, nor recognising her at once.

His mind attacked the problem of explaining the *Racer's* presence here in the eastern Caribbean after he had last seen her six hundred miles away. It was necessary to be wary, to consider every step, in these conditions when any step might lead to destruction.

Murray was at his elbow, seeking his attention.

'Shall I load with round shot or dismantling, sir?'

'Canister in the carronades. Round shot in the long guns,' said Peabody, 'if you please, Mr. Murray.'

Each of the eighteeen carronades which the *Delaware* carried fired a thirty-two-pound missile, and a thirty-two-pound round of canister contained five hundred musket bullets. He would close with the *Racer*, sweep her deck with canister, and board her in the smoke. That would be the cheapest way of overpowering her, he decided and would give her least chance of disabling the *Delaware*; not that such a lightly armed ship had much chance of permanently disabling the *Delaware*, and slight damage aloft would be unimportant in the present situation, where, unlike during the attack on the convoy, seconds would not be vital.

The chances were that her presence in these waters was a

mere matter of routine – Peabody knew how easy it was to suspect an enemy of some deep design when all he was doing was merely something for his own comfort. There had been a notable instance just before the attack on Tripoli. But on the other hand, he must be cautious. He must not run the *Delaware* into a trap. He had spent nearly every waking moment since he left New York on the watch for traps, and his alertness had not diminished with time.

'Deck there!' came the cry from the masthead. 'Please, sir, there's another sail to leeward!'

Atwell caught a nod from Peabody, and rushed aloft with his night glass.

'Yes, sir,' he hailed. 'I can see his royals sure enough, sir.'

'What is she?'

'Can't tell you yet, sir. But the chase seems to be making for her, sir.'

If the *Racer* was employed in guarding some small convoy, the last thing she would do would be to draw pursuit towards the ships she was escorting. It was unlikely that the new sail was a merchantman, then, unless she were a chance comer.

'I can see her better now, sir,' came Atwell's voice. 'She's ship rigged, and heading close hauled to cross our course. And – and – she's a British ship of war, sir.'

'Mr. Hubbard! Put her on the starboard tack, if you please.'

The barest hint that there were British reinforcements awaiting the *Racer* over the horizon was enough to make Peabody alter his course. This might be the trap he had expected; certainly he was not going to plunge blindly into unknown dangers during the hours of darkness. By laying the *Delaware* on the starboard tack he was keeping well to windward of the enemy, so that when daylight should clear the situation he would be in a position to be able to offer or refuse battle at his own choice. As Hubbard roared 'Belay!' to the hands at the braces, Atwell appeared on the quarterdeck.

'I'm not sure about that second ship, sir,' he said, 'but – but she might be *Calypso*, sir.'

A ship whose masts and sails had been so thoroughly torn to pieces as had the *Calypso's*, might well not be recognisable the next time she was seen. New masts and sails would disguise her as much as beard would disguise a man.

'It seems likely to me,' said Peabody steadily. 'Perhaps the brig's over there, too.'

'I don't think she was in sight, sir. Shall I go aloft again and see?'

'If you please, Mr. Atwell. Mr. Hubbard! The watch below can sleep at the guns.'

If there were to be a battle to-morrow, Peabody had no intention of fighting it with a crew weary after a sleepless night. He would need all his strength if he were to fight the *Calypso* and the *Racer* together; in fact he knew already that he would only engage if he could make, or if chance presented him with, a favourable opportunity. And after their experience in the Windward Passage he could be sure that these two ships would do their best to offer him no opportunity; he could be surer of it with them than with any other two ships out of the whole British Navy.

Meanwhile, he must consider his own position. On this tack he would weather Martinique not long after dawn tomorrow; if he were to fight the British it would be somewhere between Martinique and Dominica. If he did not, then the Atlantic would be open to him. If he wanted to escape he could do so; the *Delaware* could work to windward, out to sea, far faster than the British could – she would have as much advantage over them as that mysterious schooner had displayed over the *Delaware* herself. He could run the British ships out of sight, and free himself for his next move. Having drawn them to this end of the West Indian chain, logically his best course of action would be to run down to leeward, take the Mona Passage, say, and make a fresh drive at the Jamaica trade, unless he crossed the Atlantic – as he had considered doing once already – and tried to make havoc in the Channel. As long as the British were reduced merely to parrying his thrusts he was doing his duty. Two years of anxiety in America had already taught Peabody the disadvantages of the defensive.

'If you please, sir,' hailed Atwell. 'The brig's in sight. Right ahead, sir, and on the same tack as us.'

'Thank you, Mr. Atwell.'

That was decisive, then. He would not fight if he could avoid it, or unless the British acted far more foolishly than he hoped for. Out of three ships, in a close fight, one would be able to cross his bows or his stern and rake him while he was engaged with one of the others. Even the little *Bulldog* in such a position would do the *Delaware* enormous damage. He could not fight three ships at once. The *Calypso* and the *Racer* were well out of range to leeward, silently paralleling his course; he thought for a moment of bearing down to interpose between them and the *Bulldog*, and put the thought aside – the interposition would not save his having to fight all three simultaneously. He decided to maintain this course; the British ships on the larboard bow could come no closer to him and by his superior speed he would gradually head-reach on them, and possibly he might overtake the *Bulldog* and force a fight on better terms than might be the case. He would chase her until dawn and reach his own decision then.

Peacefully through the night the four ships held their steady course; on board the *Delaware* there was only the low music of the rigging and the creaking of the woodwork as seas came rolling up to her weather bow. The watch on deck talked only in whispers, while the watch below snatched an uneasy sleep on the hard planking between the guns. Peabody stood tireless by the rail, listening to the whisper of the seas going by, watching the faint shadows of the British ships to leeward, and the dim outline of the mountains of Martinique on the horizon to windward.

At eight bells the relieved watch quietly took their turn to try to sleep; there was no bustle and small excitement. This crew was a seasoned one; there were men on board who had fought, sixteen years ago, all through the night under Nelson at the Nile, and others who remembered the long chill night watch waiting to attack at Copenhagen. There were a couple of Dutchmen who had watched the British line come bearing down on them at Camperdown, and even if those men who had fought under other flags in fleet actions were only few, the majority had fought pirates off Penang, or had stood to their guns against privateers on the African coast. Heterogeneous the crew may have been once, but their recent career of success had given them a common enthusiasm, and they were bound together by a common chain of discipline, whose master link was the silent figure who stood with his hand on the quarterdeck rail.

To the eastward the sky grew pink. All of a sudden the mountains of Martinique changed from vague shadowy slopes to sharp hard outlines which might have been cut from black paper and laid against the brightness. Round the sides of the outline the light came seeping like flood water round an obstruction. To the westward the sky was still dark, the British ships were still vague, and then suddenly the light reached up into the sky above them and revealed them, all sail set, in line ahead, *Calypso* leading, *Racer* astern, the *Bulldog* four miles ahead and to windward of them.

As the seconds went by, the mountains of Martinique took on a new solidity. The bald crown of Mont Pele caught the sunlight and reflected it, while the hues of the sunrise faded, pink and lavender and green sinking into the blue. Still the sun was behind the mountains, which cast their long black shadow far out to sea, until with a kind of wink the edge of the yellow sun looked over the saddle between the mountains to the north and those to the south, and instantly it was full day. The mountainsides were green now, and broad on the starboard beam opened the bay of Fort de France, with the steep pyramid of the Diamond Rock on the starboard quarter. Behind it, through Peabody's glass, showed the coloured sails of the fishing boats making for the town with their night's catch, and, beyond, the white roofs and walls of Fort de France itself. The dwellers in the town would have a fine view of the battle, if one were to be fought soon. Perhaps the Marquis and his womenfolk were already being roused with the news that a battle was possible.

Peabody swung his glass back to the British squadron. They were holding their course steadily; during the night the *Delaware* had fore-reached upon them only a trifle, although she had perceptibly cut down upon the *Bulldog*. He had only to give the word for the wheel to be put to starboard and in twenty minutes he would be upon them, amid the roar of the guns and the clatter of battle. The temptation was grave, like that of a bottle two-thirds full. There was an analogy between the two prospects, too. In either case there would be an hour's mad satisfaction, and then, at the end, oblivion. Peabody knew the full force of that temptation, but he put it aside. He must play the game out to the bitter end, preserve the *Delaware* so that she could continue her career of destruction.

Beyond Mont Pele lay Cape St. Martin; he could weather it easily on its present course, and, once through the straits, he could go about and vanish into the Atlantic distance. Shaking off pursuit, he would be free once more. Port of Spain or Port Royal or Bantry Bay; the British would not know where to seek him until he should announce his presence by further sinkings and burnings.

The shadow of the mizzen shrouds moved a little across his face, and in a vertical sense, too, not in the circular way which was the continual result of the pitch and roll of the ship. Her course was altering a little; if that were due to the quartermaster's negligence the shadow would move back in the next second, but it did not. In that one second Peabody's subconscious mind, trained in twenty years at sea, had made the whole deduction. His glance swept the pennant at the masthead, the spread of the maintopsail, the man at the wheel. The helmsman had not been negligent; the wind had backed northerly a trifle, and he had had to change course a trifle to keep the ship on the wind. Hubbard was already beside the wheel, along with Poynter, the acting master.

A faint uncertainty came into Peabody's mind, and he could see from Hubbard's attitude as he talked with Poynter that his first lieutenant felt the same. With the rising of the sun it was not unnatural that the wind should grow fluky. Another puff breathed on his cheek and the *Delaware's* bow came farther round still as the helmsman yielded to it. On this course it was by no means a certainty that the *Delaware* would be able to weather Cape St. Martin, and with every point the wind veered by that much was he deprived of the advantage of the weather gauge. Until now the British ships had been powerless to get within range of him without his co-operation, and he could choose his own moment for battle. Now the freakishness of the West Indian wind was depriving him of the advantages which his forethought had won for him.

It was a random puff of wind which had been responsible for the *Constellation's* overtaking the *Insurgente* when he was a lieutenant under Truxtun. Thirty years ago at the Battle of the Saintes a flaw in the wind had been responsible for the breaking of the French line and for Rodney's victory – which, if it had happened six years earlier, might well have postponed indefinitely the independence of the United States. Tremendous events sometimes resulted from the unpredictable vagaries of the wind. At this very moment the fate of the *Delaware*, his own life, depended on them. But as the vagaries were unpredictable, as they were dictated by a quite inscrutable Providence, there was no reason to allow them to anger him; it would be childish as well as irreverent to break into recriminations over them, the way Hubbard over there was doing. Hubbard was looking at the trend of the land, and then out to sea at the British squadron, and up at the pennant which told the direction of the wind, and the long black curses were pouring from his lips. Hubbard found it hard to bear the tension when it was obvious that if the wind veered another single point the *Delaware's* escape round Cape St. Martin would be impossible.

'Mr. Hubbard! Hoist the colours, if you please.'

Peabody still stood by the rail, his lean face and his hard eyes expressionless as he awaited his fate, and within them he was just as unmoved, thanks to his self-mastery.

The British ships had hauled to the wind as it veered, keeping parallel with the *Delaware's* course. Across four miles of blue water the *Calypso* and the *Racer* maintained their rigid line ahead, all sail set and drawing; as the Stars and Stripes went up to the *Delaware's* peak the White Ensign rose to theirs, fluttering jauntily, and at that very moment Peabody felt the shadows move across his face again. The wind had veered one more point – two more points.

Now the *Delaware's* bow was pointed straight for the foot of Mont Pele. The *Calypso* and the *Racer* must be exultant to see her cut off from the open sea. There were signal flags going up to the *Calypso's* weather yardarm, and the *Bulldog* was answering them. Next moment she hove in stays and went about. On the opposite tack she was heading just for the spot where the *Delaware* would have to change her course if she were not to go aground – just for the spot where the *Calypso* and *Racer* would intercept her so that all the four ships would come together at once. Peabody studied the blank sky, the expressionless sea. He was trying to guess what the unpredictable wind would do next. If it were to back, he still would have a chance to reach the open sea, and to pound the *Bulldog* into the bargain while the other ships looked on helplessly. The wind was as likely to back as it was to veer; more likely, perhaps, as it had veered so far. Peabody held his course and issued no orders. He caught his fingers in the act of nervously drumming on the rail before him, and he peremptorily stilled them.

Five minutes went by. Ten minutes went by, and at the end of ten minutes the wind had veered half a point more. Peabody broke into action again. He made his body stand stiff and immovable, and he kept his voice at a conversational pitch, not for the sake of the example it gave, but because these servants of his mind must act without weakness.

'Mr. Hubbard! Tack, if you please.'

Even a losing battle must be fought out to the end; if Providence had declared against him he must fight Providence to the last, for that was the only way to earn the approval of Providence. By tacking he would delay the encounter with the British squadron and have a chance of fighting at a better advantage than if he fought at present. Something might always happen. Providence might relent, the British might blunder, the wind might change or might drop altogether. Tacking would prolong the chase and give Providence a chance. The canvas slatted and the blocks rattled as the *Delaware* came up into the wind, and stilled again as she caught the wind on the other side. Now her bow was pointed straight towards the Bay of Fort de France with its rocky islets and its white cubes of houses; that was the corner into which he was being driven.

The *Calypso* had tacked the moment the *Delaware* did, and the Racer tacked in succession behind her, neatly backing her topsails for a second to maintain her interval – the British could handle ships, without a doubt. Astern came the *Bulldog*, revelling in the safety which the veering of the wind had given her. It was she who was to windward now, who held the weather gauge, who could select her moment for battle. Peabody could not turn and tack up to her without having the other ships upon him before he reached her. In the Windward Passage he had had all the advantages, the advantage of the weather gauge, the advantage of surprise, the advantage of the fact that the British ships were separated to guard a convoy, the advantage that the power of his ship was unknown – all of these advantages which he had won by his own foresight, but which had given him the opportunity to defeat his enemies in detail.

In the present encounter the wind had been unkind, and the British had learned caution. They were keeping their squadron massed while he was being driven upon a lee shore where he could not refuse battle to their united forces. But the game was not lost yet; he still had some miles of sea room in which to prolong the chase. Standing out towards the Diamond Rock ahead was a white sail. Peabody whipped his glass to his eye; it was neither a friend nor another enemy – it was the *Tigresse*. Coming to see the sport, he supposed, a little bitterly. It would be an unusual experience for the French in these war-torn islands to witness a battle which did not affect them. Well, he could imagine the way boats would have poured out through the Narrows filled with sightseers three years ago if the rumour had gone round New York of an approaching battle between English and French off Sandy Hook.

He could claim the protection of French neutrality if he wanted to – run for Fort de France and shelter under the guns and laugh at the British. He was sure that the Marquis would do his best to protect him, because he remembered what the Marquis had said about maintaining strict neutrality. Since he had given the order to tack, the idea had come into his mind more than once, and he had put it on one side, guiltily. It was what he ought to do, logically. If it were best to keep the *Delaware* afloat and as a fighting unit, it would be better for her to be blockaded in Fort de France than sunk or captured. But he would not do it, not even though it were his duty. He would rather fight – or to word it better, he was set on fighting in preference to accepting French protection, and he felt guilty about it because he fancied that an honourable defeat was the wrong choice from the naval point of view. On his vital matter, for the first time for twenty years, he was going to allow his personal predilections to outweigh his sense of duty. He was tired of running away.

He looked over at Fort de France and at the approaching *Tigresse*. Time was growing short, and if he were going to fight it would be best to do it now while there was still a little room to manoeuvre, although God knew that once he was locked in battle with three British ships there would be small opportunity for a manoeuvre.

'Mr. Hubbard,' he said, and in his determination to allow himself no emotion, the New England drawl which his Navy service had done much to eradicate was more pronounced than ever. 'Clew up the topgallants and royals, and then heave to, if you please. We'll wait for them to come up.'

Hubbard's dark-complexioned face showed his sardonic smile as the meaning of the words penetrated his understanding; he turned and bawled his orders, and the hands came running to the braces. The *Delaware's* way diminished as the yards came round, and she lay there in the blinding sunlight, submitting to the waves instead of riding purposefully over them. Peabody turned to watch the British ships swooping down on him, and as he did so he heard a sound on the deck behind him. Somebody was cheering, and the cheering spread, echoing from the maindeck under his feet, taken up by the fighting parties in the tops. The whole crew was cheering and leaping about at the prospect of instant battle, and Peabody smiled as he looked over his shoulder at them. They were a fine lot of men.

But this was no time for sentiment. Peabody turned back again to his duty of observing the approaching attack; when the time should come he must have the *Delaware* under way again, handy and under control for the fight. The *Calypso* and the *Racer* were already shortening sail for action, while the *Bulldog*, still under all canvas, was moving so as to take station astern of them. Their plan would be to try to engage the *Delaware* all on the same side; he must do his best to prevent it. He eyed the narrowing stretch of blue water across which his fate was approaching.

He was surprised by the sudden appearance of the *Tigresse* close under the *Delaware's* stern – she came by under all sail, tearing through the water only at pistol-shot distance away; in fact what first distracted Peabody's attention to her was the sound of her bows cleaving the waves as she approached. Startled, he looked down at the smart little sloop. She was cleared for action, her guns' crews standing ready round the dozen pop-guns which stood on her deck, and aft there was a glittering party in blue and gold. Standing out among them was the Marquis, conspicuous with his blue ribbon over his shoulder and the orders hung on his coat. He held a speaking-trumpet in his hand, and as the *Tigresse* slid by he raised it to his lips.

'Stay where you are!' he shouted. 'I'll come back to you!'

That was damned insolence, if ever there was such. Peabody's mouth opened a trifle in his astonishment, and he stared after the impertinent little vessel as she sailed by, heading straight for the British squadron with the white flag with the golden lilies fluttering at her peak. Peabody watched her round-to to square in the *Calypso's* path, and he saw the white puff of smoke as she fired a signal gun, and directly afterwards the *Calypso* had to throw her sails aback to avoid an actual collision. The British squadron bunched and lost its rigid line as the three vessels clustered together.

'What's on his mind, sir?' asked Hubbard, as much in the dark as Peabody.

'Square away, Mr. Hubbard. We'll go down and see.'

Possibly this might be a chance of catching the British off their guard. If the *Tigresse* got hurt in the melée it would only be her own fault. But the yards had hardly been braced round before a smart little gig dropped from the *Tigresse's* side and began to pull towards the *Delaware*, the white flag at her bows. Dupont was in the stern, standing up signalling with his hand for attention. Peabody looked over at the halted British squadron, at the *Tigresse* between him and them.

'Oh, back the mizzen tops'l again, Mr. Hubbard,' he said. His exasperation showed itself in the omission of the formal 'if you please.'

They dropped a rope ladder for Captain Dupont – in a ship cleared for action there was no way of offering him a more dignified entrance – and the fat little man came strutting aft to where Peabody had come half-way to meet him. At six paces he took off his hat and bowed; Peabody merely uncovered. To make a leg and double himself in the middle did not seem to be a natural thing to do on the deck of his own ship.

'His Excellency sends you his compliments,' said Dupont.

'Yes?'

'And His Excellency would consider it a favour if Monsieur le Capitaine Peabody would be kind enough to visit him aboard the *Tigresse*.'

'Oh, he would?' said Peabody. There were all sorts of replies possible, every one crushing, every one well designed to convey to the Marquis exactly what Peabody thought of this gratuitous interference. Peabody was making his selection when Dupont neatly spiked his guns.

'The British Commodore is there already,' he said, pointing over the blue water. Alongside the *Tigresse* bobbed a smart red gig, the straw-hatted crew fending her off. The sight left Peabody wordless.

'It would give me great pleasure,' said Dupont, 'if Mr. le Capitaine would make use of my boat, which is ready.'

'I'll come,' said Peabody. It was a mad world, and something madder than usual may have happened.

He slid down into Dupont's gig and took his seat beside the

French captain, and the swarthy French sailors bent to their oars. On board the *Tigresse* every preparation had been made for the reception of officers of high rank, and beside the guard of honour stood the Marquis, bare-headed.

'Good morning, Captain,' said the Marquis. 'I trust you are enjoying the best of health?'

What Peabody wanted to say was 'Damn my health,' but he forced himself to mutter some form of politeness.

'I must present you to my other guest,' said the Marquis. His handsome mouth wore a smile, his bearing was one of perfect deference, but somehow there was the hint of the mailed fist within the velvet glove. 'Captain Josiah Peabody, United States' Ship *Delaware* – Captain the Honourable Sir Hubert Davenant, His Britannic Majesty's Ship *Calypso*, Senior Officer of the British Squadron.'

Davenant was a man in his early fifties, grey-haired, with a hard straight mouth like Peabody's and plainly in a very bad temper indeed.

'Morning,' said Davenant. 'The Frogs want to stop us fighting.'

He talked English with the gobbled 'o's and the hot-potato accent which Peabody had last heard used by certain exquisites at Valetta.

'His Most Christian Majesty's Government,' said the Marquis, politely, 'is determined to maintain its neutrality.'

Peabody looked from one to the other, and the Marquis took up the tale. He pointed across the water to the Point des Negres on one side of the ship, and to Cape Solomon on the other.

'You are within French territorial waters,' he said. 'I can permit no fighting here between any belligerents whatever.'

'But damn it, sir—' said Davenant.

'I shall fire,' went on the Marquis, 'into any ship disobeying my instructions while within my jurisdiction.'

Davenant snorted and Peabody grinned. There was not any particular menace about the *Tigresse's* pop-guns, but the Marquis was quite unmoved and continued placidly.

'I left orders on shore,' he said, 'that the guns of Fort

Bourbon and those of trois-Islets were to follow my example. There are twenty thirty-two pounders trained on us at the present moment, I have no doubt.'

That was a very different story indeed. No frigate in the world could stand being knocked about by thirty-two pounders. The chances were that every ship in the bay, British and American, would be dismasted in a few minutes' firing. The Marquis still smiled, his manner was perfectly polite, but the mailed fist was quite obvious. He had every intention in the world of carrying out his threat.

'God rot all Frenchmen!' said Davenant, petulantly. His gold epaulettes flashed in the sun as he swung back and forth looking at the batteries. Then he rounded on Peabody. 'You came in here because you knew this would happen, damn you!'

'I did not, damn *you*, sir!' snapped Peabody.

'Then come out of the bay and fight me, then.'

'I was going to say the same thing,' blazed Peabody, shaking with wrath. 'Come on!'

'Gentlemen!' said the Marquis. There was an edge to his voice.

'Mind your own business!' said Peabody.

'Gentlemen!' said the Marquis again. 'Don't forget the twenty-four-hour rule.'

That halted them in their stride. A vague recollection of his reading of the almost forgotten laws of neutrality came into Peabody's mind.

'When the ships of two belligerents enter a neutral harbour,' said the Marquis, 'an interval of twenty-four hours must elapse between their respective departures. I cannot stop your leaving, but I can, and I will, stop your leaving together. I have to consider His Most Christian Majesty's dignity.'

It was perfectly true. In a world which had known no neutrals whatever for years the rule had been forgotten, and furthermore during earlier years Britain's overpowering naval might and the desperate exigencies of her position had forced her officers to ignore neutral susceptibilities – as Peabody well remembered. But here was a neutral with both the will and the power to enforce her neutrality, with a couple of batteries armed with thirty-two pounders loaded and pointed and ready. He caught Davenant's eye, and the British captain was so obviously crest-fallen that he could not help smiling. And with his smile his hot-headed passion evaporated, and his native shrewdness returned along with his clear common sense.

'Please do not consider it presumption on my part, gentlemen,' went on the Marquis. 'I must apologize in advance for any appearance of trying to advise you. But may I remind you that I do not expect either of your Governments would be too pleased if any offence were offered to that of His Most Christian Majesty?'

'Damn His Most—' began Davenant, and then he bit the words off short. The ways of statesmen were strange and inscrutable. There was a peace congress being summoned at Vienna, and a lively incident between the British and the new French Government might perhaps wreck some of the politicians' dealings. And in that case God help the career of the officer responsible! Peabody could see the struggle in Davenant's face as he tried to control his peppery temper and be tactful. The Marquis ignored the unfinished sentence, as a gentleman should ignore all unfinished sentences, while Davenant began to reframe his plans in accordance with this totally new situation. An idea clearly struck him, and he turned to Peabody.

'You can't go out first,' he said. 'There's nothing you'd like better than a twenty-four-hour start.'

Peabody was in agreement. Two hours start would be enough, for that matter. Once the *Delaware* was over the horizon the business of catching her would be far more complicated for the British. To the American Government a frigate loose on the high seas was worth two – was worth two dozen – in harbour or with their whereabouts known. But he kept his face expressionless; he was not going to yield any points in this argument if he could help it.

'I'll have to go out first,' said Davenant, thoughtfully. 'I'll wait for you to-morrow.'

Peabody was quite taken aback by this calm assumption.

He felt he had never heard anything quite so British before in his life.

'*You'll* go out first?' he said. 'Why shouldn't *I* go out first? I came in first.'

'That's nothing to do with it,' replied Davenant tartly.

'I'll make it have something to do with it,' said Peabody.

'You will, will you?'

Davenant braced himself stiffly, his chin protruding as he put his head back to meet the taller man's eyes.

'That's what I said,' answered Peabody.

Then at that moment the ludicrous nature of the argument and of their attitudes suddenly struck him. He was reminded of the preliminaries to his first fight at sea, when he and Grant – the Grant who subsequently was killed at Tripoli – were squaring up to each other at the age of twelve on the foredeck of the coastguard cutter, *Beagle*. Peabody laughed, uncontrollably, and Davenant began to dance with rage. Only for a second, for his own sense of humour came to the rescue of his dignity and he laughed as well. The first round closed with the two of them grinning at each other. Davenant was the first to regain his composure.

'Seriously, sir,' he said, 'I don't know what the Admiralty would say if they heard I let you out of here after chasing you in. I'd be court-martialled – I'd be broke – I'd be on the beach for the rest of my life if they didn't shoot me.'

'And what about me?' said Peabody, this presentation of the case revealing a new light to him. 'What would they say about me in Washington? What would the Navy Department say if I let you got out of here on better terms than you came in? We have court-martials in our service, too, sir.'

'Yes, I suppose you have,' said Davenant thoughtfully. 'Damn all admiralties.'

Peabody had the feeling that each of them was sparring for an opening in this second round, after the heated exchanges of the first.

'Gentlemen,' said the Marquis. 'May I make a suggestion?'

They both turned and looked at him, suddenly reminded of his presence after some minutes of oblivion.

'Yes, sir,' said Davenant. Peabody noticed the hauteur of

his manner – the irritating manner of one who represented the most powerful navy in the world.

'Can a question of this importance be decided in five minutes' conversation?' asked the Marquis. 'I must confess that I myself can see no way out of this impasse at the moment. And I might remind you that our five valuable ships are all of them hove-to on a lee shore. Why not drop anchor in Fort de France for to-night at least? You gentlemen may not be specially busy, but as Governor of this island I have other things to do besides listening to your arguments, educational though they are.'

Davenant looked back at Peabody, and Peabody looked at Davenant.

'How's your water?' asked Davenant.

'I've enough,' said Peabody cautiously.

'So've I. But I'd like some fresh. And I could do with some fresh vegetables after chasing you round the islands for five weeks. Is there any sign of scurvy among your men?'

'They'd be all the better for a run ashore,' admitted Peabody.

'I don't let my men ashore in a neutral port,' said Davenant. 'At least, only the few I can trust not to desert.'

He checked himself on the tempting edge of the abyss of professional conversation.

'I'm delighted to see you in agreement, gentlemen,' said the Marquis.

At first that seemed to be taking a good deal for granted, but the more the two captains considered the statement, the truer it appeared to be. To each of them the moment appeared to offer a golden opportunity to give his men a rest while at the same time conferring no advantage on his opponent.

CHAPTER TWELVE

'A letter for you, sir,' said the midshipman on duty, after knocking at Peabody's cabin door.

The seal on the back was elaborate – a coat of arms of

many quarterings. Peabody broke it with care, and unfolded the paper.

THE GOVERNOR'S HOUSE,
PORT DE FRANCE,
May 30, 1814.

His Excellency the Governor and the Countess d'Ernée request the pleasure of the company of Captain Josiah Peabody and of his Lieutenants to-night at the Governor's House at 8 p.m.

Dancing.

Peabody scratched his big nose as he read this invitation. Certainly his instructions from the Secretary of the Navy enjoined the strictest regard for the susceptibilities of neutrals.

'Shore boat's waiting for an answer, sir,' said the midshipman.

There was no reason in the world why he should not accept, and every reason why he should. Peabody sat down at his desk and painstakingly repointed his quill before writing.

U.S.S. *Delaware*,
May 30, 1814.

Captain Josiah Peabody, Lieutenants Hubbard, Murray, and Atwell, and Acting Lieutenant Howard, have much pleasure in accepting the kind invitation of His Excellency the Governor and the Countess d'Ernée.

'Washington! Bring me a candle.'

It would be far more convenient, and, in a wooden ship a good deal more safe, to use a wafer to seal the letter, but there was the dignity of the United States to consider. Peabody melted the wax and impressed the ship's seal upon it with the thoughtless dexterity of his long bony fingers, and yet with the utmost deliberation. He was slow in handing the thing to the midshipman, slow in dismissing him. It was only when the door had closed, when the fussy Washington had tidied the desk and gone out, that he reached the moment which he had deliberately postponed while waiting for it impatiently, and abandoned himself to his thoughts.

He knew who would be there, whom he would see, to whom he would undoubtedly talk. He knew now that she had not been out of his thoughts since he had seen her. He had struggled honestly against those thoughts. They not only might have interfered with his duty, but they were sinful – twenty years at sea had not eradicated from his mind the idea of sin implanted in him during twelve years of childhood in New England. And now it was no use struggling against them any longer. He gave way to them. He would see those black curls and those blue eyes. He would feel her palm against his – there was sinful pleasure in that thought. The cabin suddenly became too cramped for him, too stuffy, and he went out with long hurried strides, up to where everything was illuminated by the rosy sunset.

On deck he addressed his four lieutenants, gravely, and yet with the lopsided smile which he always employed; Peabody had never seen any particular advantage to be gained from impressing it upon his subordinates that his requests were orders to disobey which involved a maximum penalty of death. Gravely they listened to him, just as they had done when he had been giving orders for the raiding of Nevis.

'You will all, of course, wear full dress,' said Peabody, after telling them of the invitation he had accepted on their behalf. 'Epaulettes, silk stockings, swords. Have you a silk cravat, Mr. Howard?'

Howard had been only a midshipman when the *Delaware* commissioned, and Peabody knew by experience that midshipmen often sailed with inadequate outfits.

'Well, sir—'

'I'll see that Mr. Howard has everything, sir,' interposed Hubbard.

The dandy from Charleston might be expected to have at least two of everything, even though when the voyage started the odds had been ten to one that defeat and death lay at the end of it.

'Very well,' said Peabody. He was racking his brains to remember what Truxtun had said in similar circumstances, when he was a young lieutenant. Truxtun had taken his young officers ashore to receptions, too, had worked conscientiously to educate them in the niceties of a society of which perforce they saw little enough, and of the necessity for which Peabody was still only convinced against his will.

'You will dance with every lady who needs a partner,' he said. 'I don't have to remind you of that. And there'll be plenty of wine – you'll be careful how you drink.'

'Aye aye, sir.'

'And – oh, that'll do. Dismiss.'

There were bright lights over at the quay when Peabody took his place at the tiller of his gig that evening among his officers, and as the boat made its way over the quiet water the lights gradually resolved themselves into flaming torches held by coloured servants in blue and white livery. A footman stooped to help the officers from their boat, and they climbed out. The solid stone of the jetty felt strange under their feet, for it was eighteen weeks since they had last trodden earth; they all stamped a little curiously as if to reassure themselves. The coloured footman welcomed them with a few words which none of them understood, and under the guidance of two torch-bearers they began their walk up into the town. On the far side of the jetty there were other torch-bearers, another boat coming in, and Peabody, glancing across, saw the red light of the torches reflected from gold epaulettes and buttons. Apparently the British officers were also attending the Marquis's reception; the Americans passed within a couple of yards of the waiting group, and on both sides a sudden silence fell over everyone, conversation dying away guiltily. No one knew whether or not to say 'good evening' to his enemies, and the situation was complicated by the fact that only Peabody and Davenant had been presented to each other. In the end the British officers looked out across the dark harbour while the Americans hurried by awkwardly.

There were lights at every window of the Governor's house, and long before they reached it they could hear music; at the open door stood a dozen coloured footmen, appearing strange to Peabody's eyes in their knee-breeches, their smart livery, and their white hair-powder. The Americans handed over their boat-cloaks and stood eyeing each other in the dazzling light as they adjusted cravats and ruffles; Peabody was conscious of a dryness of the throat and queer feeling, comparable a little with hunger, in the pit of his stomach. Howard was as nervous as he was, he was glad to note – the boy's hands were not quite steady as he tried to shoot his cuffs. The calmest one among them was Atwell, who looked about him quite unabashed.

'I've a wife in New London,' said Atwell, with a grin on his homely face, 'who'll never forgive me if I can't tell her all about this evening. Please God I can remember what the women are wearing.'

At the head of the stairs stood three figures, the Marquis with a torrent of lace running from his chin to his waist, his blue ribbon crossing his breast, an order dangling from his neck and a star over his heart, as handsome a picture as one could see anywhere. Lace and ribbons and stars; Peabody thought of them all with instinctive suspicion, but when the Marquis wore them they had not that meretricious appearance which he expected. On the Marquis's right was the Countess d'Ernée in her black, her white shoulders a little solid, the smile with which she greeted the guests a little forced – so Peabody thought. And on the Marquis's left was Anne.

When Peabody looked at her all the rest of the glittering scene faded out; it was as if her face alone was standing out against a grey and misty background, like some miniature portrait. All Peabody's vagueness as to her appearance vanished with startling abruptness. Of course, he knew, he had always known, exactly what she looked like. He had been so sure of it that the minutest change would have been instantly apparent to him. He found himself smiling as their eyes met, the whole of his body singing with happiness, which, he told himself, was due to the extraordinary identity between her present appearance and what he remembered of her. There was something hugely satisfactory about that, like the solution of some involved mathematical problem, or like picking up moorings in a crowded harbour with a gale blowing.

Something that Atwell had said echoed in his mind, and

he tried to force himself to take note of what she was wearing. But it was difficult; it was hard to focus his gaze upon her, just as it had been hard in the old days to focus upon the candle-flames of the mess table when he had been drinking. There was a white throat and white shoulders; Peabody's head swam as his gaze went lower down and he saw that Anne's gown did not begin until there was more than a hint of her bosom revealed. He expected a sudden consciousness of sin at the revelation and was a little taken aback when it did not come, as when an aching tooth suddenly ceases to hurt. There was something black and something red about her gown; he was sure of that. And there were pearls in the picture, too, which were just as mathematically satisfactory, but whether because of the pink-and-white skin or because of the contrast with the black curls, he could not decide.

He came to himself with the realization that there were other guests on the stairway and he must lead his party to the ballroom; Captain Dupont was there to do the honours. Presumably it was his meeting with Anne which had made him hypersensitive, but Peabody felt himself suddenly in sympathy with the people in the room, telepathically aware of the sensation their entrance caused. The five officers, with their rolling gaits and their mahogany complexions, close-cropped hair and plain dress – despite their epaulettes and gold – were like a breath of sea air entering a hot-house. Round the room were many languid exquisites, many lovely and fragile women, and the men looked at the Americans with vague contempt, the women with awakening interest. Peabody was suddenly glad that his neckcloth was of plain pleatless silk, and that his sword-hilt was mere cut steel, unjewelled and ungilded.

At one end of the long room there were wide-open double doors through which could be seen a supper-room glittering with silver; at the other end was a low dais on which a negro orchestra was waiting. Captain Dupont had hardly begun to make presentations when the orchestra broke into a swinging, lively tune, and Peabody gaped a little as the dancers came on the floor. Each man took a woman in his arms, and each woman clasped her partner, perfectly shamelessly. The couples circled round the floor, each with a sort of wheel-like motion which reminded Peabody of the movement of the tiny water animalcules which he had observed as a boy in the stagnant water of summer pools; but it was not the motion which appeared so strange, as the cold-blooded way in which the embraces were publicly performed, the women looking up into the men's faces and talking as collectedly, as if they had no sense of shame whatever, regardless of clasped hands, of arms round waists, of hands on shoulders, of bosom against breast, or very nearly.

'That's the waltz,' said Hubbard between his teeth to Peabody. 'I heard it was all the rage in Europe.'

A languorous beauty in her late thirties to whom Peabody was being presented, overheard the remark.

'Indeed it is,' she said. 'All the world dances it. All the world has met together in Paris now, I hear. Excepting for us poor souls, doomed to an eternity of boredom on this little island. Tell me, Captain, do you intend to give your young officers a day ashore? It will be a pleasure to me to do what I can to make their visit enjoyable. I can send horses for them down to the port – my estate is St. Barbara, six miles away from town.'

She flashed dark eyes from behind her fan at the circle of officers.

'That is extremely kind of you, ma'am,' said Peabody. 'Unfortunately I have no knowledge—'

There was so much bustle in the hall at this moment that he was compelled to break off his speech and look round. The English officers were entering the hall, Davenant in the lead, the naval officers in smart uniforms with the new white facings which Peabody had heard about and never seen before, the two marine officers in red coats and high polished boots.

'You mean,' said the languorous beauty, 'that you do not know when you are going to fight those gentlemen there. Well, it's in poor taste, now that the rest of the world is at peace. You should be ashamed to deprive us of the society of your charming Americans – it is years since we set eyes on one. We are accustomed to Englishmen, after the long English rule here. The sight of a red coat no longer rouses a thrill in our blasé hearts, Captain. But you Americans—'

'Yes, of course, ma'am,' said Peabody, as she obviously awaited some kind of answer, but there must have been a fount of hidden humour in the trite words, for the lady said 'La!' and flashed her fan again.

Peabody's eyes met Davenant's across the room. There was a moment's hesitation on the part of both parties of officers, and then they bowed to each other formally, the juniors copying the example of the seniors, and Peabody was glad to see that the gesture was performed just as badly by the English lieutenants as by his own, and that their gait was just as rolling and unfitted for a ball-room. Even Davenant, with his high fashionable neckcloth, and his red ribbon, and his star, was obviously someone straight off a quarterdeck.

Here came Dupont, very preoccupied.

'Captain Peabody, your commission as captain is a recent one, I fancy?'

'I have two years' seniority, sir.'

'Captain Davenant is the senior, then, his commission dating back eighteen years. Then he will dance the cotillion with Mme d'Ernée, and you, sir, will stand up with Mlle de Breuil.'

'Mamzelle d—?' asked Peabody, and was promptly annoyed with himself. Even if he could not pronounce Anne's name he ought to have recognised it instantly. To cover his confusion he fell back on formality. 'Of course I shall be delighted, sir.'

This was a serious moment. Not more than six times in his life had Peabody attended a ball, although in view of the occasional professional necessity of doing so, he had studied the conventions of dancing seriously enough, resolutely putting aside the nagging of his conscience on the matter. But this was something he had to go through, something unavoidable and inevitable; it was, therefore, no moment for doubt. The Marquis and Anne and the Countess were already entering the room, and Peabody braced himself, made a final adjustment of his cuffs, and strode over. He managed his bow, but try as he would, to his great surprise the formal request for the pleasure of the cotillion was a mere mumbled jumble of words. Anne smiled and curtseyed.

'I shall be delighted, Captain Peabody.'

In something like a dream he offered his arm, and she rested her hand on it. Walking in that fashion was a new experience. There was no sensation of weight; in fact it was quite the reverse. His arm felt all the lighter for the touch, as though a Montgolfier balloon were tied to it. She glided along beside him as weightless as a feather. Peabody had a feeling which reminded him of those few occasions when drink had exhilarated him without stupefying. In front of him Davenant was speaking to the Countess.

'I fear I don't know the drill, ma'am,' he was saying. 'As a matter of fact I'm damned awkward in a ball-room.'

'Never mind about that,' said the Countess. 'Charles will lead. All we have to do is to follow.'

That was doubly comforting, both to know that Davenant was nervous and that the Marquis would carry the responsibility; the Marquis was already leading out the languorous beauty of St. Barbara, and the lines were falling in behind them. Peabody had recovered sufficiently to dart a quick glance round and to see that each of his officers was leading a lady into the dance. The band played a warning chord, and he turned to his partner and took her hand in his.

For Peabody that was his last clear recollection. The rest of the dance was just a divine madness. He was drunk with music and with the proximity of Anne. Awkwardness and the restraints of conscience vanished simultaneously. He bowed and scraped, he capered when the necessity arose, he strode with dignity, while sheer instinct – it could have been nothing else – saved him from allowing his sword to trip his partner or himself. The Marquis and his lady certainly knew how to lead a cotillion, and the orchestra did its part to perfection. A perfect wave of light-heartedness flooded the ballroom, everyone presumably infected by the gaiety of the Marquis. Everyone was smiling and laughing, even the elderly chaperones against the wall.

Peabody's mind was a whirl of tumultuous impressions, of pearls, and black curls, of white teeth between red lips when Anne smiled, of blue eyes and black lashes. When the dance ended he had an impression of awakening from some innocent and delightful dream, dreamed in a feather bed of unbelievable comfort. Yet his head was singularly clear.

'May I offer you some refreshment, ma'am?' he said, remembering his manners.

'The most grateful refreshment would be fresh air, don't you think, Captain?' said Anne.

She turned toward that side of the room which had no wall, opening on to a side porch, where the last breaths of the sea breeze were entering; her hand was on his arm again, and she glided along beside him across the ball-room. Out on the porch, with the light streaming behind her, she rested her hands on the rail and looked out across the town to the sea. The moon illuminated the bay, and the ships riding there at anchor, while from the garden before them arose a dozen strains of music – an orchestra which rivalled that of the ball-room – as frogs and crickets and a drowsy bird or two all chirped and croaked in unison.

'You dance very well indeed, Captain,' said Anne.

That singular clearness of head which had come over him saved him from imperilling the good impression with a mock modest reply.

'No one could dance otherwise with you, ma'am,' he said.

'And you pay a pretty compliment, too,' said Anne; there was more music in her chuckle, and Peabody was drunk with music.

'I speak the truth,' said Peabody, with a sincerity which was a greater compliment still.

'You must save those pretty speeches for Madame Clair,' said Anne.

'And who is she?'

'How hurt she would be to hear that, after ogling you from behind her fan for five minutes! She is the lady who danced with my father.'

'I remember her now.'

'She is looking for her fourth husband.'

'Where is he?'

'On earth somewhere, I have no doubt. But I do not know

who he is, nor does Mme Clair, yet. Nevertheless, she will meet him soon enough. Perhaps she met him this evening.'

'God forbid!' said Peabody, fervently at the prospect of becoming Mme Clair's fourth husband.

'She waltzes beautifully. You should ask her for the pleasure of a dance.'

'I can't waltz.'

'Now that is serious, Captain Peabody. Naval officers should never visit neutral harbours without knowing the waltz. As ambassadors of good will – as diplomats on occasion – the knowledge would be of the highest advantage.'

Mlle de Breuil's expression was demure, but somewhere there was a hint of a twinkle, and Peabody could not tell whether he was being teased or not.

'I shall take lessons at once,' said Peabody.

As he spoke, there came low music from the violins in the ball-room.

'At once?' asked Anne.

It was a waltz which the violins were playing; Anne cast a hesitant glance behind her, for etiquette demanded that she should return to the ball-room the moment the next dance following the cotillion began. And yet – and yet—

'I am ready to learn,' said Peabody.

This extraordinary clarity of mind was quite amazing; it was intoxicating enough almost to defeat its own purpose.

'*One* two three *four* five six,' said Anne. She held up her arms as if she were in a partner's hold and danced by herself to the music. 'You slide the feet. You make the turn smooth as you can.'

She stopped, facing him, her hands still raised, and Peabody automatically held her.

'*One* two three *four* five six,' said Anne. 'Turn smoothly. Oh, that's better.'

If walking with Anne on his arm had been an amazing sensation, dancing with her in his arms was more amazing still. Peabody had not only been honest, he had been right when he said no one could help dancing well with Anne. She was like an armful of thistledown. The mere touch of her took off the weight from one's feet in a mysterious way;

perhaps she was subtly guiding him so that he did not bump into the furniture on the porch, but if so she did it without his knowing, perhaps without her knowing. They slid smoothly over the mahogany floor, the violins inside wailing their hearts out under the bows of the negro musicians. Anne ceased to count aloud; her expression as Peabody looked down at her was a trifle distracted, as if she were seeing visions. The sight of her face, the round, firm chin and the soft mouth, the strange inspired calm of her expression, gave new lightness to Peabody's feet. He was a man inspired.

The music came to a heart-broken end.

'Oh!' said Anne, standing still in his arms, looking up into his face.

Next moment Peabody kissed her, quite unaware, until lip met lip, that he was doing so. She kissed him in return, her hands on his shoulders; for Peabody everything had the awesome clarity of a dream; the touch of her, the scent of her, had an excruciating pleasure for him such as he had never known or dreamed of before. He looked down at her bewildered; he had never thought of a love affair being as simple as this, as free from the implications of sin, as inevitable and as natural as this.

'Oh!' said Anne again, but this time there was no disappointment in the voice, only wonder.

'I – I kissed you,' said Peabody. He was surprised at himself for being able to use such a word to a woman; it was like those dreams where one found oneself naked and unashamed amid a crowd of people.

'Yes,' said Anne, 'and I kissed you.'

They were still in each other's arms, the one looking up, the other down; with her left hand still on his shoulder she began to rearrange his neckcloth with her right.

'Shall I tell you?' she went on, her eyes no longer looking into his, but instead intent on the neckcloth.

'Shall you tell me what?' asked Peabody.

'That other time when I saw you – on board the *Tigresse* – when you looked at me – I said to myself: "that is the man that I would like to kiss.' And then I said to myself that I was foolish, because – I had kissed no one except my father, and how should I know? But you see, I did know.'

She looked up again at him, a little fearful as to the effect of this confession, and Peabody's senses deserted him. All that boasted clarity of mind, all that extreme consciousness, vanished utterly. It was like a wave closing over his head, as he kissed her again. He found himself trembling as the wave subsided; he was a little frightened as he suddenly realised, for the first time, the depths of passion that there were within him. With a hint of panic he released her, and stood staring at her in the faint light. He was so intent on his own problems that he paid no attention to the footsteps that he heard approaching, and that was as well, because it saved him from betraying himself with a guilty start when one of the newcomers began to speak.

'Anne!' said Mme d'Ernée; she began to speak in French, but corrected herself and went on in English. 'I did not know you were here. Mme Clair will look after you while I am not in the ball-room.'

Peabody blinked at her, recovering his wits. The Countess was not angry. It even seemed incomprehensibly as if she were a little embarrassed, and then Peabody saw clearly again and realised that she actually was. Standing behind her was Davenant, and Davenant was a little awkward and self-conscious, too. He twitched at his neckcloth and shot his cuffs. It certainly was not to look for Anne that the Countess and Davenant had come out on to the porch.

'Yes, Aunt,' said Anne, perfectly steadily, albeit a little subdued. 'Shall we go in again, Captain Peabody?'

She put her hand on his arm, and they began to walk back. Davenant made way for them with a bow not quite of the perfect polish he had usually displayed.

CHAPTER THIRTEEN

Captain Dupont was arranging the guests for what he announced as a 'contre-danse.'

'It's nothing more than a Virginia reel, sir,' said Hubbard, side-long to his captain whom he found at his side; Hubbard's wary glances were darting up and down the line and observing everything, quick to make deductions. Hubbard had no intention whatever of being betrayed into any uncouthness or of displaying provincial ignorance.

Peabody really did not know how he had come to be in that file of dancers, nor how he had come to be opposite the pretty girl who was his partner. Anne was farther down the line with a glow on her cheeks and a sparkle in her eyes. Craning his neck, Peabody could see that she was opposite the red-coated British marine officer, and as to how that had come about he was just as ignorant. All about him there was a babble of chatter, French and English intermixed, and some of the English he heard was strange enough. Not only was there the London accent of the naval officers, but there was the West Indian accent of the residents which was far more difficult; and Peabody guessed that the Martinique French which was being spoken around him was just as marked a dialect as West Indian English. Captain Dupont was performing prodigies, calling the figures first in French and then in English.

Peabody recaptured all the light-heartedness of the earlier part of the evening as the dance progressed. He felt no twinge of jealousy when he saw Anne's hand in the marine's; everything was extraordinarily natural as well as being merry. Once or twice she caught his eye – she was smiling already, but that did not detract from the smile she had for him; and when in the chain her hand touched his he was conscious of a message whose good fellowship surprised him. He had always thought that a love affair would contain a certain bitterness, or a certain remorse, which was certainly not the case at present.

The dance ended, and Peabody found himself in the supper-room with his new partner. The latter fell upon the food provided with a healthy appetite – over and over again Peabody had to intercept one of the numerous footmen who were circulating through the crowd and relieve his tray of something which had caught his partner's eye. Peabody himself found the food not so interesting. There were only made dishes to be had, things so fluffed up and maltreated as to be unrecognisable. There were little pies whose crusts were so fragile as to be unsatisfactorily ephemeral, and which contained a couple of mouthfuls of some meat or other, so minced and muddled as to be completely distasteful. There were stews of one sort or another, and Peabody took one look at them and decided not to venture farther – just anything could be concealed in them, and Peabody would rather have tried a stew produced in a ship six months out, which at its worst could hold nothing more than the rats and cockroaches to which he was accustomed. There were piles of fruit; his partner, dismayed at his lack of appetite, tried to press some on him, and secured for him a dish of some dismal pulp extracted from something like a vast orange – a 'shaddock,' his partner called it, otherwise known as the 'grape fruit,' rather inconsequentially. She even went on to explain that learned men had come to the conclusion that this thing was the veritable forbidden fruit which Eve had given to Adam, and yet Peabody did not find it attractive. Despite the damp heat he was hungry, but there was nothing to take his fancy, no honest roasts or grills, not even a dish of beans.

Corks were popping incessantly, and the footmen bore trays loaded with wide glasses filled with a golden wine; the bottles were cooled by being wrapped in wet cloths and hung in the draught, so the girl explained, her eyes looking at him over the rim of her glass. There was something enchanting about that wine, as Peabody admitted on tasting it. It was bubbling merrily as he drank, just like the sparkling water which Dr. Townsend Speakman had for sale in Chestnut Street, Philadelphia. The light-heartedness of that wine re-echoed his own – the lamentable supper had done nothing to damp his spirits.

Davenant entered the supper-room at that moment, his eyes meeting Peabody's as though the pair of them were crossing swords. Each of the two instantly decided to look away again and not risk a further interchange of glances. Peabody's eyes travelled round the room; wherever he looked he could see the blue and gold and white of the British Navy, as well as the red coat of the Marine officer who was offering refreshments to Anne. Evidently the British Navy followed the same practice as the American, of leaving the watch in harbour in the charge of the master and the master's mates, so as the free the lieutenants; most of the lieutenants, at least, who could be serving in the three British ships must be present.

It was when he had formed that conclusion that Peabody decided on a new plan. It was so simple that he wondered why he had not thought of it before – except that all simple plans are exceedingly hard to think of. At one moment his mind had been void of ideas; at the next he had the whole scheme ready in his mind, its advantages and disadvantages balanced against each other, and his decision was taken for action. Quite without thinking he rose to his feet, rather to his partner's surprise, so that he sat down again. The essence of the plan lay in his not calling attention to himself, in his awaiting his opportunity to act unnoticed. He looked across at Hubbard, conversing in a lively group of mature females with all his Southern courtesy, and at Howard who was blushingly supping with Mme Clair. Murray was just in sight at the far end of the room, but Atwell was nowhere to be seen; Peabody wondered with extraordinary tolerance whether he was forgetting, somewhere out on one of the wide porches, the existence of that wife of his in New London. The four of them would be surprised when they knew what he had done.

'I don't think you heard what I said, Captain,' said his partner, a little tartly, breaking into his thoughts.

'I beg your pardon, ma'am,' said Peabody hastily. 'I can't think what came over me.'

'I can guess the cause of your distraction,' she said. 'It was either war or a woman.'

'Maybe so,' smiled Peabody.

He did his best to be conversational and natural, but the spell was broken, and his attention was not on the present. His partner was a trifle mortified, for here she had secured what was perhaps the greatest prize of the evening, in supping with the American captain, only to find she had no chance whatever of conquest. It occurred to her that it was still not too late to try again and see whether any of the lieutenants were not more susceptible, on the principle of a lieutenant in the hand being better than a captain in the bush.

'I think, Captain,' she said, 'that I had better be going back to mother.'

Peabody did his best to express regret, though only half convincingly. He escorted her out of the room and to her mother's side, and he forced himself to make the conventional remark and to bow leisurely when he left them – anything, rather than allow anyone to guess that he was in a hurry. He did not look back over his shoulder as he left the ball-room, for he knew that would be the surest way of calling attention to himself. He walked slowly down the deserted staircase, and slowly out to the main door. The coloured footman there addressed some remark to him in island French which he did not understand.

'Oh, yes,' he replied with a drawl. 'I guess so.'

He was through the main door now; the fact that his cloak was still in the house ought to persuade the footman that he was only intending to be absent a short time. He would have to abandon the cloak, just as he was abandoning his four lieutenants. A miracle might bring them back to him, but otherwise he would have to get along without them as best he could. There were some other capable midshipmen who might make useful acting lieutenants, and his master's mates were all of them experienced seamen. The *Delaware* might not be so efficient, but at least she would be free – if he got her out of the harbour to-night the British ships would be compelled to stay for another twenty-four hours, and he would have a whole day to forestall pursuit. There would be an outcry among the British, he could guess. They would condemn his action as a slick Yankee trick, without a doubt. Let them. He had made no promises, he had passed no parole, nor had he made any appearance of doing so. This was war; Davenant would be court-martialled and broke when it came out that he was at a ball when his enemy gave him the slip – that was hard luck on Davenant, but war always meant hard luck for somebody.

By now he had passed the sentry at the gate, had picked his way across the dark square, and was on his way down the steep street to the waterfront. Another thought made him hesitate in his stride, not because he had any idea of returning, but because it knocked him off his balance. Anne! He had forgotten all about Anne! He had had her soft lips against his hard ones. He had kissed her. Not only had he kissed a woman, but the woman he kissed was Anne. He was not the same man as had walked up that evening from the boat. There was a tremendous upheaval within him, even though he still hurried down the dark street.

It was perfectly likely that he would never see her again. Even if death did not come to him, the exigencies of the service and the chances of war would more likely than not keep him from her. An infinite sadness overcame him at the prospect. He had not even said goodbye to her – he knew that why such a notion had not occurred to him was because he never would have imperilled the success of his plan by doing anything of the sort. Peabody felt pain like a cancer in his breast as he thought of leaving Anne. Life had been gay and hopeful a few minutes ago, and now it was depressing and cruel. He was leaving Anne; he was sneaking away in the darkness, like a thief, to resume a hunted life, to go on ruining small traders and harmless fishermen, to be disquieted by every sail that showed on the horizon, slinking round the Caribbean like a wolf in the forest, and with destruction awaiting him at the end, and he would never see Anne again. In the darkness the hard lines deepened beside his mouth as he hurried on, stumbling over the inequalities of the street. The puff of warm wind that came down with him told him that the land breeze had just begun to blow – the land breeze which he had counted on to take him out past the Diamond Rock to freedom, to destruction.

At the waterfront the moon revealed his gig still waiting for him against the quay; most of the men were dozing uneasily, wrapped in their cloaks and doubled against the thwarts; three of them, including his coxswain, were standing on the quay chatting with a group of dusky women whose peals of laughter, he knew, must have been tempting to men who had been at sea for so long. But he knew there had been no desertion; he had selected his gig crew himself. As he approached, and the men recognised his tall figure looming in the darkness, they broke off their conversation abruptly and a little guiltily, although the women, unabashed, went on laughing and talking in their queer island French. Muggridge, the coxswain, sprang down into the gig to assist his captain, and the boat pushed off.

'Don't say I'm in the boat when they hail,' said Peabody quietly.

'Aye aye, sir.'

The boat glided over the moonlit water towards the phantom shape of the *Delaware*; on the other side of the bay the three British ships rode at their anchors. A little to seaward the remembered silhouette of a French coastguard cutter showed that the French Preventive Service was still awake, but it could not legally interfere with what he had in mind.

'Boat ahoy!' from the *Delaware*.

'No, no,' hailed Muggridge back.

That indicated there were no officers on board, just as 'aye aye' would have been warning of the presence of officers, or the answer '*Delaware*' would have announced the coming of the captain himself. Muggridge, like a sensible man, directed the course of the gig to the *Delaware's* larboard side – only officers could use the starboard side. The boat hooked on, and Peabody went up the side in two sharp efforts. O'Brien was in the waist and peered through the puzzling light at the apparition of his captain arriving unannounced on the port side.

'What the hell—?' he began.

'Quietly!' whispered Peabody. 'I don't want a sound. Turn up all hands – quietly, remember. Ask Mr. Poynter to come to the quarterdeck.'

'Aye aye, sir.'

His period of duty in a raiding frigate had already accustomed O'Brien to the strangest orders and occurrences. He turned to do his captain's bidding, while Peabody made his way to the quarterdeck. The drowsy hands stationed there started in surprise when he appeared; Peabody was aware that none of the men had had a proper night's sleep the night before – at best an hour or two snatched by the guns – but he clean forgot that he himself had not closed his eyes since he had been awakened twenty-four hours ago. Poynter loomed up before him; there was only the smallest noise as the hands came trooping to their stations from their broken sleep.

'I want all sail loosed to the royals, Mr. Poynter,' said Peabody to the acting-master. 'Every stitch ready to set when I give the word. Have the cable buoyed and ready to slip. Mind you, Mr. Poynter, I don't want a sound – not a sound, Mr. Poynter.'

'Aye aye, sir.'

'The four lieutenants will not be returning on board,' went on Peabody. 'See that the warrant officers are warned. You will take over Mr. Hubbard's duties.'

'Aye aye, sir.' Poynter waited in the darkness for any further surprising orders, and when none came he volunteered something on his own account. 'A letter came for you from the shore an hour or two back, sir.'

'Thank you,' said Peabody. He held the note in his hand while he hurried to the rail to stare through the darkness at the British squadron. He could see nothing and hear nothing suspicious, but this was a nervous moment. If the *Delaware* should get clear away it would be a resounding triumph for the United States Navy, and the British would be a laughing stock from the Caribbean to Whitehall. With a flash of insight Peabody realised that probably the most potent action he could take with the small means at his disposal, was to set the world laughing at the British. The land breeze was blowing well – the *Delaware* would be able to make a straight dash out of the bay.

'Cable's ready to slip, sir,' reported Poynter. 'Sail's all ready to set.'

'Thank you, Mr. Poynter. Slip the cable.'

'Aye aye, sir.'

Poynter was of a plethoric type; Peabody could hear his laboured breathing, and could guess at the strain Poynter was undergoing at having to give in a whisper orders which he was accustomed to bawling at the top of his voice. Men were scurrying up the rigging in the darkness like rats in a barn, while Poynter vanished forward again, and Peabody remembered his letter. He opened it in the shielded light of the binnacle.

BUREAU DU PORT,
FORT DE FRANCE,
MARTINIQUE.

The captains and masters of ships of belligerent powers in the ports of His Most Christian Majesty are informed that to avoid incidents of an international nature no movements of such ships will be permitted between sunset and sunrise. Ships violating this ordinance will be fired on.

GODRON,
Capitaine du Port.

Contresigne

Son Excellence le Gouverneur-Général, le Marquis Charles Armand de St. Amant de Boixe.

So that was that. He felt he should have foreseen this, but it would not have been easy to have guessed at the promptness of the decision which the French authorities had taken. They were quite within their rights to take any measures they chose within reason for the proper control of their port and without a doubt the guns of the batteries were trained to sweep the sea on the exit to the bay. The avenue of escape which he saw before him was blocked. That cursed preventive cutter was probably waiting with rockets to signal any movement.

'Snub that cable!' he roared forward at the top of his voice, the sound breaking through a mystical stillness; he had to repeat himself before they heard or understood him. And there could only have been a fathom or two of cable left by the time the purport of the order penetrated their minds.

'Mr. Poynter,' yelled Peabody, and Poynter came puffing aft; the spell of previous manoeuvres still bound him so closely that although Peabody spoke loudly, Poynter tried to puff quietly.

'Make all secure again, Mr. Poynter, if you please,' said Peabody coldly, 'and then send the hands below.'

'Aye aye, sir,' said Mr. Poynter. Discipline fought a losing battle with curiosity in Mr. Poynter's breast, as could be guessed from the intonation of the monosyllables, but Peabody was not in a mood to gratify it.

'That will be all, Mr. Poynter,' he said. Then Poynter turned away completely mystified. Peabody could accept the inevitable. He was not going to explain it to Poynter.

A moment later, a gig under oars went tearing by. Peabody saw in the stern sheets gold glittering in the moonlight, and he heard Davenant's voice.

'Pull, you bastards! Pull, you sons of bitches!'

Davenant's voice was cracking with anxiety – Peabody saw him leaning forward beating the air with his fists as he exhorted his men; Davenant must have had a tremendous fright at the prospect of the *Delaware* getting to sea without his knowledge. Peabody grinned to himself while the hands were shortening cable, and two minutes later another boat shot out of the darkness and came alongside, spewing on to the *Delaware's* deck a quartette of excited officers in full dress.

'Were you going without us, sir?' asked Hubbard.

'That was in my mind,' snapped Peabody. He found himself on the verge of venting his ill-temper on innocent victims; he had done that once or twice in his career, and had found it an evilly attractive habit, like indulgence in strong drink. His iron self-restraint came down on him again and then allowed free play to his natural kindliness.

'Get below, the four of you, and get some sleep.'

CHAPTER FOURTEEN

After the moon had set there was half an hour or so of utter darkness. Peabody was still on the quarterdeck with his hand on the rail, ignorant of his fatigue and want of sleep. In this dark interval there might be a chance of escape, but

Peabody hardly dallied with the idea for a moment. The French harbour guard was by now thoroughly aroused, and so, presumably, were the British. He had no doubt whatever that the big guns in the batteries were loaded and trained to converge on the exit, and that accursed cutter would send up her rockets. The *Delaware* would be badly knocked about; furthermore, if she violated harbour rules, the British might attack her at once and plead that in justification. It would not do.

But on the other hand the port captain's regulation distinctly laid it down that movement was permitted between sunrise and sunset – indeed, the French authorities could hardly say otherwise. That started an interesting train of possibilities. And the land breeze blew strongest at dawn. Peabody turned to the midshipman of the anchor watch with a series of orders, at the same time as he settled himself into a delightful calculation of what was the exact moment of sunrise on the morning of May 31st in Latitude 14° 20′ North. At three bells his orders began to bear fruit. The hands came up from below, while the dark sky above began to take on the faintest tinge of lilac, and the mountains of the island began to assume a sharper definition against it. The crew kept out of sight below the bulwark as they moved to their places under the direction of the petty officers; they were like the starters before a race – as indeed they were. Hubbard came up on deck and stood beside his captain. His eyes were a little red with fatigue, although he had had a full four hours' sleep in the last forty-eight.

'D'you think we'll do it, sir?' he asked.

'We'll know in ten minutes,' said Peabody.

There was enough light now for the British ships to be visible, and Peabody and Hubbard turned with one accord to look at them. They showed no sign of any activity – but then, neither did the *Delaware*. Peabody looked at his watch, put it back into his fob, and buttoned the flap with his usual care.

'Very good, Mr. Hubbard,' he said.

The last syllable had not left his lips before Hubbard was pealing on his whistle and the ship broke into life. The cable roared out, the jibs shot up, the ship shied away from the wind. A second later courses and topsails and topgallants and royals were spread, and the *Delaware* jerked herself forward as the land breeze swelled the canvas. It was only a matter of moments before she was tearing through the blue water, under the brightening sky, at a full nine knots.

'Hurry up with those stu'ns'ls, there!' roared Hubbard. 'Are you asleep?'

On both sides, from royals to main and foreyard, the studding sails were being set, almost doubling the canvas which the *Delaware* had spread. The resultant increase in speed was perceptible – the *Delaware* leaped to the additional impulse.

'Look there, sir!' said Hubbard suddenly, but Peabody had seen some time ago what Hubbard was pointing to.

The three British ships had all sail set as well, had slipped their cables, and were racing for the open sea, on courses which would converge upon the *Delaware's*. If even one of them crossed the line limiting territorial waters before the *Delaware* should, Peabody would have to turn back and stay twenty-four hours, while they could cruise outside and wait for him at their leisure.

'Clear for action and run out the guns, Mr. Hubbard, if you please,' said Peabody.

With courses converging in this fashion, it would not be at all surprising if guns went off without orders, and if they should, Peabody had no intention of being caught napping. Should the British violate French neutrality he would give as good as he got. Ahead of them lay the *Tigresse*, periodically spilling the wind from her mainsail as she awaited their coming – she must have got under way long before dawn. And that accursed cutter was out, too, to see the sport. The *Calypso*, her bows foaming white against the blue of the water, was drawing closer and closer. She, too, had her guns run out and her men at quarters; Peabody could see the red coats of the marines drawn up on the poop. Her bows were a trifle ahead of the *Delaware's*, but the *Delaware* was gaining on her perceptibly. Peabody recognised Davenant; he had leaped upon a carronade slide and was bellowing through his speaking-trumpet at the *Delaware*.

'I lead!' he yelled. 'Peabody, you'll have to go back.'

Peabody snatched his own speaking trumpet.

'You be damned!' he shouted. 'We're overtaking you.'

They were closing on the *Tigresse* now. She, too, had her pop-guns run out as she lay right across the bows of the charging frigates, and there were present all the ingredients for a violent explosion. There was a puff of smoke as she fired a gun.

'That was across our bows, sir,' said Hubbard.

'Across *his* bows, too,' said Peabody, with a jerk of his thumb at the *Calypso*. She showed no sign of heaving-to in obedience to the command, and Peabody would not give way before she did. He could see Davenant looking forward at the *Tigresse* with something of anxiety in his attitude. Something rumbled through the air over their heads and raised a fountain of water a cable's length from their port bow; they swung round in time to see a white puff of smoke from Fort Bourbon. It was an argument nothing could gainsay.

'Bring her to the wind, Mr. Hubbard,' said Peabody.

As the *Delaware* came round, he saw the *Calypso's* yards swing too. It might have been a well-executed drill, the way the two ships rounded-to exactly simultaneously. A moment later the *Bulldog* and the *Racer* did the same, and all four ships lay motionless in the bay while the *Tigresse* bore up for them. They saw a boat drop from her side as she hove-to, and pull towards the *Delaware*, and directly afterwards Captain Dupont was being piped on board by the hurriedly assembled boatswain's mates.

'His Excellency,' said Dupont to Peabody, after the formal greetings had been exchanged, 'would esteem it an honour if you would visit him in the *Tigresse*.'

'His Excellency?' said Peabody.

The last time he had seen the Marquis was at the ball the night before. It seemed probable that no one had had much sleep last night.

'It would be a favour as well as an honour,' said Dupont gravely, creasing his rounded belly in another bow.

'Oh, I'll come,' said Peabody.

It was just the same as yesterday; it seemed as if nothing had happened during the last twenty-four hours as Peabody took off his hat once more to the Marquis on the deck of the *Tigresse*, and then bowed to Davenant. The Marquis was elegantly dressed in a buff-coloured coat with a pink and blue fancy waistcoat beneath it, and showed no sign of a disturbed night; Peabody, conscious of the disordered full dress which he still wore, and of his unshaven face, was glad to see that Davenant, too, was red-eyed and untidy, the grey sprouts of his beard showing on his cheeks.

'It is most pleasant,' said the Marquis, 'to have the honour of repeated visits from you two gentlemen like this.'

'You don't find it pleasant at all,' said Peabody. He was in no mood for airy and long-winded nothings.

'Hospitality would forbid my saying that even if it were true,' answered the Marquis. 'But your suggestion naturally encourages me to speak more freely. I must confess that I did not succeed in getting a wink of sleep last night owing to my anxiety lest the guests of France, for whose reception I am responsible to His Most Christian Majesty, should unconsciously violate any of the accepted conventions.'

'Look here, Your Excellency,' said Davenant, 'what we both want to know is why you stopped us this morning. We weren't breaking any of your rules.'

'I had reason to fear that one or other of you might do so shortly,' answered the Marquis. 'It was a very close race which you were sailing.'

'Well, what of it? There's nothing wrong in that. One or other of us, as you say, would have got out first.'

'And would the other one have stopped then?' The Marquis's expression was severe as he looked at them. 'You would have crossed the line almost together, and in five seconds you would have been fighting. How would the neutrality of France have appeared then, to have allowed such a thing to happen? It is my duty, gentlemen, to use every means in my power to prevent such an occurrence.'

There was much solid truth and common sense in what

the Marquis was saying; Peabody stole a glance at Davenant and saw that the British captain was impressed by the argument – naturally the fact that the argument was backed up by twenty-four pounders gave it increased cogency.

'I must give you notice that whenever I see there is any possibility,' went on the Marquis, 'of your two ships leaving the bay together, I shall stop you, without hesitation.'

Davenant rubbed his bristling chin.

'I'm damned if I can see,' he said, 'why we ever gave Martinique back to you at all.'

The Marquis ignored the implied rudeness, which he could well do in his present position of authority.

'It has caused us all the loss of a night's sleep,' he said.

Meanwhile Peabody had been digesting the facts of the situation with results which were surprising him.

'But how are we ever going to get out of here?' he asked.

'That's what I want to know, by jingo,' said Davenant.

The glance which Davenant and Peabody exchanged showed that both of them saw the difficulties of the position. British and Americans would watch each other like hawks, and at the first sign of one making ready to leave the other would rush to forestall him. During daylight, at least, neither side would have a moment's leisure or relief from tension.

'I cannot see any answer to that question myself,' said the Marquis. 'I must apologise for it.'

'But dammit, sir,' said Davenant, 'you can't keep us here indefinitely.'

'I appreciate the pleasure of your company, Sir Hubert,' said the Marquis, 'but I assure you that I am making no effort to detain you. Please do not think me inhospitable when I point out that your presence here occasions me a considerable personal inconvenience. I should, of course, be delighted to oblige you two gentlemen in any way possible, if I might act as intermediary in any arguments you might care to enter into.'

Once more Peabody and Davenant exchanged glances.

'You might perhaps spin a coin for it,' suggested the Marquis.

The struggle apparent on the faces of both the captains at the suggestion made first the Marquis and then themselves, smile. It was tempting at first – an even chance of success or failure. But Davenant thought of the damage the *Delaware* might do if the spin of the coin were unlucky for him, and Peabody thought of the fact that the *Delaware* was the only United States ship of war not closely blockaded in an American port.

'I'm damned if I do,' said Davenant.

'I wouldn't have agreed if you'd wanted to,' said Peabody.

The Marquis sighed, as a very gentle reminder that his patience was being tried.

'You gentlemen can't agree upon anything?' he said.

'Why the hell should we?' said Davenant.

'Then I shall have to keep the *Tigresse* out here all day long and every day, and the battery guns manned and pointed,' said the Marquis. 'Really, gentlemen, you have very little consideration for your host.'

'That's nothing compared with what we'll be going through,' said Davenant irritably.

'Well, perhaps,' said the Marquis, tentatively, 'there is another course possible.'

'And what is that, sir?' asked Peabody, his curiosity roused.

'I was going to suggest, gentlemen, that perhaps you might agree on a short armistice. You might, for instance, give each other your promise not to make any attempt to leave Fort de France for some definite period – a week, might I say? That would give you an opportunity to water your ships and rest your men, and give me a chance to get some sleep. You would benefit and I would benefit and Martinique would benefit.'

'By Jove!' said Davenant. To him it was obviously a new idea, and Peabody, watching him closely, saw that he was tempted. He was tempted himself. There was a good deal of the *Delaware's* standing rigging which needed resetting-up, and he might perhaps heave her over and do a good job of work on the troublesome shothole, forward. But then Davenant shook his head.

'But what would happen at the end of the week?' he asked.

'At the end of the week you would be no worse off than now,' said the Marquis. 'You might even be better off. You might even have received orders from your Admiral which would take some of the responsibility off your shoulders.'

That made the suggestion far more tempting still to Davenant.

'There's something in what you say, Excellency,' he said. In the tone of his voice, Peabody could hear the grudging underlying admission – unconvinced, of course – that for a Frenchman the Marquis was showing extraordinary intelligence.

'I'll promise if you will,' said Peabody, cutting the Gordian knot. He was weary of fencing, and his matter-of-fact mind saw the essentials clearly enough despite the unusualness of it all.

'But any moment I might get other orders,' said Davenant in a sudden wave of caution.

'That can be allowed for,' said the Marquis. 'An armistice can always be denounced on giving notice.'

'That's so,' admitted Davenant.

'Then, perhaps you two gentlemen will promise that for a week neither of you will make any attempt to leave the harbour. This promise will be subject to the condition that it can be terminated on – shall we say twelve hours' notice on either side?'

The two captains nodded.

'Then let me hear you promise,' said the Marquis.

Davenant's expression revealed a fresh struggle within him as he looked at Peabody. Davenant knew the worth of his own promise, he knew he would never do anything that would bring dishonour on the British Navy, but for a moment he knew doubt as to Peabody's promise. He found it hard to believe that a new nation and an upstart navy could be trusted. It was quite a plunge that he was taking, but at length he took it.

'I promise,' he said.

'So do I,' said Peabody.

'That's good,' said the Marquis, and then, abruptly changing the distasteful subject. 'I hope we shall be seeing a good deal of you two gentlemen at my house during the coming week – I am speaking not only on my own account, but for my sister and daughter.'

CHAPTER FIFTEEN

Captain Josiah Peabody was conversant with the usages of good society; at Malta, during the Mediterranean campaign he had served a hard apprenticeship, and it was then, when national rivalries culminated in a series of duels between American and British officers, that he had learned that the stricter the regard for the conventions the easier it was to avoid trouble. Those weeks at Malta had actually rubbed the lesson in more effectively than years of living in cramped and crowded quarters on board a ship.

So that in the afternoon, when he had set one watch to work upon the ship, and made arrangements for shore leave for the other watch, he had Washington get out his second best uniform coat, and he ordered his gig and went ashore to pay his digestion call upon the Governor, as good manners dictated. Always as soon as possible after a dinner party or a ball, one paid a personal call or at least left cards upon one's host, and in view of the fact that he would be representing all the five officers of his ship, he decided it would be more fitting to call in person. That was what he himself honestly believed; it did not cross his conscious mind that he might be at all influenced by the desire to see Mademoiselle Anne de Breuil again.

It might be pleaded for him that his usual keenness of mind was blunted by the fact that he had had no sleep for two nights, that he had gone through a good deal of emotional strain during the past forty-eight hours. It was only yesterday morning that he had turned with the intention of fighting his last fight against the British squadron; it was only last night that he had kissed Anne, and since then there had been the two attempts to break out of the harbour. Adventures had come in a flood, as they always did at sea. And the heat of the bay was sticky and stupefying, and the light was blinding in its intensity; Peabody, as he was rowed ashore, knew that he felt dazed and not as clear-headed as usual.

He landed at the quay and walked up into the town; the two hundred liberty men of the *Delaware* seemed to fill every corner of the place. They were to be seen at all of the out-of-doors drinking places, sitting at the little tables roaring remarks to each other, pawing the coloured girls who waited on them. Half of them would be quietly drunk and some of them – who would be unfortunate – would be noisily drunk when they came on board again. Shore leave to them meant rum and women and subsequent punishment one way or another. Sailors were like that; Peabody knew it and made allowances for them. He had conquered drink himself and had never allowed lust to overmaster him, but he knew that others had not been as fortunate as himself. The only lack of sympathy he displayed was with regard to their drinking publicly at tables on the street – he simply could not understand that. To him it appeared axiomatic that drinking should be done privately, and as little public attention as possible called to it. He knew that if ever he started drinking again – although he never would – it would be secretly, with hurried intoxicating nips out of a private bottle which no one would ever know about.

The sentry outside the Governor's house saluted him smartly as he passed, and he raised his hat in acknowledgment. At the front door the coloured butler recognised him and smiled. What the butler said in reply to his inquiry if the Governor were at home, he did not understand in the least. He was aware that the butler changed from Martinique French to Martinique English, but it did not make the butler more intelligible. But the butler was certainly ushering him inside, and he followed. The transition from the dazzling sunlight outside to the cool darkness within, quite blinded him. He stumbled over something in his path, trod on a mat which slipped treacherously under his foot on the polished floor, retained his balance with difficulty, and heard, as if in a dream, Anne's voice saying: 'Good afternoon, Captain Peabody.'

His eyes grew accustomed to the darkness, and the sudden mist which befogged them cleared away. There was Anne, in cool white, sitting gracefully in an armchair. He bowed and he mumbled; certainly his wits were not as clear as they should be. Something in Anne's attitude called his attention to another part of the room, and there was Davenant, newly risen from another armchair, and standing stiffly with his hat under his arm, and – possibly – feeling a little awkward, although there was no certainty about it. This meeting of one's country's enemies on neutral ground was embarrassing. But the suspicion that Davenant was not quite at ease was reassuring. Peabody was able to smile politely and bow formally in consequence.

'Very warm for this time of year,' said Peabody, utterly determined not to be discountenanced.

'Yes,' said Davenant. The way he pronounced it was more like 'yas.'

'But not as warm as it was last week,' said Anne.

'No,' said Peabody.

'No,' said Davenant, and conversation wilted. Peabody was momentarily distracted by the queer thought that if he met Davenant anywhere except on neutral soil it would be his duty to pull out his sword and fall upon him; that he would be liable to court-martial and to the severest penalties if he did not do his best to kill him as speedily as possible. He forced himself to abandon that line of thought.

'I have called to thank His Excellency on behalf of my officers and myself for the extremely pleasant evening we enjoyed yesterday,' he said.

'I'm glad to hear you enjoyed it,' said Anne, composedly, but as she said it her eyes met Peabody's and the next moment there was red colour flooding her cheeks and neck.

'Nice evenin',' said Davenant. 'There were some pretty women, by George. None of 'em a patch on you and Madame your aunt, though.'

'You are very kind, Sir Hubert.'

As if the mention of her had brought her in, the Countess entered on the words.

'Good afternoon, Sir Hubert. Good afternoon, Captain Peabody. I hope my niece has been entertaining you.'

'Delightfully, I assure you, ma'am,' said Davenant.

'His Excellency is still engaged with the Council,' went on the Countess. 'I was wondering if this would be a good opportunity while it isn't raining, to show you my orchids which I was telling you about last night, Sir Hubert.'

'Oh, yes, of course,' said Davenant.

'Sir Hubert is interested in orchids, you see, Captain Peabody,' explained the Countess, 'and His Excellency's predecessor in office, General Brown, made a most interesting collection. The British occupation of the island had its brighter side, we must admit.'

'Surely,' said Peabody.

'Anne,' said the Countess, 'will you offer Captain Peabody some tea?'

'Yes, Aunt Sophie.'

'Until we meet again, then, Captain,' said the Countess.

Next moment she was gone, through the glass door which Davenant opened for her and through which he followed her. The room was suddenly quiet, except for the faint whine of the fan in the ceiling – an ingenious arrangement by which a cord was taken over a pulley through a hole in the wall, so that a negro child outside the room could keep the air in motion without intruding on the privacy within. Peabody admired the contrivance for some seconds as if it were as fascinating as a snake. As the Countess and Davenant were leaving the room he had suddenly felt that he could not, for some unexplained reason, meet Anne's eyes. He remained on his feet, his left hand on his sword hilt, sliding the blade half an inch in and out.

'You went away!' said Anne suddenly, in the silence of the room.

He looked down at her, and she was looking up at him reproachfully.

'Anne!' he said, and he melted. There was never anything

like this, like this unrestrainable surge of emotion. His head swam, and he came down on his knees at her side – he had never knelt to any woman before, but it was the most natural thing he had ever done in his life. She put her two hands into his, and they kissed; and when they drew back from each other he went on looking into her eyes.

'Anne!' was all he could say. He did not know what a volume of meaning he put into that monosyllable.

'I didn't mean what I said,' explained Anne.

'I had to go,' said Peabody. 'I had to try to go. I didn't want to.'

'I know, my dear,' said Anne.

She kissed him again, and then her lips left his and strayed over his mahogany cheek, fluttering as she murmured something to herself, some endearment or other.

'What am I going to do with you?' said Anne. 'This – this – I can't bear to have you out of my sight.'

She took one of her hands from him and put it on her breast where the emotion surged. Peabody knew just how she felt. He sawed at his stock with his free hand in a struggle against the passion which threatened to choke him. It seemed to be the last straw that she should so frankly admit to her emotion.

'Darling!' he said.

Her lips were the lips of innocence, of a sweetness and a simplicity which left him breathless in the delight which they conferred. There had never been anything like this in all his experience. Within him subconsciously stirred a twenty-year forgotten memory of his mother's tainted caresses, and he clung to Anne's hands and put his face to hers in the violence of the reaction.

'I couldn't bear it,' said Anne. 'You were gone. I thought I might never see you again.'

He looked into her eyes, and he remembered that death was awaiting him outside the bay, just beyond the Diamond Rock. The realisation shook him, and he tore himself from her and got to his feet.

'I'm a fool,' he said. 'I shouldn't ever have done this.'

It was a second or two before Anne answered, the fear that

she felt revealing itself in her face and in her voice.

'Why not?' she whispered.

'Because—' said Peabody, 'because – oh—'

It was hard to put it all into words, the *Delaware's* homelessness, the peril in which he stood, the losing fight which he was going to wage against the mightiest sea power the world had ever seen. Ironically, the love he bore for Anne crystallised his determination not to survive the eventual inevitable destruction of the *Delaware*; he did not say so to Anne, but it showed through the halting sentences with which he tried to explain his situation.

'I understand,' said Anne, nodding her head. It was odd, and yet it tore at Peabody's heart-strings, to see this very young woman contemplating problems of life and death, of war and peace.

'There is only this one week,' said Peabody.

'One week,' said Anne.

The little round chin under the soft mouth was firm for all its allure. Peabody had a moment's piercing insight; this was the sort of woman who would load her husband's long rifle while savages howled outside the log cabin, no more than twenty years old and yet willing to face anything beside the man she loved. He shook off the mental picture from before his eyes.

'That's all,' he said simply. 'I'm sorry.'

But all Anne's twenty years of life had been spent in a world in a turmoil of war. She had learned to think clearly through it.

'My dear,' she said, and her eyes met Peabody's unflinching. 'If we are lucky enough to have a week granted us, why should we waste it?'

Peabody's jaw dropped at that, and he looked at her with surprise. It was a view of the case which his farseeing New England mind had not seen at all; he had paid so much attention to next week that to-morrow had escaped his notice.

'What do you mean?' his voice choking a little as the explication flooded in upon him.

Anne did not have the chance to explain, because the Marquis came in at that moment.

Peabody did not start at the sudden noise of the latch – his nerves were steady enough despite this present ordeal – and Anne retained her seat in the arm-chair with composure, but it would have been asking too much of them that their attitudes should not have revealed something of their preoccupation. The Marquis looked keenly from one to the other, and like a man of breeding he was prepared to pay no attention to the fact that his entrance had been at a difficult moment, but Peabody gave him no chance. He swung round on the Marquis, his brain labouring hard under the handicaps of strong emotion and recent sleeplessness.

'Good afternoon, Captain Peabody,' said the Marquis.

'I want to marry your daughter,' said Peabody, and even the Marquis's breeding was not proof against the surprise the statement occasioned. It was the sight of his discomposure which most helped Peabody to collect himself. The Marquis looked at them both again, as if during the last two seconds their appearance had undergone some radical change, and he waited some time before he spoke; even if Peabody's abrupt statement had taken him sufficiently off his guard to make him change countenance, years of training had taught him not to make an unguarded reply, and in theory, if not in practice, to count ten before he said anything decisive.

'The fact that you want to marry Mlle de Breuil,' he said, fencing for time, 'is a recommendation of your good taste, if not of your knowledge of the world.'

'Surely,' said Peabody. Now that he was in this affair he was not going to flinch, not for all the Marquises and Excellencies in His Most Christian Majesty's dominions.

'I know very little about you, Captain,' said the Marquis. 'Please forgive me – I intend no rudeness – but the name of Peabody does not enter into my genealogical knowledge. Can you tell me something about your family?'

'My father was a Connecticut farmer,' said Peabody sturdily, 'and so was his father, although he came from Massachusetts. And I don't know who *his* father was.'

'I see,' said the Marquis. 'You are not a man of great fortune, Captain?'

The question very nearly nonplussed Peabody. He was almost at the head of his profession, and he enjoyed a salary of one hundred dollars a month in hard money – a salary quite large enough to maintain a wife with dignity in New York or Philadelphia. But it was only now that his attention was called to the fact that this income – imposing enough to him – was insignificant compared with European fortunes, and it called for an effort on his part not to allow the realisation to unsettle him.

'I have my pay,' he said with dignity.

'I see,' said the Marquis again. 'Mlle de Breuil is a lady of fortune. She will have a very considerable *dot* – dowry, I think you call it. Did that influence you in reaching this rather surprising decision?'

'Good God!' said Peabody, completely thrown out of his stride this time. The idea had never occurred to him for a moment, and his face showed it. His astonishment was so genuine that it could hardly fail to make a favourable impression upon the Marquis – the latter's experiences might have accustomed him to American unconventionality, but they had not been able to eradicate the Frenchman's natural tendency to look upon matrimony as an occasion for financial bargaining.

'It is usual,' said the Marquis, 'when a marriage is being arranged, for the prospective bridegroom to match, franc for franc, his bride's fortune in the matter of settlements. You apparently had no intention of doing that?'

'No,' said Peabody. 'I didn't know that Mlle de Breuil had any money. I never thought about it, and I don't want it.'

He was conscious that he had made a frightful hash of the pronunciation of Anne's name, and it did not improve his temper, which was steadily rising.

'Josiah,' said Anne quietly. As far as Peabody knew, that was the first time Anne had ever spoken his name. It quieted him a good deal, and he made himself speak reasonably.

'All Anne and I want to do,' he said, 'is to get married. In my country we do not think about money in that connection. And one free man is as good as another.'

The Marquis suddenly became confidential.

'Do you know,' he said, 'it is my impression that just as

many unsuccessful marriages result from the one system as from the other.'

Peabody grinned.

'You don't think our marriage is going to be unsuccessful, Father?' asked Anne.

'How long have you known each other?' continued the Marquis. 'You've seen each other twice—

'Three times, then—' said the Marquis, but he had been just sufficiently checked in the full flow of his argument to cause him to stumble, and his final words were a little lame. 'It's just madness, madness.'

The glass door opened to admit the Countess with Davenant, and the Marquis swung round on his sister.

'These two ridiculous people want to get married, Sophie,' he said.

'We are going to get married to-morrow, Aunt Sophie,' said Anne.

The Countess expressed her surprise in French; Davenant's face bore such a comic expression, of mixed astonishment and envy at this American who had carried off a prize in this fashion that Peabody was immensely comforted. He even began to enjoy himself. But Davenant was of stern stuff, and not for long would he ever allow himself to be discountenanced. If the right thing was there to be said, he was going to say it.

'I wish you joy, Mamzelle,' he said. 'Sir, my heartiest good wishes and congratulations.'

'Thank you, sir,' said Peabody.

'But—' began the Marquis.

'You are very kind, Sir Hubert,' said Anne, neatly interrupting him, and then she turned to her aunt with a torrent of French. The Countess's face softened, and she came towards her niece – Peabody had a clairvoyant moment, when telepathically he was aware of the sentimental appeal an imminent marriage has for any woman. Probably aunt and niece were closer together spiritually than ever before.

'But—' said the Marquis again.

'Father,' said Anne, turning from her aunt for a moment,

'I'm sure the gentlemen are thirsty. Won't you pull the bell?'

Not even his disapproval of his daughter's marriage could weigh in the scale against a lifetime of training in hospitality, and the Marquis broke off his speech to walk across to the bell-pull.

'Now listen to me—' he began as he returned.

'The white gown will do if we use a veil,' Anne was saying to her aunt, and Peabody was careful to pay the strictest attention to her, so that the Marquis had only Davenant to whom he could address his remarks, which naturally died away undignified.

'Anne!' exclaimed the Marquis exasperated, 'don't—'

The entrance of the butler was the culminating interruption. The Marquis swung round upon him, and was immediately engulfed in orders to him. He actually never succeeded in giving any voice to his objections to the marriage.

CHAPTER SIXTEEN

Peabody came back on board the *Delaware* just at sunset. He looked round the familiar decks, and at the familiar faces, out at the red sun sinking in the blue Caribbean, and aloft to where the men were just finishing their work for the day. It was all so real, so ordinary, that for a moment he felt that the situation he had left behind at the Governor's house was an unreal one. It called for all his common sense to act normally in a world where at one moment he could have Anne's soft lips against his own, and at the next he could be putting the *Delaware* into shape for her last fight.

'Mr. Hubbard,' he said, as his first lieutenant lifted his hat, 'we'll heave her over to-morrow. Run the even numbered starboard side guns over to larboard – that ought to be enough. You'll double-breech the others, of course. That'll bring her over by a couple of strokes and you can get at those shot-holes.'

'Aye aye, sir,' said Hubbard.

'I am going to get married to-morrow, Mr. Hubbard,' went on Peabody.

'I didn't understand you, sir?'

Peabody repeated his words, but even so they did not convince Hubbard for a minute or two.

'Who is the lady, sir?' asked Hubbard, swallowing, and eyeing Peabody with some anxiety.

'Mamzelle Anne de Breuil,' said Peabody, and then he grinned, 'and the sooner she's Mrs. Peabody, so that we don't have to try to say that name any more, the better.'

Hubbard's swarthy saturnine face grinned in response as the little human touch about the joke thawed him completely.

'She's a lovely lady, sir,' he said. 'I wish you joy, sir, and happiness, and prosperity.'

'Thank you, Mr. Hubbard. Now what about that second best suit of sails? What did the committee of inquiry decide about them?'

There was a great deal to be done – there never was any ship yet in which a great deal did not have to be done, even when there was not the additional prospect of having to fight for her life within the week. Peabody went round the ship with his heads of department, his first lieutenant and his carpenter, his boatswain and his cooper and his purser and his gunner. The ship was noisy with the return at sunset of the tipsy liberty men whose last stragglers had been swept up by Atwell and a small party from the grogshops and the brothels, but Peabody like a sensible man, turned a blind eye and a deaf ear to the strange sights and sounds around him. His petty officers were the pick of all America, who could be relied upon not to incite trouble and to suppress it as soon as it showed – he paid no attention to the drunken figures which were being lashed into their hammocks like giant cocoons that could hurt neither themselves nor anyone else.

Washington was far more trouble than any drunken sailor; Peabody snapped the news at him as sternly and as unemotionally as he knew how, but that did not prevent the talkative negro from indulging in a long orgy of sentiment.

That post of old family retainer was maddening to Peabody; so long had he been solitary, so long dependent on his own sole exertions that he resented bitterly Washington's continual attempt to establish himself in his intimacy; equally irritating was Washington's bland self-deception as he deliberately tried to make a god out of his master. Washington was uncomfortable without someone to worship, and paid small attention to Peabody's discomfort at being worshipped.

'Shut your mouth, you fool, and let's see those shirts,' growled Peabody.

'Yessir, yessir, immediately, sir,' protested Washington. 'Pity we haven't got a shirt of Chinee silk for the wedding, sir. And I haven't never seen the lady yet, sir, and—'

'Shut your mouth, I said!'

A little more of it and Washington would completely unsettle him – already Peabody was holding on to his self-control with a drowning man's grip. He had been two nights without sleep, and a third would leave him fit for nothing to-morrow, he told himself as he lay down on his cot in the sweltering night. He called up all his self-control, all his seaman's habits, to try to make certain of sleeping as soon as his head touched the pillow, grimly emptying his mind of all thoughts in the manner which up till now had proved infallible. Yet to-night sleep did not come at once. He turned over, once, twice, in his bath of sweat, fighting down the images which awaited their chance to flood into his mind like hungry wolves. He heard six bells strike, and seven, and it was nature which decided the struggle in the end. At eight bells she asserted herself, struck him unconscious as though with a club, as she demanded her rights, her usurious repayment for the demands Peabody had made on her during the last forty-eight hours – forty-eight hours without sleep, of ceaseless activity, of continual mental strain of every possible kind. Once he was asleep his seaman's habits reasserted themselves to the extent of giving him every ounce of benefit from the six hours granted him.

So his hand was steady when he shaved next morning, and his eyes had not fulfilled their threat of being bloodshot, and he could listen without attention to Washington's ecstatic maunderings. He was as unobtrusively well-clad a figure as heart could desire as he went down the ship's side and took his seat in the stern of the gig along with Jonathan and Murray, and Providence was kind, for the prodigious midsummer rain of Martinique held off during the short passage to the quay, although they were hardly inside the carriage which awaited them there when it roared down upon the roof thunderously enough to drown speech.

It was a pretty compliment which his men were paying him. The watch which had come on shore a few minutes earlier had resisted the temptation of drink and women – after eighteen weeks at sea! – and were waiting for him. They ran shouting and yelling beside the clattering carriage, whooping and capering in the rain, scaring the coloured girls who put their heads out of the windows. Cheering, they thronged the carriage when it halted, so that Peabody, smiling, had to push his way through them. Their cheerful antics directed the vast crowd of Martinique, of all ages, colours, and attire who had come hurrying at the amazing news of the immediate marriage of the Governor-General's daughter. They crowded the vast audience hall, and their cheerful babble rose to a deafening height, to die away magically when everyone peered on tiptoe to catch a glimpse of Anne in white when she entered. The Marquis asked Peabody and Anne grave questions, first in French and then in English as, in his capacity as magistrate, he carried through the civil ceremony.

Things grew vaguer and vaguer in Peabody's mind – he was only conscious of the warmth and perfume of Anne beside him, and then, with a slight shock of surprise, that Anne's brows were straight and level black above the blue. It puzzled him that he had not realised before how straight they were.

There were more ceremonies; there was the signing of documents, there was a half-formal procession into the big room which he had last seen cleared for dancing. There were toasts and then there was laughter. There were endless presentations. There was a brief moment when he saw Jonathan across the room, wine-glass in hand, laughing boisterously with Mme Clair.

It all passed, and he was back in the carriage with the rain thundering on the roof again, but this time Anne was beside him, and he was more delirious with happiness than ever before, even at his most drunken moments. There was a small house – what house it was he had no idea – where there were eager coloured servants who giggled excitedly when Anne spoke to them in their queer tongue. There was a bedroom with a mosquito-net hung over the bed in the vastest dome Peabody could ever remember seeing, and Washington was there, unpacking things and chattering feverishly about a variety of subjects, from his master's future happiness to the surprising differences between coloured girls in New York and in Martinique – an endless flow of babble which only ceased when Peabody turned on him and hurled him from the room like Adam from Eden.

Anne came to him, and came to his arms like a child. Time was brief; life was short, and happiness was there to be grasped, as elusive as an eel and as hard to retain once caught. The little French words which Anne used were elusive too, and no drink he had ever drunk was as madly intoxicating. An hour before dawn he had, he knew, to start his preparations for leaving Anne for the day. He wanted to be on the deck of the *Delaware* at the first peep of daylight to attend to the work of the ship.

CHAPTER SEVENTEEN

Lieutenant Hubbard clearly had something unpleasant to report, after he had given an account of how the work on the ship progressed. He held his lanky figure rigid as he stood in the stuffy cabin, and he looked over the top of Peabody's head as he said the words.

'Midshipman Jonathan Peabody, sir. Absent without leave.'

'He didn't come back last night?'

'No, sir.'

Hubbard was saying no more than the formalities demanded.

'He was with Mr. Atwell. What has Atwell to say about it?'

'Shall I pass the word for Mr. Atwell to report so that you can ask him, sir?'

'Yes.'

Atwell's ugly face showed all the signs of anxiety.

'After the – wedding, sir—'

'Yes, go on.'

'We was all invited to another house. Madame Clair's, sir – I don't mean that sort of house, sir.'

'I know Madame Clair. Go on.'

'I didn't see much of Mr. Peabody while he was there. To tell the truth, sir, there was drinking going on and skylarking.'

'Yes.'

'But at seven bells I thought I'd leave, sir, and I looked for Mr. Peabody and I had to look a long time. And when I found him—'

'Where was he?'

'He was with Madame Clair. She was very merry, sir. To tell the truth, she had her arms round him.'

'Go on.'

'I said it was time to go back to the ship. And he said—'

'Go on.'

'He said he'd be eternally damned if he'd ever go back to the damned ship again. He said I could go back to hell on water if I wanted to, but he wasn't such a damned fool as me.'

'What did you say to that?'

'I said I'd forget his insolence if he'd only come back with me. I'd let bygones be bygones. I could see he'd been drinking, sir.'

'And he refused to come?'

'Yes, sir. I tried to make him, sir, but—'

'But what?'

'To tell the truth, sir, Madame Clair called the servants and – and I had to go without him.'

'Very good, Mr. Atwell. No blame attaches to you. Thank you, Mr. Hubbard.'

This was added bitterness in his strangely mixed cup. Jonathan had deserted in the presence of the enemy, and if Jonathan had his deserts he would be dangling at the yard-arm if he could once lay his hands on him. If Jonathan came back voluntarily he would spare his life after the severest punishment he could devise – but he knew Jonathan had no intention whatever of coming back. Nor, in a neutral port, could any attempt be made to recapture him, for Jonathan could stand on the quay and merely laugh at them. Probably that was what he would do. Peabody reached for the log-book and wrote in it. 'Midshipman Jonathan Peabody deserted.' Peabody's expression as he wrote reflected his mood; it was that same mood in which Cato put his sword point to his breast. He did not spare himself any of the agony.

The pain was still there at the end of the day, when his gig carried him over the reddened, sunset-lit water to the quay where the carriage with its ridiculous little horses stood waiting in the shade of a warehouse. His shoulders were a little bowed with it as he set foot on shore, and the hard lines from nose to mouth were deeper than ever. Washington – trust that fool to be there! – was standing by the carriage door and pulled it open the instant Peabody appeared. There was a flutter of bright colours, a whirl of petticoats, as Anne sprang down and ran to him. He made no move to take her in his arms, but she put up her hands to his lapels and drew him to her as close as his rigidity would allow, smiling up at him, and she made herself smile despite the unrelenting hardness of his face. Whether he would have kissed her in the full light of day and in sight of all Fort de France, if he had not been oppressed with the thought of Jonathan, was not to be guessed – public kissing was sinful.

'Where does Madame Clair live?' were his first words.

'Over towards Ducos. Five miles away. Six, perhaps, dear.'

'Can we go there?'

'Of course, dear. Dinner can wait.'

Peabody was not experienced enough fully to appreciate the transcendent loyalty of that speech.

'Let us go there, then,' he said.

Washington elaborately guarded Anne's skirts from the wheel; Anne gave her orders to the coachman in a steady voice which forbade any comment even from Washington who thirsted to make some. The carriage lurched over the cobbles.

'I know about Jonathan, dear,' said Anne and there was sympathy in her voice. Atwell and Hubbard had not offered sympathy, had perhaps been repelled from offering it; nor, in his drab existence, had Peabody been aware until that moment that he would be grateful for sympathy. And in his mind Peabody had drawn a sharp dividing line between the familiar realities of his professional life and the delirious unrealities of his dream life. It was the first indication that the line could be crossed, that Anne – a woman, and French, and the leading figure of the dream life should be able to know instantly what it meant to a United States captain that his brother should be a deserter.

'I don't know whether you've heard everything, dear,' went on Anne, gently. 'The island's full of the news.'

'What news?'

'They were married to-day. Jonathan and Madame Clair.'

'No,' said Peabody. 'I hadn't heard that.'

It did not seem likely in that case that a personal appeal would have any effect in persuading Jonathan to return to duty, then. Jonathan must have found a new career for himself.

'She's the richest landowner in the whole island,' said Anne. 'There's another estate on the windward side, near Vauclin, which came to her from her second husband. Jonathan will be a rich man – there are four hundred slaves.'

It was quite certain that Jonathan would not return to duty. Peabody was suddenly left without a doubt about it; he was able now to see his brother's character perfectly clearly. He could understand his passionate resentment against any kind of discipline, and the slyness which had enabled him to evade it. But that a Peabody should have deserted, that his own brother should have disgraced him like this, was almost more than he could bear. He did not know how he could face the world. He was tempted to turn and go back again, but it was not in him to give up any enterprise, however hopeless, once he had begun upon it. The stuffy interior of the carriage, the stifling heat, and the irregularity of the motion as the carriage rolled unsteadily over the inequalities of the surface, were all depressing. Then the rain came to make matters worse, and the little horses laboured in the mud of the road, and more than once they had to be checked as the wheels verged upon the ditch in the darkness.

And the meeting with Jonathan was a shameful thing – Jonathan red-faced with wine, his arm round his new wife on whose cheeks the rouge was smeared and striped with sweat, the two of them laughing and jeering at him like obscene animals at the entrance to their inaccessible cave. Peabody was conscious of the sword at his side and was tempted to slash and carve at this loathsome brother of his, but the coloured servants closed round him and he was forced to break off the hideous interview.

It was still raining when they reached the carriage door.

'We'll go straight home, Washington,' said Peabody.

'Yessir, cert'nly sir, whatever you—'

'Shut your mouth and get on the box.'

The carriage lurched and squelched back through the mud. In the darkness Anne spoke. There was the faint French flavour in her accent combined with the London accent which Peabody found so irritating in every voice except Anne's.

'I hate him,' said Anne. 'He's your brother and I hate him.'

'So do I,' said Peabody bitterly.

'Dearest,' said Anne, 'what can I say? What can I do? It breaks my heart that you are unhappy.' There was a catch in her throat as she spoke and Peabody knew she was crying in the darkness, and it was more than he could bear.

'Don't – don't,' he said.

'I hate him more than anyone on earth,' said Anne. 'But – but I love you more, ever so much more. I couldn't hate as much as I love you.'

Her soft hand touched his horny one, and that changed the mood of both of them.

Peabody in the darkness knew that all this was madness. To snatch at a moment's happiness like this, when all the world was against him, was as foolish as to heave a sigh of relief during the ten seconds' calm in the centre of a hurricane. It was not merely foolish, but it savoured of the sinful. And yet – and yet – there was no help for it. He could not control himself, and the minority party in his mind was vociferously informing him that the very briefness of his happiness was a further argument in favour of snatching at it. There was an additional fearful pleasure in comparing his own actions with those of the sinful man who said, 'Eat drink and be merry, for to-morrow we die.' Logic on the one hand and unwonted recklessness on the other combined with his own wild passion to force him into forgetting for a space the *Delaware* and the *Calypso*, his brother's defection and his own approaching end, even the history of the world in which he was playing a major part and even the peril of his own country. Anne's lips were sweet.

The torch which lit them from the carriage to the little house was hardly as bright as the white fireflies which winked on and off in hundreds all about them; the whine of the fan in the ceiling did nothing to mask the song of the frogs and the crickets in the wet undergrowth outside the dark windows. Across the table Anne's sweet face swam in a mist; the glass of wine which stood before him stood untouched and unthought of. It might be madness; it might even be sin, but it was happiness, and the first he had ever known.

The coloured maid who was wise only in the ways of Martinique brought him rum to drink in the dark morning of thunderous rain, and her white teeth accented her amused surprise when it was refused. The dawn which burst upon him as he rowed out to the *Delaware* was the dividing line between the two worlds – their world where happiness was so acute as to be distrusted, and the other world where there were hard facts to be clung to, comforting as soon as the mind had grown accustomed to them again like eyes to light.

CHAPTER EIGHTEEN

The gig which rowed over from the *Calypso* was a smart little craft, with the White Ensign fluttering above the head of the supercilious midshipman in the stern who answered Hubbard's hail.

'Message for Captain er – Peabody,' said the midshipman, and his manner implied that the name in his mouth was as distasteful as medicine.

The gig hooked on to the chains, the British sailors looking up curiously at the American ones hard at work about the ship while the midshipman scrambled to the deck. He touched his hat to the quarterdeck in the new off-hand British fashion that compared so unfavourably with the American rule of uncovering, and handed over the note.

H.M.S. *Calypso*,
FORT DE FRANCE.

Captain the Hon. Sir Hubert Davenant, K.B., presents his respects to Captain Josiah Peabody, U.S.S. *Delaware*. He would esteem it a favour if Captain Peabody could find it convenient to meet him as soon as his duties permit. Captain Davenant ventures to suggest that Captain Peabody should visit him aboard *Calypso*, and wishes to indicate that he is aware of the honour Captain Peabody would confer upon *Calypso* in that event. However, should Captain Peabody decide that he cannot do so, Captain Davenant would be delighted to wait upon Captain Peabody at any point on neutral territory that Captain Peabody may be pleased to indicate. But the matter is urgent.

Peabody read this missive in the privacy of the cabin.

'You say the midshipman's waiting for an answer?'
'Yes, sir.'
'Tell him he'll have it soon.'
'Aye aye, sir.'

Peabody's matter-of-fact mind dissected the clumsy wording. In the first place, it did not need the final sentence to impress upon him how urgent the matter was – if Davenant should eat humble pie to the extent of making the first advance that was proof enough in itself. In the second place, the note did not ask him to commit himself to anything. It did not ask him to make any promises; he was at liberty to get any advantage out of the invitation which was open to him and to make no return. There was a chance of gaining something – he knew not what – and no chance of losing anything. Clearly the thing to do was to accept, and Peabody cut himself a fresh pen and addressed himself to the task.

It was not so easy as that. Peabody found himself making innumerable erasures as he floundered in the pitfalls of the third person singular; he made a fair copy, and then had to do it all over again when carelessly he allowed sweat to smudge the completed note – it was just as well, he discovered, on recopying, because he had forgotten to put in the 'K.B.' after Davenant's name, and he was certainly not going to allow a United States captain to be outdone in the game of formal politeness by a British one.

U.S.S. *Delaware*,
FORT DE FRANCE.

Captain Josiah Peabody presents his respects to Captain the Hon. Sir Hubert Davenant, K.B. He will be honoured to wait upon Captain Davenant at three p.m. this afternoon, if that will be convenient to him.

Washington brought a candle and he sealed the note and sent it on deck.

'Get me out one of my best shirts, Washington.'
'Best shirt, sir? Yes, indeed, sir.'

These last few days had been a perfect orgy for Washington. It irked him inexpressibly that his master should ever wear the second best of anything, however neatly patched and darned, and now for days Peabody had been wearing a succession of the precious best shirts which had rested unworn in the locker since leaving Brooklyn. On deck Peabody was aware that Hubbard's keen observation had detected that he was wearing his best clothes.

'I'm going on board the British frigate, Mr. Hubbard. Call my gig's crew, if you please. I shall inspect them before I start.'

'Aye aye, sir.'

Hubbard passed on the order and turned back anxiously to his captain.

'Did you say you were going on board the British frigate, sir?'

'I did.'

Hubbard realised at the same moment as his captain that there was nothing more to say. The British might be domineering, ruthless, inconsiderate, but neither Peabody nor Hubbard could for a moment imagine them capable of false dealing. If at their invitation Peabody visited them, he could be perfectly certain of being offered no hindrance when he wanted to leave again.

Muggridge formed up the gig's crew abaft the mainmast, and Peabody walked forward and looked them over.

'Can't have that patched shirt,' he said. 'Go change it. Those trousers aren't the right colour. Well, go draw another pair from the purser. You, Harvey, straighten that hair of yours.'

No lover preparing to visit his mistress ever paid so strict an attention to his appearance as did Peabody to that of his gig's crew at the prospect of having them looked over by a rival service. He even looked sharply over the gig itself, at the spotless white canvas fendoffs and the geometrically exactly arranged oars and boat hook, even though he knew Muggridge to be too conscientious a sailor altogether to allow the slightest fault to be found with his charge. At precisely four minutes before six bells he stepped into the stern sheets;

on board the Calypso the striking of six bells accompanied the hail of 'boat ahoy!' from the officer of the watch.

'*Delaware*!' hailed Muggridge in return.

There was the most formal reception on the deck. The red-coated marines presented arms like a score of mechanical wooden soldiers; their pipe-clayed crossbelts and bright badges echoed the gleam of the spotless decks and metal work. The officer of the watch held his hand rigidly to his hat brim while the boatswain's mates twittered wildly on their pipes; the sideboys had the freshest imaginable white gloves and their infant faces had been scrubbed into preternatural cleanliness. Peabody took off his own hat in salute, and kept it off as Davenant advanced to meet him.

'Good afternoon, sir. This is a great honour. Would you be kind enough to accompany me below?'

The great cabin of the *Calypso* was smaller than that of the *Delaware*, as was only to be expected, and its permanent fittings were if anything even more spartan. Peabody had an impression of a multiplicity of ornaments – objects collected by Davenant during thirty years of commissioned service – but he had no attention to spare for them because his attention was held by the persons in the room. There were two other British naval officers there, on their feet to welcome him – he recognized them as having been present at the ball – and looking over the shoulder of one of them was, of all people in the world, Hunningford the spy, Hunningford whom he had last seen sailing away from the secret rendezvous after giving him the information regarding the Jamaica convoy. As their eyes met Hunningford's left eyelid flickered momentarily; but Peabody's wits were about him and he kept his face expressionless and with no sign of recognition.

'Allow me to present,' said Davenant, 'Captain Fane, His Majesty's corvette *Racer*, Commander Maitland, His Majesty's armed brig *Bulldog*, and Mr. Charles Hunningford, one of our most respected Kingston merchants – Captain Josiah Peabody.'

Everybody bowed.

'There's a mixture of rum and lime which is popular on this island and which ought to be better known,' said

Davenant. 'The secret lies in a grating of nutmeg, I fancy. Will you sit here, Captain Peabody? Maitland – Fane – Mr. Hunningford.'

Peabody realised in an amused moment that Davenant was actually shy, oppressed by the strange circumstance of entertaining a hostile captain, and endeavouring to carry it off with bluff and bustle.

'Your health, gentlemen,' said Davenant, raising his glass, and everyone sipped solemnly, and then looked at everyone else, the ice still not broken.

'Haven't had the chance to congratulate you on your marriage, sir,' said Fane, stepping into the breach. 'Devilish lovely wife you've got.'

'Thank you, sir.'

'Here's to the bride,' said Maitland, and everyone sipped again, and then sat silent. Peabody was enjoying himself. He felt he had a position well up to windward, and had no intention of running down to meet the others. Let them beat up to him. Davenant cleared his throat.

'The fact is, Captain Peabody,' he began, 'we are all wondering how long this damned ridiculous situation is going to last.'

'Yes?' said Peabody. He could not have said less without being rude.

'Our armistice – if that is what you are pleased to call it – comes to an end shortly. And then what happens?'

'We each have ideas on that point,' said Peabody.

'You get up sail. I get up sail, just as we did before. We start out of the bay together, and that Jack in office of a French Governor – I beg your pardon, sir. I was forgetting he was wour father-in-law, but all the same he threatens to turn the guns on us. Back we go and try again. You see what I mean?'

'Yes,' said Peabody. He had followed the same line of thought himself – so, for that matter had everyone in Martinique with any ideas in his head at all.

'So we sit and look at each other until we all go aground on our own damned beefbones?'

'My men like pork better,' said Peabody drily.

Something was coming of this interview, and he was prepared to wait indefinitely for it. His frivolous reply drew a gesture of impatience from Davenant.

'I might have guessed what your attitude would be, sir,' he said.

Peabody nearly said: 'Then why did you ask me to come?' but he kept his mouth shut and preserved his tactical advantage. He looked round at the three sullen British faces and the enigmatical expression of Hunningford, and it was the last named who broke the silence.

'Perhaps,' he began deferentially, with a glance at Davenant, 'if I told Captain Peabody my news it might influence him?'

'I want you to tell him,' said Davenant, and Hunningford addressed himself directly to Peabody.

'There are pirates at work in the Caribbean,' he said.

'Indeed?' said Peabody politely. 'I've never known the time when there weren't.'

That was true; minor piracy had flourished in the Caribbean from the days of Drake.

'Yes,' said Hunningford, 'but never on the scale of to-day. Now that peace has come half the privateersmen in the world are out of employment. Spaniards – negroes from Haiti – Frenchmen—'

'I can understand that,' said Peabody.

'Losses are heavy already and will be heavier still. The Cartagena packet was taken last week.'

'Oh, tell him what happened to you, Hunningford,' said Davenant impatiently.

'Yesterday my cutter was chased by a pirate schooner. It was only by the mercy of Providence that I got into St. Pierre.'

'I'm glad you escaped,' said Peabody politely.

'I've been chasd by pirates before. Big row boats putting out from San Domingo, and guarda costa luggers whose crews have been starved into piracy by the Spanish Government. One expects that. But when it comes to a big schooner, ten guns on a side, and heavy metal at that—'

'I know the schooner you mean,' said Peabody, surprised

into his first helpful remark.

'You've seen her?'

'Yes. I chased her off Dominica. She looked Baltimore built to me, and French rigged. I thought she was an American privateer.'

'Baltimore built and French rigged is nearly right. She was the *Susanna* of Baltimore, dismasted in a hurricane two years back and put into Port au Prince. A French syndicate bought her there. They put Lerouge in command – he's a Haitian negro who served in Boney's navy – and manned her with blacks.'

'What else do you expect of Frogs?' interposed Davenant bitterly.

'They'll never see a penny of their money, if that's any satisfaction,' said Hunningford. 'Lerouge has been nothing more than a pirate for months back. And now with all the Americas on the move against Spain he'll have plenty of plunder and plenty of chance to dispose of it, which is just as important to him. God knows how much he took out of the Cartagena packet. But there were three women on board – two of 'em young.'

'He'd look well at a yardarm,' said Davenant.

'But what has all this to do with me?' asked Peabody.

'How can I catch him and hang him when I'm tied up here in Fort de France with all these French neutrality laws and harbour rules and God-knows-what?' asked Davenant in reply. 'Let me get my ships out and he'll hang in a week.'

'D'ye think you'd catch him?' said Peabody.

'Catch him? Catch him? Why – why – what do you mean, sir?'

'The *Susanna* was one of the fastest schooners which ever left Baltimore, sir,' said Hunningford.

'She got to windward of the *Delaware* and was hull down in half a day,' said Peabody.

'The *Delaware*! He'd never get away from *Calypso* on a bowline,' said Davenant, but even as he said it the lofty confidence in his tone ebbed away. He had not commanded British frigates for eighteen years without learning something of the deficiencies of the vessels, and he was quite enough of a realist to be able to allow for them. It was a wrench to have to admit their existence to an American captain and a civilian, all the same.

'I take it, then,' said Peabody, keeping the argument on a practical plane, 'that what you want me to do is to give you a free passage out of the bay to deal with this pirate?'

'That is correct, sir,' said Davenant. He had known beforehand that his plea would not have one chance in a hundred of being granted, which was probably why he had deferred stating it in plain words.

Peabody thought for a full minute, twisting his glass in his fingers and paying careful attention to the powdered nutmeg afloat on the surface.

'I think it is quite impossible,' he said slowly. 'I will give you my definite decision later.'

'But see here, sir,' expostulated Davenant, and then he changed his tone. 'It's what I might have expected of a Yankee skipper. You fellows can't see farther than your noses. Here's all America in a flame, as Hunningford has said. That fellow Bolivar's on the rampage through Venezuela – he licked the Dagoes at Carabobo last spring. These waters will be swarming with letters of marque and privateers with commissions from Bolivar and Morelos, flying the flags of Venezuela and New Granada and Mexico and God knows what next. Pirates? How long will it take a Venezuelan privateer to become a pirate? Give 'em a lesson now and it'll save two dozen next year.'

'Your country's trade with these islands is nearly as big as ours,' said Fane.

'Yes,' said Peabody, rising to his feet. He was not going to be rushed into a hasty decision by any eloquent Englishman. 'I'll think about it.'

He turned to Davenant and repeated the formula he had heard Preble use after an official reception at Valletta.

'I must thank you, sir, for a delightful entertainment.'

As he turned to bow to the others Hunningford was catching Davenant's eye.

'Take Mr. Hunningford with you, sir,' pleaded Davenant.

'His business connections with the United States should enable him to put the case clearer than I have done, perhaps. You will be able to question him freely in private.'

Peabody made himself hesitate while he counted ten inside himself before he spoke.

'I really don't see the use of it,' he said. 'But if Mr. – er – Hunningford would accompany me in my gig—?'

'I'll come gladly,' said Hunningford.

Down in the gig Hunningford looked up at the sun.

'Devilish hot even for this time of year,' he said.

'So I thought,' said Peabody politely.

It was not until they were safely in Peabody's cabin and the skylight was shut that Hunningford allowed himself to relax. He ran his finger round inside his collar.

'That feels better,' he said. 'Whenever I am on board a King's ship I feel a peculiar sense of constriction in the neighbourhood of my larynx.'

'What the devil were you doing there?' demanded Peabody.

'It is part of my duty to be where there's trouble,' said Hunningford. 'Naturally I paid my respects to the British Commodore in the hope of acquiring information which might be useful to the United States Navy in the person of yourself. But I must admit I did not anticipate all the subsequent developments.'

'Is it true about the pirate?'

'Yes, curiously enough it is. I made my little adventure with the *Susanna* the pretext for my visit to the *Calypso*. I was naturally going to wait for a dark night on shore before I saw you next. I had not made sufficient allowance for the excitement a mention of piracy rouses in the British Navy. I wish I could take all the credit for this present admirable arrangement, but, much to my regret, I cannot. My native honesty forbids.'

'And now you're here, what's the news?'

'Plenty. And some of it's bad. Decatur's gone.'

'Decatur? Is he – dead?'

Hunningford shook his head.

'No, he tried to escape from New York in the *President.* They caught him off Sandy Hook and he had to haul down his colours.'

'Good God!' Peabody thought of Decatur eating his heart out in Dartmoor Prison. It was a horrible mental picture. 'What else?'

'The *Argus* is lost, too. I don't know how, yet, except that she was taken in British waters.'

With the *President* and the *Argus* gone the same way as the *Chesapeake,* the United States Navy was diminishing to minute proportions. There were only the *Essex,* somewhere in the Pacific, and the *Delaware* left to display the Stars and Stripes at sea.

'What else?'

'A British force took Washington. The militia ran, and the Capitol's been burned, and the last I heard they were moving on Baltimore.'

Peabody had nothing to say now. He had no words left at all.

'But there's good news as well. You knew of Perry's victory on Lake Ontario? Yes. That was before you sailed. Now Macdonough's won a battle on Lake Champlain. The Canadian frontier's safe.'

Tom Macdonough was Peabody's immediate junior on the captain's list – Peabody remembered him at Tripoli under Decatur's command. Peabody called up before his mind's eye the map of the Canadian frontier. With the American flag triumphant on Champlain and Ontario there was nothing more to be feared from the north, as Hunningford had remarked. Perry and Macdonough could both of them be relied upon not to allow the local command they had attained to slip through their fingers again, and the strongest sea power in the world would for once be baulked on water.

'That puts a different complexion on it,' he said.

The long Atlantic seaboard was exposed to British attack, it was true, but it was hardly possible that the British should attempt serious conquest. The raid on Washington assumed smaller proportions immediately.

'And one more thing,' said Hunningford. 'Mr. Madison

has sent to Europe to discuss peace.' Hunningford's voice as well as his face were quite expressionless as he said this.

'Well?' said Peabody drily. 'That makes no difference to my position here.'

He was right. If he did his best to fight a war he would be doing his best to influence an advantageous peace, and if the peace discussions proved inconclusive he would not be found to have wasted any opportunity.

'It is my business to tell you all there is to know,' said Hunningford. 'Thank God I don't have to instruct you on how to act on the information as well. To say nothing of the fact that you'd see me damned before you allowed me to.'

Peabody grinned his agreement.

'I'd see you worse than that,' he said.

'What are you going to do about this proposal of Davenant's?'

'Nothing, I fancy,' said Peabody. 'I'm not going to let him out of here because of a pirate on better terms than I'd give him at any other time.'

'You're right,' said Hunningford. 'Not that you mind what I think, of course. But it's irksome, all the same, to think of that black devil, Lerouge, raising hell in the Caribbean.'

'I have the United States to think of first,' said Peabody.

'When honest men fall out,' said Hunningford, 'rogues come by other people's property. The world is at peace except for us. The Americas are open for trade for the first time since the world began. Every merchant in the world wants to start business again – I hope, Captain, that you will not take too violent objection if I inject a little treason into what I say. There's no reason on earth left why we should go on fighting. Trade with Europe is open again – or would be if the British Navy was not in the way. They don't want to press our men any more. They don't want to search our ships. And yet you and Davenant sit in Martinique watching each other like dogs across a bone. What is more, you allow gentlemen like Lerouge to run off with the bone while you watch each other. And I, who flatter myself that I might be a useful member of society, spend my days with a rope round my neck facing the imminent possibility that at any moment it may grow much tighter than is convenient. Please don't for a moment think I am complaining, Captain. I am merely commenting at large upon the inconsistencies of the situation. From my reading of history I would rather continue to court the end I have just mentioned than the usually much more unpleasant one of the man who sets out to put the world to rights.'

CHAPTER NINETEEN

Mrs. Josiah Peabody was at work with her needle in the candle-lit drawing room of the little house on the hill. Beside her stood her empty coffee cup, and opposite sat her husband. For once in a way his usually clear-thinking mind was in an extraordinary muddle. He had thought about the string of events which had helped to change the unpronounceable Mlle Anne de Breuil into Mrs. Josiah Peabody. He had thought about the coincidence that those same events enabled him to sit here watching her, under the monotonous swaying of the fan, secure in the knowledge that the British squadron, restrained by its senior officer's pledged word, would make no attempt to steal a march on him for two more days. Naturally he had thought about the *Delaware*, for he was never awake five minutes consecutively without thinking about her. She was fully stored with provisions and water again, her crew rested, her rigging newly set-up, ready for a six months' campaign. The gold which he had taken from the *Princess Augusta* had paid for everything – the fresh provisions, the fruit which had got his men back into health, the shore leave which had utterly reconciled them to a fresh voyage. He was a lucky man, and what he could see of Anne's cheek and neck as she bent over her needlework was lovelier than the set of the *Delaware's* foretopsail. And Lerouge was hanging about off Cape St. Martin, paralysing shipping, and which his duty really was regarding him—

Anne looked up as Peabody stirred in his chair.

'Father told me about the pirate,' she said. Already it had ceased to be a surprise to Peabody when Anne's remarks exactly chimed in with his own thoughts.

'Yes, dear,' he said. There was still a pleasant novelty about using the endearment.

'And Aunt Sophie told me about what Captain Davenant wants to do,' went on Anne.

'Oh, did she?' said Peabody.

He felt a slight shrinking of the flesh at the words. This was a hint of something he had feared, deep down within him. Women were interfering in man's business, and that meant trouble. The phrase 'petticoat government' drifted into his mind; much as he loved his wife he would never give her the smallest opportunity of discussing – which meant diverting him from – his duty.

'Captain Davenant and Aunt Sophie are growing very friendly,' went on Anne.

And Davenant is trying to get the women to do his dirty work for him, thought Peabody, but aloud he only said: 'I suspected as much myself.'

'He's quite furious about the pirate. And the people here are distressed as well. I suppose you've seen the ships in the bay which daren't go out. They're the first ships to leave Martinique for France for eleven years, and it's going to cause a lot of trouble to everyone. Monsieur Godron was telling me that he's afraid he'll lose the market in France and it'll ruin him.'

'Wars often ruin people,' said Peabody unhelpfully. He felt all the irritation of a fighting man, whose life is in peril from day to day, against the man of peace whose worries about his money merely complicate the issue.

'But I can't help feeling sorry for Monsieur Godron all the same,' said Anne.

'Now look here,' said Peabody. 'I can't do anything about it, dear. That's as precise as I can make it. I've got to—'

He restrained himself. He had almost allowed himself to tell his wife of his intention to hang on in Fort de France, watching for an opportunity to escape, keeping the British squadron eating their heads off there, and hoping for some shift in the circumstances of which he could take advantage. But he shut his mouth tight; he was not going to allow even a hint of his military intentions to escape him. He had not told Hubbard, and he would not tell Anne.

'It's very difficult for you, dear, and I know it,' said Anne.

Peabody saw the softness in her eyes. He had the sudden fresh realisation that his problems were as important to her as to him; that the peril in which he stood was far more of a strain upon her than upon him. The knowledge was liable to lose its reality with the passage of time. He spent necessarily so many hours thinking about the inevitable eventual end to the adventures of the *Delaware*; he had to calculate upon the destruction of the *Delaware*, upon the extreme likelihood of his own death, upon the probable termination of his own professional career. Long thinking about his approaching ruin and death made them loom even larger in his emotion than they deserved, and made it hard to realise – what was undoubtedly true – that they meant to Anne as much as or more than they meant to him. And it was hard when he allowed childish resentment against Providence to master him, not to be resentful at the same time against Anne who had only to sit back and have no worries about the proper employment of the *Delaware*, no insidious inward thoughts about the round shot which would one day dash him in red ruin on his own quarterdeck – smash him into pulp as he remembered Crane the master smashed into pulp beside the wheel.

But Peabody knew again now that thoughts like that were not nearly as painful to him as Anne's thoughts were to her, and that she shut her mouth as firmly over them as he did over his military plans. He bent forward towards her and touched the hand with the long slender fingers.

'I love you so much, dear,' said Anne.

Peabody did not say 'I love you,' in return, as he well might have done. He gave instead the most positive proof of it, by allowing the inertia of his previous train of thought to carry him on into a technical discussion with a mere woman whose knowledge of ships was of course negligible.

'Davenant couldn't do anything even if I let him go,' he said. 'That schooner of Lerouge's is Baltimore built and as fast as anything that sails. He'd never catch her with that tub of a *Calypso* – not even the *Racer* would do it. I chased the *Susanna* myself, a week back— By God!'

He had broken off what he was saying and was staring at her. It was odd that even at this moment when a fresh plan was forming in his mind, with a rapidity and a completeness which startled him, that he should still be able to note simultaneously with a thrill of pleasure how straight her brows were and how steady were the blue eyes below them. They smiled at him now.

'You've thought of something interesting,' said Anne.

'Yes,' said Peabody.

He got to his feet and walked back and forward across the room. Davenant would agree, he was sure. Peabody's logical and essentially matter-of-fact mind brushed aside the fact that the plan he had in mind was probably unprecedented. That was no argument against it. On the surface the plan was ludicrous, too – and that was an argument in favour of it. And – there were new aspects, new developments, revealing themselves as he thought about it. He smacked his right fist into his left hand to clinch the argument with himself, and stopped short in his pacing of the room to look down at Anne who was looking up at him.

'I beg your pardon, dear,' he said.

'I like it,' said Anne, simply.

Peabody caught her up to him and kissed her, and she kissed him back, her lips moving against his. This was stranger and more delightful than ever. It had never occurred to Peabody that plans for war and passion for his wife could coexist. He would have said earlier that it was as impossible that two masses should occupy the same space at the same time. The one thing was perfectly possible, as the present moment proved, and everything was so delirious that he would not be surprised if the other were possible despite what Euclid might say to the contrary. The excitement of caution gave an edge to his passion. Because he had thought of a method of dealing with Lerouge he could kiss Anne with added fervour; conceivably the prospect of immediate action in place of possible weeks of inactivity played its part as well. Anne saw the light dancing in his eyes and was glad. To Peabody it was all mad – mad – mad. It was mad that he should have thought of his plan while Anne's hand was actually in his. It was mad that at the same moment that his brain was seething with suggestions for the destruction of Lerouge it should be seething with warm images of Anne. It was mad that he could kiss thus, and that he should have his passions sweep him away and yet that he should feel no sense of sin. The white throat on which he set his lips was sweeter than the sweetest honey he had known in his hard childhood. The soft sleep which came at last in Anne's scented arms was something life had never given him before. The drugged, swinish oblivion that drink had given him in his youth, and which had sometimes seemed so alluring, was not to be compared with this sleep, hopeful and yet with desire all burned away. And the oblivion of death of which he had sometimes allowed himself to think longingly, blank and loveless like his life until now, could no longer be thought of. Anne, in the darkness, his face against her breast, knew that he smiled in his sleep. She loved him enough to be happy on that account, whether he was smiling because he was in her arms or because in his sleep his mind was still at work upon the details of plans to deal with Lerouge the pirate.

CHAPTER TWENTY

Captain Sir Hubert Davenant had said it was most irregular. He had gobbled like a turkey cock about it when it had been first suggested to him, mouthing his words in his queer London accent, and yet it had only taken a few minutes to convince him both of the essential reasonableness of the scheme and also of its likelihood of success.

'Fox and geese, eh?' he had said, with the chart spread before him. 'We'll chase Mr. Fox Lerouge into a tighter trap than he knows of.'

The Marquis had given the scheme his unqualified assent when he was consulted about it. He had offered the services of the *Tigresse* to stop the least obvious of the bolt holes through the Saint's Passage, and he had looked upon his son-in-law with something more than approval when the scheme was made clear to him. The military details – the need for complete secrecy to ensure surprise – he accepted as a matter of course, even though Davenant and Peabody, glancing at each other across the council table, expressed secretly to each other by their look their certainty that the *Tigresse* with her French crew would be horribly mauled if ever she found herself broadside to broadside with the *Susanna*. The Marquis had pledged his word to the execution of his part of the scheme – the issuing of sealed orders to Dupont in the *Tigresse* and the sudden reversal of orders at sunset to the captain of the port and the officers commanding in the batteries.

Night was coming on apace when Peabody in the *Delaware* began to make the first of his preparations for sea. Eight p.m., well after dark, was the time appointed for the start.

'We don't want to spoil the ship for a ha'porth o' tar,' said Davenant when the time was being discussed – in other words, they did not want to risk disclosing their plans to any possible informers in Martinique for the sake of gaining an extra half hour perhaps of darkness; besides, by that time the first puffs of the land breeze would help to get them clear of the harbour.

'Mr. Hubbard,' said Peabody. 'We are leaving Fort de France to-night.'

'Aye aye, sir,' said Hubbard, and then, 'pardon me, sir, but have you squared the port captain?'

'No,' said Peabody. 'But we'll be allowed to leave. The British squadron will be leaving at the same time. So will the *Tigresse*.'

'Geewhillikins, sir,' said Hubbard; the dark mobile face lengthened in surprise, and Peabody relented. There was no sense or purpose in keeping his first lieutenant in the dark.

'The unofficial armistice is still going on,' he said. 'All we're going to do is to catch this Haitian pirate, Lerouge.

After that we meet again in Fort de France and start again on the same terms as before. I've given my parole to that effect.'

'I see, sir,' said Hubbard. He digested the astonishing information slowly. 'It won't do the men any harm to get them to sea again for a time.'

Curiosity struggled with discipline, and curiosity won in the end.

'Pardon me, sir,' said Hubbard again. 'But was this your idea?'

'Yes.'

'It's a damned clever idea, too, sir, if you'll allow me to say so.'

'I'll allow you to.'

'The French'll be as pleased as Punch if we get this Lerouge out of the way. I suppose they've said so, sir?'

'They have.'

'And we keep the ball rolling that much longer without risk to ourselves. Oh, that's great, sir.'

'I'm glad you think so, Mr. Hubbard. We'll get under way at four bells in the second dog watch.'

'Aye aye, sir.'

The land breeze was breathing very faintly when the *Delaware* got under sail in the darkness – she crept over the black water with hardly a sound of water rippling under her sharp bows.

'There's the *Tigresse*, sir,' said Hubbard to Peabody, pointing through the darkness to where a faint nucleus of greater darkness was just visible.

'Yes,' said Peabody, and he pointed in return over the quarter. 'And here come the British.'

The *Calypso* in the van could be almost recognised; the *Bulldog* in the rear was hardly visible at all, but enough could be seen to make plain how well handled were the three ships in their line ahead. Peabody felt a queer feeling of comfort. For months he had been at sea in continuous imminent danger, with every man's hand against him and not a friend within call. Even though he knew this present interlude to be a brief one, there was something pleasant about having even temporary friends. The thought of friends carried his mind inevitably to his wife. By now she would have received his note— 'Dearest, I shall not be coming home to-night, as I have duties to perform in the ship. Please keep the servants thinking that you still expect me, as it is important that the news that I am not returning be delayed as long as possible. And will you please forgive me for leaving you like this, dear? It is my duty that takes me from you. Your father will explain why to-morrow. I shall see you again in a week.'

That note had been hard to write – Peabody had written nothing except formal letters all his life. It had been the first time he had written the word 'dearest,' and the first time he had ever written 'dear' in the middle of a letter, but it had not been that which had made the writing hard. It had been hard to face the fact that he had not admitted his wife into his confidence, that in the deep secrecy in which the move had been planned he had not made an exception of Anne. But that was where his duty lay. Military secrets must be told to no one unnecessarily, and he had told no one. Anne, waiting for him, would be hurt and disappointed – that was what made it hard. Later she might be hurt again when she realised that he had not trusted her, and that would be harder still. Peabody drummed on the rail with his fingers, and then suddenly he knew that Anne would understand.

'Course South by East, Mr. Hubbard,' he said.

'South by East, sir.'

They would weather Cape Solomon now. In three hours – less if the breeze freshened as it should – they would be rounding Cabrit. It would be a long reach back to the Caravelle, but they should be there well before dawn, and the British, weathering Cape St. Martin in the opposite direction, would drive Lerouge straight into his grasp. And in any event it was a joy to feel the lift and surge of the *Delaware* again beneath his feet, to hear the wind in the rigging and the music of the sea under her forefoot. Peabody recalled himself guiltily at the thought that at this very moment he might instead have been in Anne's arms – a wife certainly deprived life of its primitive simplicity in exchange for enriching it. It was an effort to dismiss the thought from his mind. A wife was a wife and his duty was his duty. He bellowed a sharp reprimand at the captain of the foretop, and had the weather foretopgallant studdingsail taken in and reset, and, having relieved himself of some of this unaccustomed internal stress, he made himself go below to rest for a few hours before dawn. He was a little afraid as he composed himself to sleep, lest married life was softening him.

'Eight bells, sir,' said Washington, allowing the cabin door to slam as a gust of the fresh Trades came into the stuffy cabin. 'A clear night, sir. Ship's on the starboard tack, sir. What shirt, sir?'

'The one I've got on,' said Peabody, swinging himself out of his cot. 'Bring me a cup of coffee on the quarterdeck.'

Murray was officer of the watch; he came up in the darkness while Peabody sipped his coffee and studied the traverse board and the scrawled writing on the slate which constituted the deck log.

'We're nearly up to the Caravelle, sir. You can hear the surf on the cays.'

'It's a nasty coast,' said Peabody.

With all these Lesser Antilles, practically without exception, the Atlantic side, to windward, was without real harbours, and dangerous with reefs and cays. The main life of the islands was carried on on the leeward Caribbean side where were to be found the anchorages and the large towns The rule held true from Antigua down to Trinidad.

'Lay the ship on the other tack, Mr. Murray, if you please I want to be five miles farther to windward by dawn.'

Lerouge would certainly be taken by surprise. He would be aware of the dead end which had been reached in Fort d France by the *Delaware* and the British squadron, and h would be counting on a free hand until the matter had been decided and an action had been eventually fought and repair effected; and he probably had sources of information in Martinique on which he would rely for ample warning. Th sudden appearance at dawn of the British squadron would surprise him, but would hardly imperil him; he would se all sail and leave them easily behind. But it would be a very different story when the *Delaware*, fast and handy, appeared right across his course, with the British spread wide in pursuit behind him. The moon was behind clouds and setting fast.

'Mr. Murray! I want the best men you've got at the mastheads at the next relief.'

'Aye aye, sir.'

The *Delaware* was beating to windward close-hauled; it would be safe to leave an even greater distance between her and the island. With the wind abaft the beam, Peabody fancied that she would be faster than the *Susanna*, and the courses would converge if Lerouge did not want to pile his schooner on the coast – although that might be the way to prolong his life to the maximum. The tops of the waves going by were already growing a little more visible; there was enough light from the eastern sky to show up their ghostly white. This trade wind air, clean and fresh after its journey across three thousand miles of sea, was delicious after the stuffiness of Fort de France. Along the eastern horizon now there was a decidedly noticeable line of brighter colour, almost green by comparison with the deep blue of the area above it. It was widening, too, and changing in colour; the green was shifting into yellow, and now the yellow was changing into orange and from orange to red. Miraculously the sky was brightening. During the last few minutes everything on deck had become visible. Then the *Delaware* rose on a wave, and as she rose a little fleck of bright gold was visible peeping over the horizon to the east. It disappeared as she sank again, but at the next wave it was there, larger and plainer, and at the following wave it was clear broad day, with the sun fully over the horizon.

'Now,' said Peabody to himself. 'Where's our friend, Lerouge?'

It would be a disappointment if he had doubled back on his track to run into the *Tigresse* in the Saintes' Passage; it would be a far worse disappointment if he had got clear away from the British altogether. But he had done all he could do, and he had nothing for which to blame himself in that event. He looked up at the masthead to make sure that the lookouts were attending to their duty; the *Delaware* was as close to the wind as she would lie, thrashing away with the big Atlantic rollers bursting under her bows and bright rainbows playing on either side of her. Far back on the lee quarter lay the mountains of Martinique, a pale purple against the blue sky. On the far side of them Anne was waking alone in the big bed with the vast dome of mosquito netting over it. Beween the ship and the island were the innumerable cays and reefs of the windward shore, revealed mainly by the white surf which burst continually against them – the long peninsula of the Caravelle showed itself as a green chalk mark along the dazzling white.

'Sail on the weather beam!' came a hail from the masthead. Hubbard raced with half a dozen midshipmen up to various points of vantage aloft.

'She's that schooner, sir. And heading straight for us.'

'Clear for action, Mr. Murray, if you please. Quartermaster! Keep her on the wind.'

'Schooner's hauling up, sir,' reported Murray.

'Will we weather her?'

'Yes, sir. Easily.'

So that was all right. If the *Delaware* had cut off her escape to windward, and Martinique lay to leeward, and astern of her lay the British squadron, the *Susanna's* fate was sealed. It only remained to see which ship would take her – whether she would go about and face the British, or hold her course and fight the *Delaware*. The guns were being cast off and run out, the decks were being sanded, and from below came the clatter of the bulkheads being taken down. Peabody turned his glance to search the horizon on the larboard beam for any sign of the schooner, but the two ships were not near enough yet to be within sight of each other from the deck.

'If you please, sir,' hailed Hubbard, 'the schooner's put up her helm. She's come before the wind.'

''Bout ship, Mr. Murray.'

The hands sprang from the guns to help at the sheets and braces, and the *Delaware* came round like a top. As she steadied on her new course Peabody caught his first glimpse of the schooner, the rectangles of her big topsails against the sky.

'Starboard a point,' he said to the helmsman, and then, hailing the masthead, 'you can come down now, Mr Hubbard.'

'He had the schooner under his own personal observation now, and he could lay his own course. He would intercept her before either she could pile herself up on the cays or – as was probably Lerouge's hope – escape into dangerous waters where no ship would dare follow her.

'I thought I could see the *Racer's* royals just before I came down, sir,' said Hubbard. 'I wasn't sure enough to report it.'

'I expect you were right,' said Peabody.

'Hope we get her before she comes up, sir,' said Hubbard.

'We will if she holds that course much longer.'

On their converging courses the schooner and the *Delaware* were nearing each other fast. Peabody could already see the gaffs of her big fore and mainsails. She was going through the water very fast, but no faster than the *Delaware* with all sail set and the trade wind blowing hard over her quarter.

'She's a lovely little ship,' said Hubbard. 'Pity she fell into the wrong hands.'

'She'll be in the right ones again soon enough,' said Peabody. 'Mr. Murray! Load with canister. I want this done quick and clean. One broadside as we come alongside and then we'll board her in the smoke.'

'Aye aye, sir.'

But Lerouge had no intention of submitting to a close-range action without an attempt to dodge past the frigate which lay between him and life. Peabody saw the big fore and aft sails flap, saw the schooner spin on her heel as she wore round, and at the first sign of the manoeuvre he was already bawling the order which brought the *Delaware* to the wind, close hauled on the same track. Peabody knew that the schooner would not hold this course for long, heading as she was back towards the British squadron and narrowing her already small free area of sea. He saw the schooner's sails shiver again as though she were preparing to tack. No, she would not do that – it would bring her too close to the *Delaware*. It must be a feint to induce him to put the *Delaware* about so that while the big frigate was engaged in the manoeuvre Lerouge would dodge back again. He smiled to himself in the exciting pleasure of quick thinking and shouted further orders. The *Delaware* came up a little closer to the wind; the headsail sheets were brought across, and the *Delaware's* sails flapped thunderously. That was convincing enough. Lerouge was expecting the *Delaware* to tack, and now that she showed all the signs of it he put his helm up again and spun the schooner round in his desperate effort to drive past the *Delaware*. But the moment Peabody saw his masts separate he was ready with his orders. Over went the helm, back came the headsail sheets, and he had beaten Lerouge in the race. Already the two ships were near.

'We've got her now!' yelled Murray at the top of his voice, apparently without knowing he was speaking.

Peabody could make out the individuals on the schooner's deck. Aft there was a red spot – that was Lerouge; perhaps to play on his name he wore habitually a red coat looted from the baggage of some British officer. He could see the bustle on the schooner's deck – could see the guns' crews bending to their work. Next moment the schooner was wreathed in smoke and the air was full of the sound of round shot. The maintopmast stay parted with a loud snap, but that was all the damage done, and the two vessels were still nearing each other. Once more Lerouge feinted, turning the schooner to port, towards the *Delaware*, and then spinning suddenly back to starboard, but Peabody was not to be deceived by the feint. He held his course for a few more seconds and then ported his helm – all the extra manoeuvrability of the schooner availed nothing when her captain was being outguessed by a shrewd opponent.

He was on the schooner's quarter now, and the vessels were not a cable's length apart. Another broadside – a crash below and a hole in the forecourse. The schooner would have to dodge again at once, or submit meekly to having the *Dela-*

ware run alongside her. Here it came! Peabody had foreseen it and was ready.

'Hard a starboard!' he ordered to the quartermaster, and then lifting his voice, 'starboard guns!'

The neat turn brought the ships close together, heading in the same direction.

'Hard a port now,' said Peabody, and as the *Delaware's* broadside crashed out, frigate and schooner came together in the smoke.

Peabody's fighting blood was racing through his veins. He had drawn his sword and swung himself into the mizzen rigging.

'Boarders!' he yelled.

There was no need for self-control now, no need for clear thinking. He could fling himself into the fight, abandoning himself to the mad impulse of it all, and recompense himself for months of rigid caution. He scrambled down into the mizzen chains and dropped on to the schooner's deck, sword in hand. Behind him the *Delaware* swung round pushing the schooner before her, widening the gap between the vessels' sterns and closing it at their bows, while the boarders jostled each other at the main-deck ports, and he was left all alone – and unconscious of it – abaft the wheel on the schooner's deck.

The hurricane of canister had swept the schooner like a broom. There were dead men everywhere, and only a few half-naked black figures were grabbing weapons to meet the attack. But not five yards from Peabody was Lerouge in his red coat with the gold lace flashing in the sun, eyes and teeth gleaming in his black face, and Peabody leaped forward to cut him down. His sword clashed on Lerouge's guard; Peabody cut again, the cut was warded off, and then he thrust and thrust again at the bosom of the red coat. He night as well have been thrusting at a stone wall.

It dawned upon him that Lerouge was a swordsman who must have picked up the art of fencing during his service in the French Navy. He feinted and lunged; the lunge was parried, and he lunged again desperately to anticipate the ripost. That ripost would come soon, he knew already. Only while he could maintain this fierce attack was his life safe – the moment it slackened Lerouge's blade would dart forward and kill him, he knew. He beat against Lerouge's blade, thrusting first over and then under, his iron strength and long reach only a poor compensation for his lack of skill, trying to remember his early lessons in swordsmanship, and the course of a dozen hours in fencing he had received twelve years ago from the Maltese fencing master in Valetta. The blades rasped harshly together, jarring his fingers as they gripped his sword-hilt, and only in the nick of time did he beat aside the first thrust which Lerouge had made. This was death, death in the hot sun; the loud noises of battle which he heard about him reached his consciousness as faintly as the squeaking of mice.

Lerouge's mirthless grin, as his thick lips parted snarling, seemed to grow wider and wider until Peabody seemed to see nothing else. The sword-blades slipped apart, and Peabody made a wild blind effort to cover himself. There was a sudden burning pain in his right forearm, and his sword-hilt escaped from his paralysed fingers. Desperately he leaped forward; chance – or his own rapid instinctive reactions – put Lerouge's sword-blade into his left hand, low down by the guard, and he tore the weapon out of his path as he closed with his powerful antagonist. His right arm was paralysed no longer as he flung it round Lerouge. His left hand battled against Lerouge's right for control of the sword, his right behind Lerouge's back seized the golden epaulette on Lerouge's right shoulder, and his right foot was behind Lerouge's heel. He put out all his strength for the fall, was baulked, swayed to his left, and heaved again on one last insane effort. Lerouge's feet left the deck, and he fell with a crash, Peabody staggering above him with the sword in his left hand and the golden threads of the torn-off epaulette in his right.

The deck was thronged by now with American sailors cheering and shouting, and the din they were raising reached Peabody's ears now in its natural volume. Someone came rushing forward with a pike to pin Lerouge to the deck as he rolled over on his face, but Peabody kicked the weapon up in the nick of time.

'Tie him up, Harvey,' he said, recognising the man, and a dozen willing hands grabbed lengths of rope and bound Lerouge until he was helpless.

The schooner was captured – here came O'Brien running breathlessly aft with an American flag to hoist at her peak while the *Calypso* came tearing up with all sail set too late to show in the honour of the capture, and here came Captain Davenant, as fast as he could heave his ship to, and as fast as his gig could whisk him across the big Atlantic rollers.

'Congratulations, Peabody,' he said.

'Thank you, sir,' said Peabody.

It was pleasant to have made a clean job of the business before the British arrived.

'You are wounded, sir!' said Davenant.

Peabody looked down; blood was dripping slowly, in heavy blobs, down his right hand and falling on the deck. His right sleeve was heavy with blood as he moved his arm. And his left hand hurt him too – as he looked at it he saw that the horny palm had several haggled cuts across it where the nearly blunt part of Lerouge's blade had scored it.

'It's nothing,' said Peabody.

'Wounds in this climate are always important, sir,' said Davenant. 'Have you a capable surgeon? Hamilton, go back and fetch Doctor Clarke.'

The midshipman touched his cap and dashed off.

'My doctors are quite capable, thank you, sir,' said Peabody. He was conscious of a lassitude which was unusual to him and he did not want to argue about anything – the sun seemed too hot.

'They will probably be glad of Clarke's opinion all the same,' said Davenant, and then, looking round the schooner, 'and I suppose this is Lerouge?'

The burly negro in his red coat snarled again in his bonds as attention was drawn to him – Peabody remembered that snarl vividly.

'A nasty-looking customer,' said Davenant. 'Any other survivors?'

There were six of them, grouped round the mainmast, all bound. Two of them were squatting on the deck weeping aloud. Lerouge looked at the two captains and saw his death in their faces.

'St. Amant'll hang 'em if we take 'em back to Fort de France,' said Davenant. 'It'll mean a trial and evidence and depositions, though. He's a whale for the letter of the law – we both know that.'

'We've taken 'em red-handed,' said Peabody. He knew the law of the sea and the instant fate which awaited pirates. His head was beginning to swim in the heat, and there was a hint of sickness in his stomach, although Lerouge deserved nothing better than was going to happen to him – something worse, if anything. Pirates captured at sea by officers of a navy were hanged on the spot. Hubbard had turned up from somewhere, and his dark saturnine face wore a message of doom for the pirates, too; Peabody saw the two deep grooves between the bushy black eyebrows. Those grooves seemed to fill the whole seascape at that moment.

'Hang them,' said Peabody. He hardly recognized his own voice as he spoke.

His head was swimming worse than ever, and his impressions of the rest of the business were confused. He would never forget the wild struggles of the bound Lerouge as the hands dragged him away down the heaving deck, nor the screams of one of the other negroes and the ugly sound with which they ended. But blended with those memories were others of the doctors grouped round him, of cool bandages applied to his burning arm.

'Bind it up in the blood and leave the bandage unopened for a week, that's my practice,' said the pontifical Doctor Clarke to Doctor Downing across Peabody's recumbent body –this Clarke wore hair-powder which soiled the shoulders of his coat, Peabody saw. He did not know how he had got back to his cabin, but there he was, undoubtedly; and overhead was the clatter and rumble of the guns being secured again.

'I make it a rule never to have a rule,' said Downing. 'Open your hand, sir, if you please. Ah, no more than a few fibres severed, I fancy.'

CHAPTER TWENTY-ONE

'Turn to the other side, sir, please,' said Washington. He was shaving his captain with all the gusto Peabody expected of him. Washington had been perfectly delighted to find Peabody crippled in both arms – it gave him enormous pleasure to wait upon him hand and foot, to pass his shirt over his head and part his hair, and Peabody hated it. He had forbidden Washington to chatter while attending on him – curious how the act of shaving someone else seemed to loosen a man's tongue – but Washington side-stepped the order by asking Peabody to move his head as the operation demanded. Washington might well have suffered some internal injury as a result of accumulated pressure had he not done so, in fact – for the chance to say those few words he was willing even to forgo the pleasure of tweaking his captain's nose and turning his chin from side to side.

It was hateful to have Washington attend to him, and yet it was delicious to have Anne do so. There was enchantment in the touch of her slender fingers, always cool somehow in the sweltering heat of the West Indian autumn. There was a queer pleasure in being dependent upon Anne, for him who had made it a rule all his life to be dependent upon nobody. There was a mad shock of joy when he discovered for certain that there was pleasure for her in looking after him. She would stoop and slip the pumps from off his feet, the stockings from his legs, and she could smile while she did it. And when she took his head on her shoulder and put her lips against his forehead, troubles and anxieties and responsibilities lost their weight. Memories of a red-coated figure writhing in bonds were not nearly so acute then; even the memories were dulled of fighting a losing fight on the deck of the *Susanna*, of the imminent approach of sudden death.

That crossing of swords with Lerouge had had a profound effect upon Peabody, which even he realised. He was not the same man as had laid his ship so deftly alongside the *Susanna*, perhaps because of the unexpected nature of the danger he had encountered. He had thought of death from disease, of death among the waves of the sea, of unseen death from a flying cannon shot, but the death he had seen face to face had been at the hands of a negro pirate, and as a direct result of his own shortcomings in the mere matter of handling a sword. It had had an effect upon him similar to the spiritual upheaval of a religious experience, making him take fresh stock of himself, unsettling him; to feel his face against Anne's smooth throat, to know himself to be loved dearly – these were matters of desperate importance now in the impermanence of life. Yet even so Washington had to shave him.

The wounds healed quickly enough. Downing grudgingly admitted that in this particular case Dr. Clarke's method of binding up clean cuts in the blood and leaving them was justifiable. Downing had a theory that the inconsequential behaviour of wounds was not as inconsequential as people thought, and that whether they turned gangrenous or not depended to a certain extent on whether some foreign agency were introduced into them. He was a little nervous about this theory, because he had seen wounds heal even with a lump of lead inside them, and wounds go gangrenous and refuse to close when there was simply nothing foreign to be seen about them, so that he laughed a little deprecatingly when he hinted that the sword-blade which had transfixed Peabody's forearm and cut his hand must have been quite clean, and he saw to it that the wounds were exposed as little as possible to the tropical air.

In these conditions they healed quickly – within three days he was allowed to take his right arm out of its sling, and his ability to use the fingers of his right hand relieved him of his hated dependence upon Washington, and as soon as the cuts on his palm had closed over Downing encouraged him to use his left hand, as well. Otherwise, as Downing said, there was a danger lest the scars should prevent his being able to extend his hand fully. There only remained a soreness deep down inside his right forearm, and an angry red blotch to show where Lerouge's sword had entered. That was all – save for a mental soreness, that continual feeling of humiliation at the memeory of his helplessness before Lerouge. Peabody was wrongheaded about it; he had not felt fear at the time, and yet he suspected himself of it in the light of his present reactions. It made Anne's kisses all the sweeter, and yet their added sweetness did not mask the bitterness of the distorted memory. Anne, under the vast dome of the mosquito net, with her husband at her side, was aware – as of course she would be – of the tangled unhappiness of the man.

The convalescent captain came on board his ship to the usual compliments. She was ready for sea again, complete in every particular; it was good to look round her and lay new plans for the future. But Hubbard, who came up to greet him, was worried about something – Peabody could see it in his long face.

'We've got a couple of deserters on board, sir,' he said.

'Deserters from where?'

Hubbard jerked his head towards the British squadron which lay on the other side of the bay.

'They're off the *Calypso*, sir,' he said. 'They had a flogging coming to them and they didn't stay for it.'

'How did they get on board?'

'They swam here, sir, and climbed up through the hawsehole during the middle watch. The anchor watch ought to have seen 'em, sir. I've punished 'em already.'

'And the deserters are still here?'

'Yes, sir. Would you like to speak to 'em, sir?'

The two men were a fair sample of the sailors the British Navy had been forced to use in their desperate struggle against the whole world. Larsen was elderly, a Swede, slow spoken, and still unfamiliar with English. Williams was a Cockney, hardly more than twenty, pert and sly and with a desperate squint, a warehouse boy in a London draper's before a boating frolic on the Thames had brought him within the clutches of the press.

'What in hell did you come to my ship for?' demanded Peabody.

Williams jerked his thumb across the bay and winked with the eye which was under his control.

'They row guard every night between the ships and the quay, sir,' he said. 'I seen too many o' the boys try it, an' I seen wot 'appened to 'em arterward. We couldn't come nowhere but 'ere, sir.'

'But what did you want to desert for?'

'Me, sir? Captain's coxs'n, 'e copped me prigging from the cabin stores, sir. It'd ha' been five dozen for me this morning, sir. An' Larsen, 'ere. Well, sir, you can see 'ow slow 'e is, sir. Boatswain's mate 'ad a down on 'im, sir. Always in 'ot water, 'e was, sir.'

'Dat is zo,' said Larsen.

Peabody looked the two over again. He knew well enough what life on the lower deck of British ships of war was like – the fierce discipline necessary both to restrain the motley crews and to inculcate the unquestioning obedience which had carried the Navy through such sore trials; the bad food and worse conditions which were all that a bankrupt Admiralty could afford for its slaves; the feeling of a lifetime's condemnation as the war dragged on and on and the desperate straits of the British Government gave no chance of leave or release. And some petty tyrant had been abusing his power and making Larsen's life hell for him. He was sorry for the Swede, although he could feel no sympathy for the squinting Cockney who had deserted his colours.

'Do you want to take service with me?' he said.

'Yessir,' said Williams eagerly.

He was one of that kind, who to save his skin would even fight against his own country. Peabody dallied with the idea of returning them both, with his compliments, to the *Calypso*. For the first attempt at desertion in the British Navy the punishment was a thousand lashes. For the second attempt, a milder punishment – death, after the worse had been tried and had failed. Williams read the thought in his face.

'You ain't goin' to send us back, sir?'

'I'll think about it,' said Peabody. 'Take 'em for'ard.'

He could not send them back, of course. He could not give back two trained seamen to his country's enemies. He could not (as he would have liked to do) return Williams and keep Larsen. He disliked deserters, and he could sympathise very strongly with what would of course be Davenant's reactions when he should hear that his men had taken refuge on board the *Delaware*, but he could not, just on that account, hand them back again. From the point of view of the politicians at Washington he was achieving something worth while in weakening the British forces – that was an aspect of the case which only crossed his mind later in the day when he was making ready for the reception on shore which was being given by 'Captain Henri-François Dupont and the officers of His Most Christian Majesty's Navy.'

It was a function to which Anne had been looking forward with eagerness.

'Now the world will be able to see how well you can waltz, dear,' she said in the darkness of the carriage as they drove to the reception, and the recollection that the words called up, and the pretty trick of speech, set him smiling despite his preoccupation. It was a surprise to him to find that he, too, was looking forward to the party, to encountering the world with a wife he was proud of on his arm. He had never believed that he would ever know a pleasurable sensation while on his way to a social function.

Captain Dupont was a courteous host, when he received them in the drawing-room of his house above the quay. He asked politely about Peabody's wounds and he turned a pretty compliment about Anne's appearance. It was only when he had finished speaking to her and had turned back to her husband that he saw Peabody standing rigid, staring across the room with the hard lines carved deep in his face. He followed his gaze; there was Jonathan Peabody laughing and joking with half a dozen pretty women, his new wife watchful at his side.

'It is unfortunate, sir,' said Dupont. 'I am ready enough to admit that. But His Most Christian Majesty's Government can, of course, take no official cognition of the fact that young Mr. Peabody is a deserter. We only know him as the husband of one of the richest and most influential landowners in the island.'

'I understand,' said Peabody, and the tone he used made it clear enough that while he understood he did not excuse. He turned away; there was no pleasure in the party for him now. He nodded to Hubbard and the others, who were entering the room eagerly, with all the freshness of their white gloves and glittering lace. Behind them came the British officers, Davenant and Fane side by side and their juniors following them. Peabody bowed to them as good manners dictated – just the slightest unbending towards an enemy on neutral soil. The Marquis was entering now, the Countess beside him, and the whole room rose to its feet in deference to the embodied presence of the direct representative of His Most Christian Majesty.

A few minutes later Peabody found himself alone – the Countess had taken Anne from him and had carried her off to where she was now the centre of an eager group of chattering women. Peabody wondered what on earth they found to talk about, seeing that most of that group saw each other every day, but he tried to smile tolerantly while he wandered through the rooms. At the far end of the suite was a room where a few elderly people were sitting round card tables, and Davenant and Fane were just emerging. Peabody stood politely aside to make way for them, but Davenant halted and addressed him.

'Good evening, Captain,' he said. 'I trust you are going to return those two deserters of mine?'

The words which ended in 'g' nearly had no 'g' at all, the way Davenant pronounced them.

'I don't intend to, sir,' said Peabody. He was a little nettled at Davenant's calm assumption of certainty.

'You don't intend to?'

Davenant's face exhibited a surprise which was not in the least rhetorical. With the capture of the *Susanna*, Davenant had come unconsciously to look upon the *Delaware* as a ship of war which could work with his own in matters not connected with the war between their countries, and Davenant, after forty years at sea, had grown to believe that naval discipline was the most vital and important factor in the civilised world. Peabody's refusal to return deserters would unsettle the crews of all the British ships. If Peabody had announced a determined belief in the community of property or of the necessity for every man to have nine wives, he could not have been more shocked.

'I don't intend to, sir,' repeated Peabody firmly.

'But man, you don't understand what this means. D'you think I'm goin' to let a couple of deserters flaunt themselves within a cable's length of my own ship?'

That 'g' quite disappeared as Davenant grew more heated.

'They will flaunt themselves, sir, as you say, if the discipline of my ship permits.'

'Good God!'

The exclamation, as Davenant made it, was extraordinarily like the gobbling of a turkey, and Davenant's cheeks were deepening in colour like the wattles of a turkey. Peabody made no reply, and stood waiting to pass.

'Haven't you any sense of decency, man?' exploded Davenant.

Long years as captain of a ship had made it an unusual experience for Davenant to be crossed in his will, and for as many years he had never made any attempt to control his fiery temper. He did not stop to think what he would have said in reply to a request for the return, say, of a couple of American deserters.

'As much as other people have,' said Peabody, 'or more.'

Hubbard had miraculously appeared from nowhere, and was standing at his shoulder; Peabody was aware of the hush which had fallen about them as people listened to their words, but he did not take his eyes from Davenant's. There were strange feelings within him. He knew just whither this argument was leading, and he was strangely glad. Somewhere in the back of his mind was the memory of his fight with Lerouge, and his grim New England conscience was accusing him of fear during the crossing of swords. He must prove to himself that he had not been afraid. And life had been too good. Anne's kisses had been too sweet. With a desperate contrariness he felt he must imperil all his unaccustomed happiness to deserve it.

Fane had put his hand on Davenant's shoulder and was

trying to lead him away, while Davenant's fierce temper refused to be mollified.

'It's what one might expect of Yankee trickiness,' he said. 'It's in keeping with the way they use dismantling shot.'

That made Peabody smile despite himself, and the smile set the coping stone on Davenant's rage. He searched through his mind for the most wounding, the cruellest thing he could say to this upstart American who had dared to oppose him.

'Of course,' he said loudly. 'In the American service they marry their deserters to rich widows. Especially when they happen to be the captain's brothers.'

Peabody stepped back from the impact of the insult as if it had been a physical blow. His lean brown cheeks were white under their sunburn. When he spoke it was with an interval between the words as he exerted his will to keep himself from bursting out with undignified anger.

'Who is your friend, sir?' he asked.

Davenant's shoulders lifted a trifle as he suddenly realised into what fresh trouble his hot temper had led him. But there was no going back now; the next development was as inevitable as a rainstorm.

'Captain Fane will act for me, I am sure,' he said, and turned away, in obedience to the etiquette of the duel which demanded that he should not see his enemy again until they met upon the ground..

'Captain Fane,' said Peabody. 'May I have the pleasure of presenting Lieutenant Hubbard, first lieutenant of the United States ship *Delaware*?' Then he, too, turned away. Dupont was hurrying up, wringing his hands over this deplorable incident at his party, but Peabody brushed past him. All eyes in the room were upon him, but he only saw Anne, just as he had seen her once before, with her face outlined like a miniature against a background of mist. His acute tension relaxed as he met her eyes beneath their level brows, but the exhilaration of excitement still remained.

'Anne,' he said, coming to her, 'we shall have to go home.'

As she looked up to him she had nothing to say to this husband of hers, who in the mad manner of men had imperilled everything she loved in the world for a few words.

There was nothing she could say, nothing she could do; these affairs of honour between men were something whose course no woman could divert in the slightest. Her eyes were moist.

'I'm sorry to have spoilt your party, dear,' said Peabody, smiling down upon her. He was still too stupidly excited to appreciate how much she was hurt. Her lips trembled before she spoke.

'Let us go,' she said.

When Peabody was getting his cloak Hubbard appeared, with his usual air of quiet efficiency. He was accustomed to handling – or participating in – affairs of honour.

'Dawn to-morrow,' he said. 'On the edge of the canebrake across the stream from your house. I know the place – it's barely half a mile from there. Pistols at twelve paces. We'll use mine – they're London made and reliable. I have to go back to the ship for them, and to tell Downing and Murray – we'll need another second. May I spend the night at your house – I've still got some details to settle when I get back?'

'I'll give orders to that effect,' said Peabody.

Back in the room where the mosquito net reared its vast dome over the big bed, Peabody put his arms out to Anne. He saw that she was weeping now, and for the first time misgivings asserted themselves, though unavailingly in the face of his other emotions. That Old Testament conscience of his was grimly satisfied that he should have put this undeserved happiness of his at the disposition of Providence, and he knew now that he was no coward.

'Darling!' he said – the endearments which he had never used before came more readily now.

Anne looked at him, and both her eyebrows and her shoulders went up a little. There was no predicting what this husband of hers would do next, nor how he would feel about it. In seven short hours his life would be in terrible danger – danger that made her feel sick when she thought about it, and yet here he was unmoved. She fought back her tears; as she knew, she would not be able to divert him a hair's breadth from the course mapped out for him at dawn next day. If she were weak now she would do no good and just possibly might do harm. She must be strong, and she took a grip on herself and was strong – Peabody in his blindness knew nothing of it at the time.

As they kissed, a knock on the door made them draw apart. It was Anne's coloured maid still displaying evident signs of excitement over the affair about which the news had spread like wildfire round the island.

'Ma'ame d'Ernée,' she said.

'Madame d'Ernée? To see me?' asked Anne.

'Yes, ma'amselle.'

'I'll come,' said Anne.

Peabody was philosophic about it. He sat down in the bedroom and ran over in his mind the arrangements necessitated by to-morrow's affair. His will – he had made that, and had it witnessed, directly after his marriage. He had given orders about Hubbard, and a bedroom on the ground floor was being prepared for him. He had a black stock and cravat to wear to-morrow so that he would show no linen, and he would fight in his second-best coat without the epaulettes. Anne's aunt had probably come to see if with Anne she could not devise some means of stopping the affair – she ought to have more sense, but she was interested in Davenant, of course. Anne would not presume to meddle, naturally.

Anne came in again. There was a queer twist to her smile and an inscrutable lift to one eyebrow. But her expression softened as her eyes met his, and she melted towards him. She came warmly into his arms, and Peabody quite forgot to ask her what on earth Madame d'Ernée had wanted. He did not want to know anything, not with Anne's lips against his and this sweet passion and purity of conscience consuming him.

Later he slept heavily enough not to feel her slip away from his side and under the mosquito netting; he turned once and found she was gone, smiled in his half awakeness without any suspicion at all. He did not wake far enough to think about the morrow, and when, an hour before dawn, the maid came in to waken them, she was back at his side.

CHAPTER TWENTY-TWO

Hubbard was positively masterful.

'Don't walk too fast, sir,' he said, and the 'sir' was a most perfunctory audition. 'We can't have you arriving out of breath.'

He looked at his watch, and up at the brightening sky from which the rain still dripped monotonously.

'Just right,' he said. 'We don't want to wait when we get there. And no gentleman would keep the other side waiting, although I've known it done.'

They passed a small gang of negroes on their way to work in the fields, and the dark faces all turned to see this odd spectacle of two white men on foot in the rain before dawn. A babble of talk burst from the group – every member of it had heard the gossip about the quarrel between the English captain and the American captain, and what was to happen this morning.

'It's round this corner, sir,' said Hubbard. 'You can walk a bit slower – if you please, sir. Damn this rain.'

Round the corner Murray was waiting, and Downing with a big case of instruments resting on the ground at his feet. Their faces were pale in the brightening dawn. And here came Fane, with Doctor Clarke beside him, and in the background Peabody caught a glimpse of Davenant and Maitland.

'You're sure those gloves are comfortable, sir?' said Hubbard. 'Better to show white than have an awkward grip on the trigger.'

'They're all right,' said Peabody, passing the forefinger of his left hand between the fingers of his right. They were a pair of dark doeskin gloves lent by Hubbard; only his face would catch the light now that he had on his black stock and cravat and blue trousers. Fane was approaching, and Hubbard went to meet him, uncovering and bowing with the utmost formality. Downing and Clarke went off with their instruments into a nook in the canebrake out of the line of fire, leaving Murray alone. He caught Peabody's eye and smiled a sickly smile, so sickly that it made Peabody grin – the Baltimore lad was so acutely nervous, and this period of waiting was trying him hard, and his clothes were soaked.

Hubbard took the case of pistols from under his arm and opened it before Fane. He slid a ramrod down each barrel; each pistol was charged.

'I loaded 'em last night in case of rain this morning, sir,' he said. 'I'll draw the charges if you like—'

'Please do not trouble, sir,' said Fane.

'Would you please be so kind as to keep off the rain while I prime, sir?' said Hubbard.

Fane opened his cloak and held out the breast of it horizontally, and Hubbard held each weapon in turn under this exiguous shelter, close against Fane's bosom, while he filled each priming pan with fine powder from the small canister he produced from his pocket.

'Have you seen the new percussion caps they are making in London, sir?' asked Fane, his polite small talk tinged with professional interest.

'Too damned new-fangled for my liking, sir,' said Hubbard. 'There, sir. Is that to your satisfaction? Then please take your choice, sir.'

With the weapons under their cloaks to screen them from the rain they looked up at the sky.

'The light's fair in any direction with these clouds,' said Fane. 'Better station them with the wind abeam.'

'I agree,' said Hubbard.

They stepped out twelve paces apart and looked round at their principals who came up and were posted on the exact spots indicated. Peabody saw Davenant's face for the first time since yesterday. It was composed, stolid, philosophic. Peabody knew himself to be calm and his hand was steady, so that his heart was joyful.

'Sir,' said Hubbard, 'I must ask you if it is not possible, at this last moment, to compose your differences with Captain Davenant and prevent the effusion of blood?'

'Not a chance,' said Peabody.

Fane had posed the same question to Davenant.

'Never,' said Davenant steadily.

'Then you will please turn your backs,' said Hubbard. He raised his voice. 'I will call "one – two – three – fire!" You will remain still until the word "fire," when you will turn and fire at your leisure.'

'Captain Fane, did your principal hear what I said, or shall I repeat?'

'My principal heard,' said Fane.

Hubbard took the pistol from under his coat and put it into Peabody's hand; the butt felt reassuringly solid through the doeskin glove. Peabody made sure of his grip, made sure his finger was securely against the trigger, raised the pistol so that his eye was along the barrel, made sure that there was no chance of his feet slipping. He tensed himself ready to wheel round while Hubbard's footsteps died away.

'One!' came Hubbard's voice. 'Two – three – fire!'

Peabody swung round, careful to point his right shoulder to his enemy so as to reduce the surface presented to the shot. Davenant's face showed clear at the end of the pistol-barrel, and he began a steady squeeze on the trigger. At that moment came a bang and a puff of smoke. Davenant had fired – presumably he had fired as he wheeled. The aim must have been poor, for Peabody did not even feel the wind of the bullet. Davenant was at his mercy now, and he could take his own time over his shot. Not that there was any need, for Davenant's face, seen clearly through the rain, wa· there along his pistol-barrel. As surely as anything in this life he could place a bullet right between his eyes and kill him. Davenant's eyes looked back at him without a sign of faltering.

Peabody's first instinct was one of mercy. He did not want Davenant's life. He did not want to kill anyone except to the benefit of the United States of America. It raced through his mind that Hunningford had told him of the imminent possibility of peace – the peace of the years to come would not be helped by a memory of a captain slain in a duel. He just had time to point the pistol vertically into the air before it went off.

The four seconds came pressing forward.

'My principal has stood your principal's fire,' said Hubbard, and Peabody noticed that Hubbard's voice sounded strained. All that careful unconcern had been merely a pose, and he was off his guard now and showed it. 'He has deliberately missed. Honour is completely satisfied, and both parties will leave the ground.'

'No second shot?' asked Maitland, and Hubbard turned upon him with an icy politeness barely concealing his poor opinion of a man who could display such ignorance of the code of honour.

'Your principal had his shot and it was not returned,' he said. 'You cannot expect him to be accorded further opportunities.'

That was perfectly true – it had been at the back of Peabody's mind when he missed. A duellist whose life had been spared must remain satisfied with that.

'Mr. Hubbard is quite right,' said Fane. 'Both parties must leave the ground. But I must remind everyone that this is a most suitable opportunity, now that honour is satisfied, to make whatever concessions are compatible with honour and gentlemanly conduct. Mr. Hubbard, would you perhaps be good enough to approach your principal again?'

Hubbard strode over to Peabody and spoke in a low voice.

'You could accept an apology, sir,' he said. 'You could do a good deal more than that, even, seeing that you've stood his fire.'

'What happens if I don't?' asked Peabody. He was vague on the point – he was familiar with the code of honour, but had never come across the practical application of this particular item.

'Nothing,' said Hubbard. 'You can never admit his existence, sir, that's all, and the same with him. You never see each other when you meet. It's awkward when you're in the same ship – I saw it with Clough and Brown in the old *Constitution* – but as things are it'll hardly affect you.'

'I see,' said Peabody. It probably would not affect him much, not even though Davenant was on a familiar footing with his wife's aunt. He would probably never again have dealings with Davenant now that the affair of the *Susanna* was settled. And then at that very moment the germ of an idea came into his mind, engendered by this thought. He might be able to wring very considerable advantages for the Service if he could keep in touch with Davenant.

'Fane and I will be speaking together,' explained Hubbard further. 'Fane might be able to make a lot of concessions, seeing that the world will not know who made the first advance, so to speak.'

'I'll accept anything in reason,' said Peabody. 'I can leave it all to you, I know, Hubbard. But I don't want to be put out of touch with Davenant if it can possibly be helped. Remember that.'

'I will, sir,' said Hubbard, and turned back. Fane left Davenant a moment later and joined him, as the two talked together in low voices. Davenant and Peabody stood and fidgeted in the drenching rain – their eyes met once and Peabody had difficulty, in his present excitement over his new plan, in keeping his features in their proper expression of stony indifference. Hubbard came back.

'He's ready,' he said, 'to express through Fane profound regret that the incident ever happened. That's not a full apology, sir. It's only a half measure, and if shots hadn't been exchanged I should strongly advise against acceptance. But as things are, and remembering what you told me about wanting to remain in touch, I've taken it upon myself to accept.'

'Good,' said Peabody. 'What do I do now?'

'Merely acknowledge him, sir, before we leave the ground.'

All very well, thought Peabody, to say that so airily, but actually it was a difficult moment. Peabody felt positively awkward as he came up to Davenant. He made his stiff spine bend in the middle.

'Your servant, sir,' he said.

Davenant bowed with an equal lack of grace.

'Your servant, sir,' and then constraint suddenly vanishing : 'Dammit, man, I'm glad I missed you.'

Walking home, Hubbard and Murray and Downing were in the highest spirits despite their wet clothes.

'By God, sir,' said Hubbard, 'this'll look well in the newspapers at home. You spared his life, sir. I could see that. I could see how you had him along your pistol.'

'Davenant's a dead shot,' said Downing.

'Yes, sir,' said Murray. 'They say he can hit a pigeon on the wing.'

'I didn't tell you that, sir, before you met him,' said Hubbard, with a laugh.

No damn you, thought Peabody, a little embittered at the thought, and he said nothing.

'He's lost some of his reputation now, anyway,' said Downing.

'I can't think how he came to miss,' said Murray.

'He shot from the waist without sighting,' said Hubbard. 'That takes practice.'

'But it looked to me,' said Murray, 'as if he couldn't miss.'

'So it did to me, by God,' said Hubbard. 'Did you hear the bullet, sir?'

'No,' said Peabody.

It was a most unpleasant conversation in his opinion, although he could not have said why, seeing that the affair was over. There was Anne standing at the door of the house, and she ran down the path through the rain when she saw them. She threw herself into Peabody's arms without shame, and he kissed her without shame in the presence of his subordinates. He had purged himself of his inward doubts, he had put this happiness of his at the disposition of Providence and Providence had returned it to him, so that shame had disappeared. There was coffee waiting for them, and the usual glass of rum which they all refused to touch.

'I can drink this coffee now,' said Murray, smacking his lips. 'I couldn't swallow a mouthful in the ship before I came up this morning. I hadn't the heart for anything.'

'The captain drank his,' said Hubbard. 'I watched him. Not a sign – he might have been getting ready to come on deck at anchor in the Chesapeake.'

'The captain's an interesting physiological subject,' said Downing, and then, suddenly: 'Gentlemen, although this is only coffee, can't we drink his health?'

'The captain,' said Hubbard, raising his glass.

'The captain!' echoed the others – Anne among them – and they drank to him as he grinned awkwardly at the compliment.

'The ship's waiting for us,' he said, to change the subject. 'I'll see you on board after I've changed my clothes.'

The bedroom with its dome of mosquito netting had been put to rights while he was gone; he got himself out dry clothes from the inlaid tallboy – married life played the devil with systematic rotation of his wardrobe when he had to keep half his clothes on land. He laid out a fresh white neckcloth on the dressing table among Anne's tortoise-shell toilet things, shoving aside her reticule to do so. The things fell with a thump on the floor, and he stooped to pick it up. Two things had rolled out of its open mouth across the polished floor, and he pursued them. Marbles?

Beads? He picked them up. They were unexpectedly heavy, of a dull metallic hue. Pistol bullets! He stood looking at the half-inch spheres of lead on his palm, lost in thought.

'Anne!' he called. 'Anne!'

She came running – he heard her light step on the stairs – and as she entered the room she saw what he held in his hand and stopped short. The smile that was on her lips remained there, rigid, in shocking contrast with the terror in her eyes. If it had not been for that she might have been able to disarm his suspicions, so utterly incredible had they seemed to him.

'What are these doing here?' he asked, even now more bewildered than stern.

'You – you know,' she said. She was sick with fright at the knowledge that her terrible husband had caught her interfering with his precious masculine foolishness – imperilling his precious honour.

'I *don't* know,' he said. 'Tell me.'

'I took them out,' she whispered, faltering. 'Aunt Sophie and I.'

'But how in the name of – of anything at all—?'

'I went into Mr. Hubbard's room,' she said. 'Aunt Sophie was here. You were asleep, and I crept out. I went into Mr. Hubbard's room when he was asleep. Aunt Sophie waited by the door – I went in my bare feet, and I took the – the pistols. We dug out the – the wads with my stiletto and shook the bullets out.'

'But the pistols were loaded – I saw Hubbard test with the ramrod.'

'We thought he would. So we had to put in something hard which wouldn't hurt anybody. It was all we could do.'

'But what was it you did?'

'It took us a long time to think of something. In the end I got two bits of bread and baked them as hard as I could. I thought they'd fly to powder when the pistols went off and not do any damage.'

'You were right,' said Peabody grimly. 'And then?'

'That's all. We put the bits of toast into the pistols and stuck the wads in again on top, and I went back into Mr. Hubbard's room and put them back in the case. Mr. Hubbard snored and I nearly dropped them.'

'I wish you had,' he said bitterly. Her lips had lost their rigidity now and were trembling as he stared at her, the pistol bullets still in his hand. He suddenly remembered their existence and hurled them with a crash across the room.

'I was going to tell you about it,' she said, 'not to-day. Not to-morrow. But sometime I was going to tell you.'

'Much good that would do,' he sneered.

And then his saving common sense came to their rescue. After all, he had gone through the affair in good faith. He had stood Davenant's fire and he had not trembled. He had spared Davenant's life in the same good faith as Davenant had tried to take his. And the thought of Davenant, the man who could hit a pigeon on the wing, trying to bring down an American captain with a piece of toast, was marvellously funny. A laugh rose suddenly within him quite irrepressibly. And what made the joke more perfect was that the new plan he had in mind – a plan of whose success he was quite certain – would never have stood any chance of success if it had not been for the duel. Davenant would never have listened to his new suggestion for a moment if it were not for the mortification of knowing that all the world had heard that his life had been spared. If he had killed Davenant – and most assuredly if Davenant had killed him – the new plan would have had no chance. That was amusing as well. The laugh that was welling up inside him burst out to the surface beyond his control. He laughed and he laughed. He thought of Hubbard's grave dignity, of Murray's scared apprehension, while all the time two fragments of toast lay hidden in the barrels of the pistols, and that made him laugh the harder.

He turned grave again when another thought struck him.

'What about your aunt?' he asked. 'Can she keep the secret?'

'Yes,' said Anne, after a moment's serious reflection.

'Yes. She would always keep a secret for me. And this time it concerns Captain Davenant. She wouldn't want the world to know about this.'

'I suppose not,' said Peabody.

Mischief danced in his eyes which were so often cold and hard. Anne's steady gaze met his and she could not help smiling back at him. She smiled and she laughed, and Peabody laughed back at her.

CHAPTER TWENTY-THREE

Peabody's carefully worded letter had suggested neutral ground for the interview with Davenant, and Davenant's cautious reply had accepted the suggestion, and in the end Peabody had had to make use of 'petticoat influence' in violation of his prejudices, although by now not of his judgment. A word to Anne about his difficulties had been passed on to Aunt Sophie, and Aunt Sophie had responded with an invitation to Captain Peabody to drink a dish of tea with her at the Governor's house – a much more private and comfortable place in which to talk to Davenant than any café in Fort de France or any hill-side in Martinique. Women were of some use even in men's affairs, decided Peabody, as he walked past the well-remembered sentry outside the gate and followed the butler into the Countess's drawing-room.

Naturally there was some constraint perceptible at the

beginning of the meeting. Aunt Sophie was all charm, and she poured the tea with admirable grace, the rings on her fingers flashing back the light which leaked in past the shaded windows, but Davenant was ill at ease, displaying a British surliness vastly emphasised by a not unnatural antipathy towards the man who had condescended to spare his life. Peabody on his side was cautious and uncommunicative, a little afraid of showing his hand prematurely, so that all Aunt Sophie's conversational efforts met with a poor reception – especially as both her guests detested tea and were too polite to say so. But Peabody, noting the Englishman's ill temper, and clairvoyantly realising the reasons for it, was glad. It might be easier to induce him to agree to making a step which could only be thought of as rash – to goad the bull, so to speak, into making a charge which would lay him open to a sword-thrust.

Aunt Sophie replaced her cup in her saucer.

'Tea, Captain Peabody? Tea, Sir Hubert? No? Then if you will forgive me, I will leave you alone for a few minutes. There are some domestic trifles I must attend to.'

Davenant hurried across the room to open the door for her, and she sailed out with all her stately grace, turning before she left them with a few final words.

'I shall see personally that no one listens at this door,' she said. 'There is a sentry at the garden door who speaks no English.'

'Thank you, ma'am,' said Davenant, bowing her out and shutting the door before turning back to Peabody. 'A fine woman that. You have married into an admirable family, Peabody.'

'I thought so myself,' said Peabody, sitting down with all the coolness he could display. 'But it is most kind of you to say so, sir.'

Davenant sat himself opposite him. He, too, was doing his best to display cool indifference, crossing his right ankle over his left knee, and leaning back relaxed in his chair. But beneath his lowered lids he was watching Peabody closely, and he was drumming with his fingers on the arm of the chair.

'Well, what is it, sir?' he said at length.

'A challenge, sir,' said Peabody. 'Another one.'

Those last two words were the darts to infuriate the bull, as he could remember seeing them employed in the bullfight at Algeciras. Davenant flushed a little, but he kept his reply down to one word.

'Yes?' he said.

'I'm tired of watching you across the bay,' said Peabody, 'and I guess you're tired of watching me.'

'I'm tired of all this tomfoolery,' said Davenant.

'I'm not surprised,' agreed Peabody. 'The whole island, of course, is amused at you.'

'At me?' said Davenant, on a rising note.

'Yes,' said Peabody. 'Of course, they do not understand the whole circumstances of the case. They can only see that you have twice my force and are having to wait here just because I do.'

'They think that, do they?'

'I'm afraid so, sir. You and I know it's not true, but you can hardly blame them for judging by appearances. The mob thinks much the same all the world over.'

'Damn the mob,' said Davenant. But another shaft had gone home. He was thinking of the British mob, of the English newspapers, and the rash conclusions they might draw regarding his conduct. 'Come out and fight me, Peabody.'

'I want to,' said Peabody, with an edge to his voice. 'I said I had a challenge for you. Come out in the *Calypso* and fight me ship to ship.'

'I'd like to, by God,' said Davenant, and then, trying to keep his head: 'What about these damned neutrality laws?'

'We'll have to obey the twenty-four hour rule,' said Peabody. 'But if I go out first I'll give you my parole to wait for the *Calypso* outside territorial waters. I'd be glad to let the *Calypso* go out first on the same understanding – it does not matter either way.'

'You mean me to leave *Racer* and *Bulldog* out of the action?'

As a sailor Davenant was trying to remain clear headed even while as a man his fierce instincts were overmastering him.

'Yes.'

'Thirty-eight guns to thirty-six, and a hundred and fifty tons advantage to you.'

'I know that, sir. But it's the nearest match we can arrange. You can draw extra hands from your other two ships which will help redress the balance. As many as you care to have.'

'So I can.'

'I'll be glad to do it. My officers have been discontented ever since our last meeting because they were sure I ought to have closed and captured the *Calypso*.'

'Closed and – by God, sir, what do you mean by that? I still had every gun in service. If you had closed instead of cutting my rigging to pieces – by God, sir, you'd have learned a lesson you sadly need.'

The bull had charged.

'I'll close with you this time, I promise you, sir,' said Peabody. 'I won't have a convoy to destroy as I had before.'

The mention of the convoy brought Davenant out of his chair. Its destruction must have called down upon his head an official reprimand whose memory still galled him. He gobbled at Peabody, his cheeks flushed, as Peabody effected his last prod.

'Let's hope conditions will be fair,' said Peabody. 'When we took the *Guerriere* and the *Java* and the *Peacock* we heard afterwards that the wind or the sea favoured the British. We must see that neither of us has that kind of excuse to offer this time.'

'You're insolent, sir!' raved Davenant. 'Meet me how and when you like, if you dare!'

'I have already said I would,' said Peabody. 'We have only the details to settle. Which of us will go out first, *Calypso* or *Delaware*?'

'Have it your own way.'

'As you will, sir.'

'I'll take *Calypso* out at noon to-morrow, then you can leave next day, and I'll be waiting for you ten miles west of Diamond Rock.'

'I think that will suit admirably, sir,' said Peabody, rising to his feet.

He was hard put to it to maintain his expression of cool indifference and to conceal his elation, and he did not want to run even the slight risk of Davenant's reconsidering his decision.

'Ten miles west of Diamond Rock the day after tomorrow,' he said. 'Until then, sir, I must hope that you enjoy the best of health. Would you be kind enough to convey to the Countess my thanks for her hospitality and kindness?'

'I will, sir,' said Davenant, with his stiff bow.

Outside, in the muggy heat of Fort de France on his way to the quay, Peabody walked as if on air. The plan had succeeded. He had got the best of the bargain. His presence in Fort de France had retained twice the force to watch him – but when England had a navy a hundred times as strong as the American what did that count? An American ship loose at sea, free to ravage and destroy, forcing the British to impose all the hampering restrictions of convoy on their trade, was worth a hundred American frigates in harbour.

He knew he could defeat the *Calypso* if the latter were unsupported by the *Racer* and *Bulldog*. It would be a hard fight, but he would win it, and there would be enough left of the *Delaware* to patch up and conduct on a fresh voyage of destruction – a weakened crew – Peabody made himself contemplate calmly a total of a hundred and fifty casualties – and patched sails and jury rigging, but she would still be strong enough and fast enough to play Old Harry with merchant ships. And the *Racer* and *Bulldog* had depleted crews already, if he knew anything about King's ships; Davenant would deplete them still further to give *Calypso* a full complement for what he must know would be the fight of his life. They would not be in a position to hamper his activity very much – they would be an easy prey for him if they dared to cross his path after he had finished with the *Calypso*.

Delegates were discussing terms of peace in Europe. What the basis of peace might be he had no idea, but of one thing he was sure, and that was that it would do his country no harm during the discussions if it were known that an American frigate was at large again in the West Indies. Perhaps in the United States they were tired of the war, disheartened, despondent. The loss of the *Essex* and of the *President* would not have helped to cheer them up either; the news of the capture of the *Calypso* would act as a tonic to them – if the peace negotiations broke down and further sacrifices were required of them this victory would give them the necessary tonic. The White House – or what was left of it, if Hunningford's account of the raid on Washington were correct – would be all the better for the stimulus of a little victory, too. Mr. Maddison might be an admirable President – as to that Peabody knew little and cared less – but as a war minister he had been a woeful failure.

By the time Peabody reached the quay his step was light and he was breathing the muggy air of Fort de France as if it were the keen winter air of Connecticut. Out in the bay the pelicans flapped in their rigid formations; egrets and herons, white in the bright sun, haunted the waters of the edge of the bay, and overhead flew the manifold gulls with their haunting cries. Soon he would be as free as they. It crossed his mind that in the history books of the future he would be noted as the man who captured the *Calypso*, but the thought only crossed his mind and did not linger in it. He simply did not care whether the history books mentioned his name or not, as long as what he had done met with his own grudging approval. He knew himself to have done a good day's work for his country, and he was pleased.

It only remained – Peabody was being rowed across the bay in his gig by this time – to put the *Delaware* into as perfect shape as possible for the forthcoming struggle. He would have an hour's exercise at the guns this afternoon, before nightfall. To-morrow morning Hubbard could put the crew through sail drill while he and Murray went through the watch bill to make certain that every man was posted where he could do most good – those foreward carronades, starboard side, would not be under good supervision if Corling became a casualty and they had the poorest gun captains – and in the afternoon there would be a chance for a final polish on the gun drill.

He would come out of the bay with all top hamper sent down, every stick of it, and fight the *Calypso* under topsails alone. A fallen mast then would do least damage, with the courses furled and wetted as a precaution against fire. He would not need speed, because Davenant would try to close with him as rapidly as possible, and under topsails he could still outmanoeuvre him until the ships came broadside to broadside. Then they would fight it out at pistol shot. It would be better not to board, for *Calypso* would be full of men and his gunners were the more efficient. Pistol shot distance, with grape from the carronades and round shot from the long guns. By closing his eyes Peabody could call up the whole scene before him, the deafening roar of the guns and the choking fog of smoke, the splintering of woodwork and the cheers and the screams. *Calypso* would have to be beaten into a wreck, half her crew dead and the other half dropping with exhaustion, before Davenant would surrender. Davenant would probably be dead, too. And he himself? He might be dead. There was at least an even chance of it. But he knew that what he had done was the best he could do for his country.

As Peabody came on deck he blinked, blindly, as though he had just emerged from his dark cabin instead of having been for the last hour in the blinding light of the sun. In a clairvoyant moment he had been seeing the deck littered with wreckage and corpses, guns dismounted and bulwarks smashed. So vivid had the vision been that he was taken a little aback by the sight of the gleaming white decks and the orderly crew and the guns all snugly secured. It was a couple of seconds before he recovered and began, coldly, to give those orders to Hubbard which were to make his vision into a reality.

CHAPTER TWENTY-FOUR

Eight bells in the forenoon watch, and the hands just dismissed for dinner.

'*Calypso's* making sail, sir,' reported Kidd.

'Thank you,' said Peabody.

Since yesterday the British frigate had been under the closest observation. They had watched her top hamper being sent down; they had counted every man who had been rowed across to her from the *Racer* and *Bulldog*. Twenty marines, conspicuous in their red coats, had been sent by the *Racer*, every marine she had, probably. That meant possibly that Davenant had it in his mind to board, but the seamen who had also been ferried over were probably quarter gunners and gun captains who might improve *Calypso's* gunnery. Peabody's guess was that *Calypso* had now at least a full complement, a most unusual thing for a British ship of war. He himself had suggested to Davenant this supplementing of *Calypso's* crew, but his conscience was clear, for Davenant would have thought of it himself before the time came for sailing.

Calypso was getting under weigh in the fashion to be expected of a King's ship, the anchor hove short, every sail set exactly simultaneously, anchor up, and the ship on the move instantly. She made a brave sight, even with her topgallants sent down, as she beat against the sea breeze over the enamelled green water of the bay. Her first tack was bringing her over towards the *Delaware*, whose crew was lining the hammock nettings to watch her. There was a little murmur forward, swelling instantly into a deep-chested roar. The crew of the *Delaware* was cheering their opponent as she passed, cheering wildly. From the deck of the *Calypso* came one single stern cheer in reply; Davenant was visible on his quarterdeck, conspicuous with his red ribbon and his epaulettes, and he raised his cocked hat in acknowledgment of the compliment. Then the noise from the *Calypso* ceased abruptly as discipline took hold again and the crew stood by for their ship to go about.

Peabody found himself swallowing, and the iron depths of him were even a trifle shaken, for he was luring those brave men over there to their deaths, and to-morrow the brave men here under his command would be dying at his word. His thin, mobile lips were even thinner during the brief space that he allowed himself to think about it. There was no written word between himself and Davenant either, no public parole. He realised with a start that it had not occurred to him to doubt the other's good faith for a single moment, nor had it occurred to Davenant to doubt his. A single sentence had sufficed to settle the details of the combat, and to come to an agreement far more binding than any treaty between statesmen. He bore no rancour against Davenant, and he knew – allowances being made for Davenant's fiery temper – that Davenant bore none against him. He remembered something of the 'treason' which Hunningford had talked at their last interview, and he felt a twinge of regret that fine men and fine ships should be doomed to destruction on the morrow. In a sudden panic he shook the thoughts from him, consumed with misgivings as to whither they were leading him.

'Well, Mr. Styles?' he said to the purser more sternly than usual.

Mr. Styles produced his lists to prove that the *Delaware's* stores were complete in every detail, that every water butt was full, that every brine cask was charged with meat – bought with the *Princess Augusta's* gold from Martinique butchers at prices which made Mr. Styles groan – and every bread bag full of biscuit. Wood for fuel, rum, tobacco, clothing; the *Delaware* was as fully supplied as the day she left Brooklyn. After the *Calypso* should be dealt with she would be free to continue her operations for months without being dependent on the shore for anything.

The *Calypso* was rounding Cape Solomon now, hull down at the mouth of the bay as she headed for her rendezvous ten miles west of the Diamond Rock. Peabody took one last look at her before he went down to the maindeck. Wooden slats had been nailed to the planking there beside the guns, to serve as pointers for concentrated broadsides, at such angles as to ensure that if the guns were laid along them their fire would all be aimed at a point fifty yards on the beam. He called for his big protractor and went along carefully checking the angles. Broke in the *Shannon* had made use of the method when he fought the *Chesapeake*, as Peabody had read in a copy of the *Jamaica Gazette* he had picked up in Fort de France; the same method might be invaluable if there were not enough wind to blow away the smoke and he laid the *Delaware* athwartships to the *Calypso.* There was no harm in learning from the enemy.

He was busy enough, and therefore one might almost say happy enough, until nightfall, by which time he had tired out his crew. He wanted them to sleep soundly that night, ready for the next day, and they perhaps would not do so in their present state of excitement without a good deal of exercise first. So he kept them hauling at the gun tackles in the sweltering heat, and he devised imaginary emergencies for them to deal with, until it was too dark to see. Then he dismissed them to rest. He looked out once more over the dark water, wondering what was happening aboard the *Calypso*, hove-to under shortened canvas out there at her rendezvous in the Caribbean, before he nerved himself to call for his gig.

He did not want to go ashore; he did not want to see Anne again. He doubted so much his ability to bear what he foresaw would be an agonising strain. The premonition of approaching death was strong upon him. This love of his, these few days of happiness, had been a tiny interlude of joy during his joyless life. Perhaps no bitterness, no disappointment, no privation, could ever be too much for his iron temperament, but he was afraid of happiness. He was afraid of himself, afraid lest he might weaken, lest this last glimpse of the happiness he was losing should break him down and betray him into some demonstration of weakness which would be sinful if anything was, which he would be ashamed of when he remembered it broadside to broadside with the *Calypso*, and which Anne would remember of him when – if ever – she thought of him in after years.

But he had to go through with it. That was all. It was something that he had to do, and so there was no use in grimacing as he swallowed his medicine.

'Good night, sir,' said Hubbard, hat in hand.

'Good night, Mr. Hubbard,' said Peabody as he went over the side in the darkness.

There was the little carriage, which had been waiting at the quay ever since sunset, and there was Anne, faintly illumined in the light of the lantern which the coachman held

She held up her mouth to be kissed, and he kissed her, and he knew then, at the touch of her lips, that all his fears regarding his weakness were nonsensical. It was a moment of fresh recognition, like the time when he had seen her again at the Marquis's house – he had forgotten what she was like until he saw her again. Anne could never be a cause of weakness; she could never be a drain on any man's strength. Rather was she a fortifiant, strengthening him and revivifying him. Peabody remembered the Pilgrim's Progress, and how Christian's burden dropped from him when he reached the Cross. His own burden dropped from him as he felt Anne's slim shoulders under his hands and her lips against his, and there was nothing impious about the comparison, not even to his morbid conscience.

Later that night he tried to tell her about it. He even mentioned Christian and the Cross a little shamefacedly, for he was quite unliterary and high-flown similes did not come easily to him, and he felt her lie suddenly still in his arms. It was a second or so before she replied, in that London accent with its French quality that he loved so dearly, and she stroked his cheek as she spoke.

'Dear,' she said, 'darling. When I'm an old woman I'll remember what you've just said and I'll still be proud of it. But you've got it all wrong, dear. It isn't me. It's *you*. To you I'm what you think I am, of course – oh, how can I explain it? You're so good yourself, you're so honest and you think no evil. It's because you're like what you are that you think other people are the same. And my dear, it's because you think that that we try to be. Oh, what a muddle I'm saying, and yet to me it's as clear as clear. Sweetheart – darling—'

The night was passing and the dawn was approaching; the maid's knock on the door awoke them as they slept still in each other's arms. When Peabody was dressed the carriage was waiting to take him down to the quay, and Peabody stood to bid his wife good-bye. Their eyes met as he stretched out his hands and she put hers into them.

'Good-bye, dear,' he said.

'Good-bye, dear,' she answered, looking at him with level gaze, unflinching. 'You'll come back to me soon?'

'As soon as ever I can,' he said; the premonition of death had not left him.

He bent his head to kiss her hands, and he felt their impassioned clasp as he did so, but her eyes were still dry when he looked up again, and her voice was steady. It was not until he had gone that she wept, bitterly, heartbroken, alone in her room.

On board the *Delaware* the early morning routine was under weigh, just as ever. Rank by rank, their trousers rolled above the knee, the hands were washing the deck, polishing metal work, scrubbing canvas.

'Good morning, Mr. Hubbard.'

'Good morning, sir.'

'It looks as if we're going to have a fine day.'

'The glass rose during the night, sir.'

The tropical sun was already glaring down at them over the hills, and one or two belated fishing boats were still returning to the bay with the night's catch. The little revenue cutter was standing out from the quay and hove-to close under the *Delaware's* quarter. Dupont was on board, in full uniform, and he hailed the American ship.

'You will be allowed to sail at fifteen minutes past noon,' he shouted, bringing out his watch from his fob. 'I keep the time, and it is now six-thirty.'

Peabody looked at his own watch. He had forgotten to wind it the night before, and even on his wedding night he had remembered it. But he managed to keep his expression nonchalant as he synchronised his watch with Dupont's, and he called no attention to his actions when he next slipped the key over the winding post and gave it a few casual turns.

'Very good, Captain,' he hailed back.

'Isn't it sickening the way these Frogs can order us about, sir?' said Hubbard.

'It's for the last time,' said Peabody. 'Mr. Hubbard, I've left duplicate orders for you should I be killed this afternoon.'

'Yes, sir,' said Hubbard, steadily. He did not cheapen himself with any conventional 'I hope not'. He was like Anne in that respect.

'One set is in my desk,' went on Peabody. 'The other is in a sealed envelope which the gunner has in the magazine in case our upper works are wrecked. However hard hit the ship may be, you are to repair her at sea.'

'Yes, sir.'

'The British have some sort of expedition fitting out at Jamaica,' went on Peabody. 'It may have sailed by now, but you are to track it down. My own guess is that they'll send it against New Orleans.'

'Yes, sir.'

'Hang on to it and do it all the damage you can. If you catch it at sea you may be able to snap up a transport or two – a couple of thousand redcoats for prisoners wouldn't do us any harm.'

'I guess not, sir.'

'But remember this, Mr. Hubbard. You are not to fight any British ship of war if you can help it.'

'I understand, sir.'

'I hope you do.'

'I'm fighting *Calypso* this afternoon because it's the only way to get out of this damned harbour.'

'And you've been damned clever to arrange it, sir.'

'That will be all, Mr. Hubbard. See that the men get their dinners at six bells.'

'Aye aye, sir.'

Peabody was aware that to an outsider the worst of having made all his preparations in plenty of time would be that now there was nothing to do except wait – Peabody remembered how careful Hubbard had been, the morning before the duel, that there should be no waiting on either side. And yet this morning waiting was a pleasure; it gave him time to enjoy his present tranquillity of mind and soul. He felt at his best; he could look up at the green slopes of Martinique and across the blue waters of the Caribbean and take pleasure in them. There was something purifying in his certainty that he was to die that afternoon. He had done everything he could, and he had left nothing undone, nor, looking back over the voyage, had he done anything he ought not to have done. America would register him among her heroes. And he would live in Anne's memory, which was the immortality he desired. He felt no shame in remembering her sweetness and the dear delights he had shared with her. That was strange, that he should feel this purity, as of a mediaeval knight watching over his arms, having known her ardent passion. It was the crowning of his present happiness.

An hour before noon the pipes of the boatswain's mates began to twitter as the men were called to their dinners. The sea breeze had begun to blow, and would reach appreciable strength when the time came to sail, Peabody decided. He looked up at the pennant at the masthead; if the wind did not shift they would be able to weather Cape Solomon in a single board. Closehauled, they would very nearly make the rendezvous – it would depend on how soon they would pick up the trade wind out in the Caribbean. He looked out again over his projected course and started with surprise. There was a ship under full sail just coming into sight round Cape Solomon. She had every sail set, studding sails as far as the royals on both sides, and was heading for the bay with the wind well abaft the beam at a speed so great that even at that distance he could see the white water under her bows. She was the *Calypso*, or so his eyes told him. His brain refused to believe any such thing. There was no possible reason for her to be returning.

'*Calypso* coming into the bay, sir!' yelled the lookout, but there was that in his voice which told that the lookout did not believe his eyes either.

Atwell across the deck had his telescope to his eye.

'Well, I'll be God-damned,' he said, turning to his captain, and then hastily added – 'Sir.'

The officers were hurrying up from below, cluttering the quarter-deck and staring at the beautiful vision as the sea breeze brought her in fast.

'Davenant must have remembered something,' said Hubbard, and one or two of those who heard him laughed.

'Sprung a leak, perhaps?' suggested Atwell, seriously. 'On fire down below? Yellow Jack among the crew?'

All the suggestions were plausible, and the laughter stilled as every eye strained to see if there was anything to be seen which might confirm one of them. She was well into the bay now, and her studding sails came in altogether.

'They've an anchor ready to let go, sir,' said Hubbard, without taking the glass from his eye.

'Heave our anchor short, Mr. Hubbard,' said Peabody.

It might be a nice legal point, as to whether the return of the *Calypso* nullified the application of the twenty-four hour rule. It still wanted twenty-five minutes before noon, but he wished to be ready to dash out of the harbour the moment the *Calypso* anchored, before *Racer* or *Bulldog* could take a hand in the game. To escape into the Caribbean without a battle was better than any hard won victory. He was prepared to go and leave the diplomats to argue the case subsequently. The loud clanking of the capstan served as a monotonous accompaniment to the excited comments on the quarterdeck.

'Turn up all hands, Mr. Hubbard, if you please. I want all sail ready to set.'

Calypso was heading straight for the *Delaware*; at no more than a cable's length's distance she rounded to. Every sail was taken in simultaneously, and the roar of the cable through the hawsehole was plainly audible from the *Delaware*.

'Nothing wrong with the way she's handled,' commented Hubbard, grudgingly. The sudden bang of a gun made them all start, and then they all felt a trifle sheepish at the realization that *Calypso* was only firing off her salute to the forts.

'Anchor's aweigh, sir!' came the yell from forward.

'Set sail, Mr. Hubbard.'

Courses and topsails were spread on the instant, as the headsails brought her round.

'*Calypso's* launched a boat, sir,' said Kidd.

So she had; a gig had dropped from her quarter and was pulling madly across to intercept the *Delaware* as she gathered way.

'Keep her closehauled on this tack, if you please, Mr. Hubbard,' said Peabody. He could think of no message whatever which would keep him in Fort de France if once he had the chance to escape.

The gig's crew were bending frantically to their oars, making the little craft fly over the surface. Peabody could see the officer in the stern gesticulating wildly as he urged the men to greater efforts. Then as they came close the men lay on their oars and the officer jumped to his feet in the stern sheets, his hands as a speaking trumpet to his mouth; it was the same supercilious midshipman who had once before brought a letter from the *Calypso*.

'Message from Captain Davenant,' yelled the midshipman as the gig was at the level of the *Delaware's* mainmast. Peabody paid no attention. If he had the chance of getting to sea he was going to take it.

'Message for Captain Peabody,' yelled the midshipman as the mizzen mast went by.

The gig bobbed suddenly as the wave thrown off by the *Delaware's* bows reached her, but the midshipman retained his balance with the practice of years. He put his hands to his mouth in one last desperate yell as the gig passed under the *Delaware's* quarter.

'It's peace!' he yelled. 'Peace!'

'Bring her to the wind, Mr. Hubbard,' said Peabody. After all, that was the one message which would keep him in harbour; and he had not thought about it before.

The gig overtook the *Delaware* as she lay hove to.

'Captain Peabody?' hailed the midshipman.

'I am Captain Peabody.'

'Sir Hubert's respects, sir, and would it be convenient for him to visit your ship?'

'My respect to Sir Hubert, and it will be convenient whenever he wishes.'

The gig turned about and rowed back, while Peabody gave his orders.

'Anchor the ship again, Mr. Hubbard, if you please. Be ready to compliment Captain Davenant when he comes on board.'

Peabody dashed below, where the gun deck was cleared

of all bulkheads and obstructions ready for action. There was only an exiguous canvas curtain hung to preserve for the ship's captain a shred of privacy up to the moment of action commencing.

'Washington! My best coat! White breeches. Silk stockings. Hurry, d'you hear me?'

'Lord ha' mercy, sir. What are you wanting those for?'

'Jump to it, damn you, and shut your mouth.'

Washington could not obey the last order, could not have done so to save his life, but he muffled his remarks in the sea chest into which he had to bend his head as he sought for the clothes, in the highly inconvenient corner of the cabin where the chest had been thrust while clearing for action. Peabody had thrown off coat and trousers and was standing in his shirt before Washington had found the other clothes; as Washington got to his feet the jarring rumble of the cable shook the ship.

'Lordy!' said Washington, and shut his mouth with a snap as Peabody turned a terrible eye on him. He could only roll his eyes when the tramp of the marines' heavy shoes sounded on the deck overhead as they poured up to the entry port.

'Tell the captain of the afterguard to set my cabin to rights directly,' said Peabody, buckling on his sword. As he set his foot on the companion he heard Hubbard's warning yell, and he reached the deck just as the boatswain's mates' pipes pealed and the marines presented arms.

'Ah, Peabody,' said Davenant, coming towards him with outstretched hand. He was smiling in kindly fashion, the wrinkles showing round his eyes.

'I am glad to see you, sir,' said Peabody, a little stiffly.

Davenant was struggling with the overwhelming curiosity which consumes a captain of a ship of war when by some chance he finds himself on the deck of a rival ship. Even at that moment it was hard to keep his eyes from straying.

'Here,' he said, opening the paper which he held in his left hand and passing it over to Peabody. 'The damned despatch boat from Port of Spain sighted me this morning and gave me this. It's conclusive as far as I'm concerned.'

Peabody read the despatch; the seal was official enough and it was addressed from the Admiralty at Whitehall—

> 'I am directed by my Lords Commissioners of the Admiralty to inform all captains of His Britannic Majesty's Ships that in consequence of peace having been concluded at Ghent between His Majesty and the United States of America hostilities will cease forthwith and to request and require all such captains to refrain from any hostile action whatsoever immediately upon receipt of this order.
>
> E. Nepean, Secretary to the Board.'

'I suppose it needn't bind you,' said Davenant. 'You can wait until you receive your orders from Washington.'

'It binds me too, of course,' said Peabody. If he went out to sea in the face of that evidence and began a career of destruction he would be in bad odour, to say the least of it, with the Secretary of the Navy.

'It's a damned shame,' said Davenant. 'No, damn it, I can't say that. I don't know whether to be pleased or sorry, damn it. We'd have had as neat a single ship action as there's been these twenty years.'

Peabody was not ready with a reply. He was looking forward into a new future, one which he had never allowed himself to think about until now. A future of a world at peace, a world of thriving commerce. His own life would be dull and without incident, and anyone who did not know him would say that the most interesting chapter of his career had finished. But Peabody – such was the nature of the man – thought that the most interesting chapter had now begun. He took control of his thoughts just as they were drifting towards Anne and brought them back to less romantic matters. There were three dozen scrawny Martinique hens in coops on the spardeck, and, boiled, a couple of them would be just edible.

'Can I have the pleasure of your company to dinner, sir?' he said.